The Harvests of War

The Harvests of War
The Prairie West, 1914-1918

John Herd Thompson

McCLELLAND AND STEWART

This book has been published with the help of a grant from the Social Science Federation of Canada, using funds provided by the Canada Council.

The Canadian Publishers
McClelland and Stewart Limited
25 Hollinger Road, Toronto

Manufactured in Canada by Webcom Limited

CANADIAN CATALOGUING IN PUBLICATION DATA

Thompson, John Herd, 1946-
  The harvests of war

(The Canadian social history series)

Originally presented as the author's thesis (Ph.D.),
Queen's University, 1975.

Includes index.
ISBN 0-7710-8560-5

1. Prairie Provinces - History - 1905-1945.*
2. European War, 1914-1918 - Prairie Provinces.
3. Prairie Provinces - Social conditions.
I. Title. II. Series.
FC3242.T46   971.2'02   C77-001835-1
F1060.9.T46

FRONT COVER PHOTOGRAPH
Western recruits in training. *Manitoba Archives.*

CONTENTS

Emergency harvest help, 1917.
Manitoba Archives.

PREFACE

The World War of 1914-1918 must be counted among the most profoundly significant events in the history of western civilization. The war's near-global scope, its staggering physical horror, and the transformations which it set in motion were so truly momentous that for a generation the English-speaking world knew it simply as the "Great War." A popular analogy likened the war to a crucible, within which nations were subjected to an intense heat, and from which none emerged unaltered. The Dominion of Canada, not yet a half-century old at war's beginning, was not excepted from this experience. Canada's shores were untouched by the violence that devastated parts of Europe, but six hundred thousand of her children took part in the military conflict. Sixty thousand of them never returned, and those who survived returned to a country very different from the Canada they had left. The seven million Canadians who had remained behind had seemingly been changed by the war, just as the soldiers themselves had been. One private soldier said simply that "the place we had left off wasn't there anymore."*

This book is an examination of the effects of the war on one of Canada's regions, the provinces of Manitoba, Saskatchewan, and Alberta, which compose the Prairie West. In 1914 these provinces formed a distinct regional entity, sharing similar backgrounds, economies and societies as well as a common geography. Each had entered Confederation as a creation of Ottawa, denied the maturity conferred by possession of its own natural resources. In sharp contrast to their neighbour, British Columbia, the Prairie Provinces depended for their livelihood on the pro-

*Norman James, *The Autobiography of a Nobody* (Toronto, 1947), p. 101.

9

duction for export of grain, and the majority of their citizens were farmers. At a time when Canadians in other regions were moving to the city, seven of every ten Westerners lived in an environment which could not be described as urban, even by the generous definition used by the census-takers of 1911. The Prairie West had become an important factor in the Canadian equation in a space of twenty years. By 1914 20 per cent of Canada's population lived in Manitoba, Saskatchewan, or Alberta, an increase accounted for by the fact that the largest part of the one and one-half million immigrants who had arrived since 1900 had chosen these provinces as their destination. Among these immigrants were almost 300,000 from Central and Eastern Europe, whose presence produced a social situation peculiar to the West. For these reasons, the West of 1914 was unique, as unlike Ontario or Quebec as these provinces were unlike each other. Because of this distinctiveness, the Great War left an imprint upon the West different from the one it left upon Canada as a whole.

Some further introductory comments are necessary. In an attempt to define "social history," E.J. Hobsbawm points out that it "can never be another specialization like economic or other hyphenated histories because its subject matter cannot be isolated....The intellectual historian may (at his risk) pay no attention to economics, the economic historian to Shakespeare, but the social historian who neglects either will not get far."* I have tried to follow his advice in writing this book and it therefore encompasses themes which might be individually delineated as economic, intellectual, or political in order to present a picture of a society during a period of crisis. The chronological scope of this study has been limited to the years of the war themselves, 1914 to 1918, although the first and concluding chapters consider, in a general sense, the situation before war's outbreak and the legacy it bequeathed to the post-war era. This is not meant to suggest that the influence of the Great War can be encapsuled neatly within the framework of five years, or that it concluded abruptly on November 11, 1918. This limitation was established to permit concentration on the war, to view it as a phenomenon worthy of study in its own right, not simply as a preface to the appearance of the Progressive Party, the general election of 1921, or the Winnipeg General Strike.

*E.J. Hobsbawm, "From Social History to the History of Society," in Felix Gilbert and Stephen R. Graubard, eds., *Historical Studies Today* (New York, 1971), pp. 5-6.

The organization of *The Harvests of War* is neither fully chronological nor fully topical, but is rather an attempt to combine the strengths and avoid the weakness of the two approaches. The initial chapter "begins at the beginning," while the closing chapters deal with the final years of the war. Other chapters, however, for example those dealing with the problems of ethnic minorities, or the use of the war by social reform movements, consider one theme in the context of the entire period. One final note of explanation: jaded by "a century of total war," we find it difficult to understand what the Great War meant to those inhabitants of a more peaceful century who found themselves confronted with it. Arnold Toynbee dismisses the war as no more noteworthy than those described by Thucydides, most of us call it "World War I" or the "First World War," and our librarians catalogue it coldly as the "European War, 1914-18." These terms of reference seem ahistorical, a barrier to any attempt to understand the Canada of 1914. For this reason, the war will be referred to throughout the text as it was christened by the generation whose future it altered, the Great War.

Many people helped me during the preparation of this book. Librarians and archivists in Ottawa and the Prairie Provinces directed me to useful manuscript collections and occasionally permitted me access to material outside regular hours. Stan Hanson, Peter Gillis, Sheilagh Jameson, John Bovey, and Doug Bocking earned individual thanks. The Canada Council and the Social Science Grants Committee of McGill University provided funds for research and travel. Helpful colleagues read chapters and suggested revisions, and Michael Cross and Jo LaPierre read the entire draft and performed vital editorial functions. Ms. Joanne Richling and Mrs. Margaret Blevins typed the manuscript in different versions and Katrin Partelpoeg was companion, typist, and editorial assistant. Finally, there are three historians to whom I wish to dedicate this book: Walter Stein introduced me to historical studies as a possible career, Ed Rea convinced me that the region in which I was brought up had a history to be discovered, and Roger Graham directed the doctoral thesis as which *The Harvests of War* began.

CHAPTER ONE

1914
Innocent Enthusiasm

"Looking back on it now, I do not think we had a care in the world," wrote Nellie McClung of the summer of 1914 in her memoir *The Stream Runs Fast*. Mrs. McClung's reminiscences were written during the Second World War, and, "looking back" from this vantage point, through an interval clouded by the Great Depression, most Canadians who remembered Canada before the Great War would have shared her wistful nostalgia. The memory of another popular Western Canadian novelist is almost identical. Writing in the midst of the 1930s, C.W. Gordon–Ralph Connor to two generations of Canadian readers–described 1914 as a blissful year when "Our life was full of rest and happy peace. It was a good world."[1]

Gordon's "good world" is the image which has coloured our impression of the period before the Great War. The early years of the twentieth century were a period of material progress for Canada, the so-called "Laurier Boom," named for the prime minister who is supposed to have promised his countrymen that the new century was to belong to them. The economic expansion which had buoyed such optimism slowed and finally ended by 1912. A tempting tendency exists, however, to extend it by means of historic licence to 1914, moving in one sweep from the "Battle about Reciprocity" to "Canada and the War," better to depict the dramatic contrast between pre- and post-war Canada. Donald Creighton's *Dominion of the North* juxtaposes an eloquent description of Robert Borden, victor in the reciprocity "battle," with "August 4, 1914, when Great Britain declared war on the German Empire." J.M.S. Careless tells readers of *Canada: A Story of Challenge* that "the long boom period was coming to a close," but opens his chapter "Canada and the First World War" in "the golden summer of 1914," returning to the image of a placid, innocent Canada thrust from peace and prosperity into the maelstrom of war. W.L. Morton argues that for Canada the nineteenth century did not end until 1914.[2]

As with most portraits of the past, the colours are too bright, the brush strokes too bold, the shading unsubtle. Canadians were indeed innocent before the events of August 1914, but many of them were neither placid nor prosperous. In fact since Laurier's fourth electoral victory of 1908 the seeds of destruction of the economic and political system he had inherited from Macdonald had sprouted, grown into seedlings, and begun to mature into healthy plants. Their growth was cultivated by the reciprocity struggle of 1911, watered by the controversy over Borden's naval policy, and fertilized by the dislocations created when the "boom" played itself out. None of Canada's regions had as much to fear from the end of this "boom" as the region that had been virtually created by it, the Prairie West. It was during the "golden summer" of 1914 which preceded the declaration of war that the West came face to face with a reality that fifteen years of almost uninterrupted prosperity had allowed her to overlook, a reality with profound implications for her future.

The West's economic problems were the most serious, particularly when viewed beside the years of expansion just ended. For Western prosperity was predicated upon this expansion and with its conclusion the Prairie economy entered an unavoidable recession. Most visible and most alarming was the agricultural situation. Agricultural expansion had temporarily ended, and had in fact exceeded its limit in places. In 1912 a stabilization of production coincided with a drop in prices to reduce the value of the wheat and oats crops by sixteen million dollars. Depressed prices continued through 1913 and by 1914 had taken their toll. The spring of the latter year saw for the first time an actual decline in the acreage devoted to the principal grain crops. Drought complicated the situation created by price levels, and by mid-July it was becoming obvious that 1914 was going to provide no improvement. Manitoba and the more northern parts of her sister provinces had received enough rain to promise some sort of a crop, but in southwestern Saskatchewan and southern Alberta crops were a total failure. After three consecutive years of disaster, homesteaders with only a quarter-section faced starvation. A member of the Alberta legislature reported to the dominion minister of agriculture "families existing on soup, the ingredients of which are gophers, Russian thistles, and a little salt," while R.B. Bennett warned Prime Minister Borden that for Westerners "the next winter will be in every respect perhaps the most difficult that has ever been faced."[3]

For the West's once-confident urban areas, present and future looked no more promising. The *London Economist*, which had warned British investors that the Western cities "in their anxiety to get big quickly" were mistakenly wagering their futures on an impossible rate of growth, saw its prophecy fulfilled as population growth and business activity in the would-be Chicagos and St. Pauls of Canada dropped off precipitously. Prairie cities and towns were of course affected by the agricultural depression, but also crippling to them was the fact that the construction industry, which had assisted at the birth of the cities themselves, had finished most of its work. Completed projects were not replaced by new ones, and railway construction, which had once fuelled the West's economic furnace, could not compensate. By 1914 both the Grand Trunk Pacific and the Canadian Northern faced financial difficulties which prevented completion of lines already surveyed. All railway companies reduced staff in the summer of 1914.

Jobless railroaders were not alone in their plight. The business recession throughout the West left severe unemployment in its wake. Moose Jaw, dependent on the railway shops, reported 2,500 men out of work in the spring of 1914. In Edmonton and Winnipeg groups of unemployed workers demonstrated to demand jobs, but city governments were without funds to finance public works programs to provide them. Western cities had had difficulty borrowing money since 1912, and like the situation in agriculture, this problem became steadily worse.[4]

With no recovery in sight, the slump added weight to the long-term economic grievances of the West, particularly those related to the protective tariff and the problem of transportation. The defeat of reciprocity in 1911 had demonstrated to Westerners that their interests were in some ways irreconcilable with those of central Canada, and that neither free trade in wheat nor a reduction in the duties imposed upon their tools of production was likely to be forthcoming. The election of 1911 has been described by W.L. Morton as "the first act in the agrarian revolt of Western Canada," and the same act was rehearsed again in the Conservative Party's budgets of 1912, 1913, and 1914.[5] The last was particularly badly received in the West. Advance publicity had hinted that it would contain concessions to Western interests, but the version presented by Minister of Finance Thomas White contained only a minuscule reduction in the duty on mowers and binders, ignoring the rest of the implement tariff structure and the question of free wheat. The *Swift Current Sun* expressed Prairie opinion when it dismissed the change as meaningless, and accused the government of "listening to the railway and milling interests, and turning a deaf ear to the producers."

The disappointing budget was announced with news of still another Eastern failure to come to grips with the problems of the West. Adequate and reasonably priced railway transportation had been a demand of Prairie farm organizations since the 1880s. In an attempt to solve this problem, the Board of Railway Commissioners had spent two years in consideration of the question of differential railway rates. Now at last it presented its report. The commissioners found reason to suggest some rate reductions, but avoided the question of discriminatory rates for the Western provinces. Issued during the week that the budget was presented, this report outraged Western opinion. The two new transcontinentals had received millions of dollars in public funds, much of it against Western wishes, and a large loan had been made to Mackenzie and Mann's Canadian Northern earlier that same year. But despite the fact that the taxpayer seemed to be paying the piper, the Board of Railway Commissioners was refusing to let him call the tune. "Far from giving the West the justice that was demanded," said the *Grain Grower's Guide*, the report had made "no attempt to equalize freight rates east and west."[6]

Economic conditions, bad enough by themselves, exacerbated a social problem for which Westerners were seeking the answer. Between 1896 and 1914, Western Canada had become the home of hundreds of thousands of immigrants, many from Central and Eastern Europe. Some of these "sturdy peasants in sheepskin coats" became farmers, homesteading quarter-sections throughout the Prairies. More visible to the English-speaking Westerner was the group which provided an inexpensive source of labour for the construction industry. This unskilled urban tip of the immigrant iceberg disturbed social commentators, who noted that these "foreigners," even when naturalized, were not adapting to the standards of citizenship expected of a Canadian. In his introduction to young J.S. Woodsworth's *Strangers within Our Gates* the principal of Winnipeg's Wesley College admonished his fellow Canadians to "educate and elevate the incoming multitudes or they will drag us and our children down to a lower level." Such voices were scarcely heard when ears were filled with the ringing of the cash registers of affluence. During the period of expansion, Westerners shared instead the confidence of Canada's most popular novelist, Ralph Connor, whose novel *The Foreigner* was prefaced with a vision of a confident Canadianism which would amalgamate the newcomers into "a race greater than the greatest of them all."

But as the economy slowed down in 1912, unemployment was nowhere more acute than among the "foreign navvies" who had worked in the construction industry. As single immigrants lost their jobs in the winter off-season, they crowded into Prairie cities which had nothing else to offer them. This influx contributed to an uneasy awareness that the assimilation of the non-English-speaking immigrant was not proceeding as it should. The comment that George F. Chipman, the editor of the *Grain Grower's Guide*, had made in 1909 was now much more relevant. "The fusion of the races in the melting pot is unceasing," Chipman had written, "and the blast furnaces are developing the new Canadian–but there is something defective in the system. The product is not satisfactory, nor is the process sufficiently rapid and sure."[7]

Those who shared this concern with the question of assimilation had little difficulty pinpointing the "something defective" of which Chipman spoke. The major factor in the process of Canadianization was the public school, "the mill that gathers all into its hopper and turns them out with the stamp of the King and the maple leaf." In the Prairie Provinces the school was especially important, for "if the school is not to represent the common Canadian citizenship, what else is there out there in the solitudes to do it?" In Manitoba, Saskatchewan, and Alberta, however, the public school was handicapped in its task by the fact that many immigrant children, if they went to school at all, were often being taught in their own language by a teacher whose knowledge of English and of Canada was no more precise than their own.

It was in Manitoba that the situation was most serious. In that province schools which operated in another language in addition to English "upon the bi-lingual system" had been legal since the Laurier-Greenway compromise of 1897. Many districts, however, were eliminating the English. In Saskatchewan and Alberta, the same type of school existed outside the law. One Alberta school inspector reported that among the Ukrainians of the Vermillion area "a strong sentiment with their language is developing....In one instance the school was conducted entirely in Ruthenian." The *Vegreville Observer* quoted one Ukrainian school trustee as boasting that "the rule of the English cowboys is finished; we are now in charge; we are a nation able to govern our own matters." Across the Prairies editors of English-language newspapers warned against "the menace of anti-Canadian nationalism," and urged that the language problem be solved.[8]

The problem of the education of the immigrant was one that could be solved within the West itself once provincial electorates were convinced that it existed. But Western economic problems required solution by the Dominion government, and by 1914 some Westerners were coming to the conclusion that this solution would have to be sought outside the traditional two-party system. Had not the problems of the tariff and of freight rates been the same under both Conservative and Liberal governments? As the *Grain Grower's Guide* pointed out in a critique of the Report of the Board of Railway Commissioners, "both political parties have evaded the question [of railway rates] in the past. It becomes more apparent," continued the *Guide*, "that the Western people will have to carry their fight for a square deal into the political field." To those who accepted the *Guide*'s analysis, the way to enter this field was to nominate independent candidates "absolutely free from obligations to either political party" who would represent their region and their constituents rather than the "special interests." One of the *Guide*'s readers pointed out the futility of the West's continuing to send to Ottawa the lawyer representatives of the Conservative and Liberal parties. "If a bunch of pigs were having a hog congress," wrote G.C. Bennett from Riddelvale, Alberta, "do you suppose they would elect a butcher to represent them?"[9]

Both Canadian parties were aware of Western discontent, and feared its political expression. The rapidly increasing population of the West would entitle her to a larger representation in the next dominion Parliament, and make her votes that much more necessary to electoral success. Neither party had cause for satisfaction in the situation which prevailed during the summer of 1914. Even a Conservative fire-eater like Minister of Militia Sam Hughes warned his leader that in a general election their party "would be swept out of the three Prairie Provinces to a man."[10] But it was questionable if the Liberals would be able to consolidate this lost support behind their own candidates. As July neared its close, both Borden and Laurier scheduled tours of the West, in the hope that their personal presence would encourage the faithful and gather the strays back into the fold.

The *Grain Grower's Guide* anticipated their coming in a long editorial. Laurier and Borden would be told, the *Guide* predicted, "in the plain unvarnished language of the soil and with true Western spirit," that

> ...the present serious condition now prevailing in the rural West is very largely due to the unjust burdens which these two gentlemen, in their capacity of political leaders, have laid upon the shoulders of the western people for the benefit of a small group of individuals in the financial centers of Quebec and Ontario. The two political leaders will not be asked to provide any special legislative favors for the western farmers. They will only be asked to remove restrictions which hamper the western farmers....When this year's crop is harvested and sold not one quarter of the farmers of the Prairie Provinces will be financially one cent better off than a year ago, and the great majority of them will be farther behind....The people of the Prairie Provinces are no longer satisfied to be herded into a legislative corral and plundered by the Barons of Special Privilege.[11]

The last phrase was reminiscent of the angry editorial with which the "bible" of the Western farmer had answered the high tariff budget of the previous April. Then it had warned whomever cared to listen that there was "bound to be a day of reckoning" between the West and the "Toronto group," the "Watered Stock Brigade." Neither the *Guide* nor its readers could have known that this "day of reckoning" was to be postponed for seven years.

Neither projected political journey took place. Even as Western farmers read the *Guide*'s stern warning to Borden and Laurier, the train of events that produced the Great War was being set in motion in Central Europe. On July 28, the Austro-Hungarian Empire declared war on the Serbs, and in the week which followed a proliferation of declarations and counter-declarations ensued. Canada was committed to the conflict by Britain's declaration of war against Germany on August 4, and the next morning headlines informed Canadians of this fact.

To most Canadians, particularly those in the West, war came as a surprise, a surprise for which they had had little preparation. The last major North American conflict, the American Civil War, had ended a half-century before, and the wars with which most Westerners were familiar were the small-scale colonial wars of the later nineteenth century. Preoccupied with the establishment of a new society, Westerners were largely indifferent to the ebb and flow of European politics, and felt a sense of security contributed to by physical isolation. Even during the naval construction race, the escalating rivalry between Britain and Germany received little attention. The only possible enemy that Canada might have to face was the United States and–since 1914 marked the anniversary of one hundred years of peace with the Americans–no Westerner took that thought seriously. Even the diplomatic crisis touched off by the assassination of Austrian Archduke Ferdinand brought no awareness of a potential European conflagration. The reaction of Manitoba's *Dauphin Herald* to the news was typical. The fate of Ferdinand and his wife was relegated to page four, and reported in a few lines without a headline. "European royalty leads the strenuous life," joked the *Herald.* "This week the crown prince and princess of Austria met their deaths by assassination." "There never has been a time when prophets have not foreseen a conflict that was to deluge the world with blood," commented the *Saskatoon Phoenix* in an editorial entitled "the Wail of the Jingo." "Generation after generation has listened to these predictions of the final Armageddon....International combinations break up, and new ones are formed, and the jingoes find fresh material for their lugubrious diversions. It is sheer stupidity."[12]

Because of their conviction that they faced no danger, Westerners had been for the most part resolutely opposed to any attempts to provide for Canada's defence. "Defence against what?" asked those who disagreed with the proposed contribution of dreadnoughts to the Royal Navy, or who annually denounced the amount and purpose of the expenditures of the Department of Militia. Paul F. Sharp has suggested that Western Canadians took this stand because of a resolute anti-militarism, and because "farmers on the Canadian Prairies were often as isolationist in sentiment as their cousins in the American Middle West." This characterization is perhaps overdrawn. Despite Sharp's claim to the contrary, few Westerners played a prominent role in the peace movements of the pre-war period.[13] Most Western complaints about things war-like tended to be pacifism of the pocketbook as much as of principle. Arguments were based on the theme that war "would cost untold millions of money" and cause "an unprecedented financial panic" more than on the fact that it would also cost "thousands of lives." It was the "incubus of militarism," wrote one Western editor, that was curbing Western development. Money spent for armaments might be better spent on such things as education. "Do you know," said Professor Mack Eastman to the convention of the United Farmers of Alberta, "that one discharge of a big gun costs as much as a four year university course?"[14]

When militarism and the purchase of armaments were being criticized, a sort of selective schizophrenia evidenced itself. European nations, especially Great Britain, were urged to drop out of the arms race, and Sam Hughes was vilified annually when his militia estimates were presented in the Commons. But the local representatives of militarism–the militia, the cadets or even the Boy Scouts–were not usually subjected to the same treatment. The same editor who complained that Canada's large militia was merely a temptation to go to war could describe in glowing terms a church parade of the local cavalry squadron, or devote a long article to the Boy Scouts' celebration of Victoria Day,

> ...not the least interesting feature of which was the forming and marching of the girl guides, scouts, and school children. The Citizens' Band was to the fore with proper martial music and the scouts assisted with bugle band and fife and drum. The scene was an inspiring one as the several hundred young people neatly dressed marched in time to the music. It is a hopeful sign when any town can turn out such a fine, healthy and promising aggregation...[15]

There is no evidence to suggest that militia units were any less popular in the West than elsewhere in Canada. The cadet branch was in fact more popular than in the other provinces. Manitoba led the country in the percentage of its school children enrolled in cadet corps, and Alberta was a close second. In Alberta school inspector J.T. Ross reported in 1914 that the cadet movement had made a "marked advance" during the year. The summer of 1914 also saw a large and enthusiastic turnout at the cadet camps held in the Prairie Provinces. Eighty-seven boys went from the Swift Current area to the Saskatchewan camp at Fort Qu'Appelle, and the local newspaper sponsored a contest for the best essay describing life at camp.[16] Thus "indifferent" is probably the best word to describe Western attitudes to the world crisis brewing in the Balkans. Rather than being resolute pacifists, most Westerners were simply preoccupied with their own lives and their own problems.

Even as war became imminent, they retained this preoccupation. Rather than tell its readers of Sarajevo's implications, the Cypress River *Western Prairie* warned them instead to tether their cattle, to ensure "less danger of the contamination of the milk from eating and drinking from garbage pails and slop barrels" as well as "a very decided improvement in the appearance of the sidewalks." Even in urban centres like Saskatoon, the activities

Boy Scout camp, summer 1914.
Foote Collection, Manitoba Archives.

of Western Canadians on the holiday Monday before war was declared displayed no awareness that their attention might suddenly be turned outwards. At the ballfield a large crowd had gathered to watch Sammy Beer, leading pitcher in the Western Canada League, try for his thirteenth consecutive win against arch-rival Regina, but the Regina hitters were not the only people in Saskatoon facing Beer that afternoon. On Third Avenue, in a grey stone church, a "Banish the Bar" convention had assembled to hear W.W. Buchanan of the Manitoba Social Service Council report on the progress of the prohibitionist cause in his home province. At the Exhibition Grounds the opening day of the Exhibition was declared a success, despite drizzling rain and a cold wind which reduced the attendance. The opening addresses of Premier Walter Scott and Lieutenant Governor George Brown both concerned the importance of agriculture to the development of Saskatchewan, a topic that was politically safe even if not very exciting. If either provincial statesman considered a European war a possibility, no hint entered his address that might spoil the fair-goers' afternoon.[17]

News that the Empire was at war reached Western Canada early the next day, touching off enthusiastic demonstrations of patriotism. Cities and towns expressed their loyalty with a series of spontaneous parades and band concerts, and an abundance of Union Jack waving. Despite the West's economic plight, provincial and municipal governments made flamboyant gestures in support of the Imperial war effort. Alberta was the first Canadian province to respond, contributing 500,000 bushels of oats. Manitoba and Saskatchewan followed with gifts of 50,000 bags of flour and 1,500 horses respectively. Both the dominion and imperial governments were somewhat overwhelmed by this largess, asking how and at whose expense the gifts were to be transported. Alberta was offended when its oats were not accepted for a week, and Manitoba was asked to withhold its flour until it was formally requested. These minor adjustments failed to cool Western ardour. Municipal councils passed resolutions of support for the imperial cause, and the city of Calgary went so far as to offer to equip a battalion of infantry. The city withdrew its offer, however, when the city fathers discovered the enormous costs involved.[18]

The city dailies went into second and third editions, printing preposterous stories of imaginary engagements. The war news that the Canadian public received from the press during the first week of war was little more than cheap sensationalism. Several papers printed reports of a full-scale naval engagement in the North Sea between the German and British fleets. Others brought the war closer to home with a "Mysterious Airship" that threatened Ottawa, or German warships shelling Cape Breton Island. The *Saskatoon Phoenix*, supposedly disgusted by such fabrications, demanded from the dominion government "a censorship which protects the people from disquieting stories which have no foundation in fact." In the same edition, however, it reported another gigantic naval battle in the North Sea![19]

These fantastic news reports were accepted–or at least not challenged–because few Canadians had any firm idea as to what direction the war was likely to take. The prevailing impression was that it would be a war of movement, swift offensives and counterthrusts, and that it would be over in a matter of months, possibly even weeks. War, after all, was too expensive to be engaged in for long periods, and if a military decision were not reached in a short time the combatants would be forced by financial necessity to terminate hostilities.[20] Men leaving their jobs to enlist expected in most cases to be back at work shortly after the new year. Professor A.C. Rankin of the University of Alberta requested a three months' leave of absence from President Tory for his war service.[21] For those inclined to wager, Lloyds of London set odds at even money that the war would be over by December 31.

Because most Canadians expected a short and decisive war, there was no realization of the role that Canada might be called upon to play. There was a general hope in the West that the war would stimulate the world demand for agricultural products. One Winnipeg lawyer confided to his partner, the Attorney-General of Manitoba, that he saw no way in which the West could "be prevented from being made prosperous to some extent by the misfortunes of countries that are actually at war."[22] The West was eager to take advantage of this opportunity to act as breadbasket to the Allied nations, but almost no one expected Canadians to take any significant part in the military struggle. Those who rushed for places in the first Canadian contingent worried lest the war end before they could take their places on the battlefield. One trooper wrote home to Manitoba from Valcartier to suggest that "some check be put on the slaughter of Germans until the Canadians are allowed to get on European soil." He recommended "game laws" which would restrict "holders of the British license" to killing one hundred of the enemy a day, with "no more than ten German prisoners to be in his possession at any one time."[23] The more realistic criticized this kind of attitude. "The people are blinded, absolutely blinded, as to what war means" editorialized the Winnipeg labour weekly *The Voice* early in August. "Those of the great majority think that it is brass bands, braid and feathers, and the throwing out of the chest, but if you have ever seen the regiments of militia on parade you will notice that the stretcher-bearer section is there."

But if Western Canada's potential soldiers had noticed the medical section, they managed to overcome their fear. A rush of eager recruits stormed the armouries, scrambling for places in battalions headed for France. Their precise motivation is impossible to determine. Viewed in terms of the West's pre-war indifference to international affairs, it is difficult to accept the arguments of those who suggest that the high rate of Western enlistments was the result of "an outpouring of the spirit of generosity and of sacrifice."[24] In an examination of the men who enlisted in the West during the first weeks of war, two facts stand out. First, a large percentage of the Westerners in the first contingent of the Canadian Expeditionary Force were men who had been born in the British Isles. Each recruit's attestation form asked for his birthplace, and the information thus yielded soon made this fact apparent. The first group of sixty-eight from the Swift Current area, for example, contained sixty-three who were British-born. The Eleventh Battalion, recruited in Manitoba and Saskatchewan later that winter, had only 250 native Canadians compared with 874 born in the British Isles. One recruit later described his battalion. "Few of us had any relatives there; the majority of us were Britishers who had left the old country to try our luck in the new land; many of us were veterans of other wars who wanted to get into the game again."[25]

The same recruit attributed the urge to join the army to "ardent patriotism for the old flag," but a second factor was as strong or stronger. Most British immigrants had indeed come to Canada to "try their luck," and for most of them that luck was bad in 1914. Those who had homesteaded faced crop failures or low prices, those who were tradesmen a hard winter of unemployment. The immediate effect of war was to create a financial uncertainty which exacerbated the already difficult economic situation. As the summer construction season drew to a close, what was derisively referred to as "hungerscription" proved one of the CEF's most effective recruiting sergeants. An unemployed worker who became a soldier had not only the promise of a trip to Britain and $1.10 a day all found, but a source of support for his wife and children if he were a family man. The severity of the unemployment situation produced demands that the government use the army as a source of at least temporary employment. This idea made strange bedfellows of Manitoba's Premier R.P. Roblin and the Manitoba labour movement, as both called for intensified recruiting "to relieve the distress of many and insure the keep of those who are practically broke." "If this were done," wrote Roblin to Minister of Labour T.W. Crothers, "our unemployment question would be solved, the Empire would be strengthened, and her common foe would realize that the Dominion of Canada, especially Manitoba, is responsive to every call that is made upon her."[26]

But it would be a mistake to think that this more pragmatic reason for enlistment, or the fact that so many of Canada's first soldiers were born beyond her shores, meant that Canadians in general or Westerners in particular were unenthusiastic in their response to the war in its early stages. Western Canada's fighting men were given an enthusiastic send-off by their fellow citizens. In each community where recruits assembled before departure, farewell ceremonies assured the soldiers that nation, province, and town would join them in spirit on the firing line. The description of the "night before the volunteers went away" was an evening of excitement in dozens of Prairie centres. In Dauphin, Manitoba, for example, "A crowd of enthusiastic men, joined by a host of boys, well supplied with Union Jacks, some Belgian and some French flags, formed in procession headed by the band. Everywhere, from doors and windows, hotels and street corners, the volunteers were lustily cheered." When the procession reached the town hall, "only a small portion of the crowd" was able to get inside, so the public meeting was moved out of doors so that all could attend. Mayor Bottomly spoke, along with members of the Council, then "the boys were recipients of a box of cigars each, some wholesome advice, and heartiest congratulations." It was, said the local paper, "truly a great night in Dauphin."[27]

For the first few dizzy weeks, the war forged the Canadian people together to create a sense of unity which had never before existed. Premier Scott of Saskatchewan wrote to an Australian acquaintance that "throughout Canada, notwithstanding the very composite make up of the population, there is only one sentiment in relation to the war–everybody is enthusiastically supporting the action and policy of the Home Government."[28] The most remarkable evidence of Scott's contention was the ceasefire that was declared on the domestic political front. Not only were Canadians of all regions and political colours supporting the policy of the "Home" government, they supported the war policy of the Borden government as well. It would have been political suicide for the Liberal opposition to have done otherwise, and its members recognized this fact. J.W. Dafoe, the West's most influential Liberal editor, urged that "the politicians be removed to the back of the stage, out of sound and hearing" so that Canada could present "an unbroken front." Politicians largely conformed to Dafoe's suggestion, in some cases, one suspects, more from a sense of political reality than a sense of patriotism.[29]

The political truce, which reflected the unity of the nation, was very much in evidence during the special session of parliament which was called in late August to set Canada upon a war footing. Only four Western members spoke during the short session, which passed the War Measures Act as well as a supplementary budget that increased the general tariff level to help finance Canada's contribution. Only Michael Clark, the irrepressible free-trader from Red Deer, was prepared to take a pot shot at the tariff increase, asking instead that Finance Minister White introduce "a good fat tax on incomes." But Clark made it plain later in his speech that, as far as he and the rest of the Western members were concerned, "the measures taken by the Canadian Government up to the present moment in this crisis have been characterized by wisdom, energy, and effectiveness." This was due, Clark said, to the fact that Canadians were no longer divided but were "today acting as one man." How long could such unanimity continue? Clark's leader, Sir Wilfrid Laurier, promised on behalf of his party that the Liberals would "raise no question,...take no exception,...offer no criticism, so long as there is danger on the front."[30] Most Westerners shared his determination. But then, they thought that it was going to be a short war.

CHAPTER TWO

Democracy and Empire: Mobilizing the West for War 1914-1917

I

In retrospect, Michael Clark's comment that Canadians were "acting as one man" in August 1914 might seem to have been an exaggeration. "National unity" is a preoccupation of Canadian historians, and because the controversy surrounding conscription did so much to disturb that always fragile structure it is easy to forget the way in which the outbreak of war created a national consensus of unusual solidarity. More often overlooked is the durability of that consensus for English Canada. Canada, as we are fond of reminding ourselves, is too diverse ever to manifest the sort of nationalism that saw the nations of Europe through the Great War and contributed so much to its occurrence. Nationalism based on faith, race, language, geography, or even on economic interest cannot flourish in the face of the contradictions within Canadian society. The largest of these contradictions is Canada's pluralistic culture, a product of the "primary antithesis" of French and English acting in combination with the effects of large-scale immigration. But the English-Canadian majority itself has barriers which divide it; barriers of region and barriers of economic class, and in 1914 these barriers had been made higher by the inequalities fostered by the National Policy.

Thus the most remarkable fact about Canadian participation in the Great War should not be the divisions which rent Canadian society at war's end, but the degree of unity which was maintained throughout most of the conflict. During fifty months of fighting, most national antagonisms remained at the simmer, and were kept there by a conviction that the war had to be pursued to a successful conclusion. This conviction did not extend to all Canadians for the entire period of the war. French Canada opposed the vigour of the war effort when one of its consequences proved

27

to be conscription. The immigrant minorities concentrated in Western Canada probably felt the same way, although no one consulted them as to their opinion, and they wisely kept that opinion to themselves.[1] English Canadians, however, overcame their regional and class differences to unite in support of the war effort. They did this despite frequent distaste for the Borden government and its domestic policies, and without giving up the right to criticize the way in which Canada made war. But English Canada's criticism of the war effort never demanded that participation should slacken or cease. Instead it took the form of demands that Canada make war more fiercely.

How did English Canadians, particularly those in the West, come to a consensus about the Great War? What made them feel sufficient commitment to create an army of 500,000 men, and to attempt to maintain this army with a policy of conscription which they knew would seriously alienate French Canada? Why did they later tolerate government which was arbitrary and inefficient, all in the name of "winning the war"? The answers can be found in the way in which English Canadians explained the Great War to themselves.

The initial explanation of Canada's involvement was to identify participation in the war as part of the duty owed to the Empire, a reiteration of Laurier's dictum that "when Britain is at war, Canada is at war." This was an accurate assessment of the constitutional situation but English Canadian sentiment went far beyond constitutional compulsion. Even in the polyglot West, a majority was British-born or of British descent. These Canadians felt what Carl Berger has called the "Sense of Power" and, when Britain declared war, answered with an unquestioning enthusiasm almost like that felt in England itself. Some of these people made no distinction between Canadian and Briton, but thought of themselves as citizens of Empire. Arthur Lower remembers that when he enlisted in the Naval Reserve he "had little or no sense of separation from Great Britain, with which, as one of the 'cubs of the lion,' I identified myself." The refrain of a Canadian wartime song captures this feeling:

From England and Scotland,
From Ireland and Wales,
They rally to the standard,
Firm till the right prevails.
From overseas Dominions,
From lands both far and near,

They rush to serve their Empire,
For duty's voice they hear.

The lyricist entitled his song "Sons of the British Empire Unite–Your Country is Calling," demonstrating the way in which "British Empire" and "Country" could be synonymous.[2]

To even the most ardent imperialist, however, it was important that the Empire's cause be just; that Britain fought, as the song put it, to see that "the right prevails." After the first few moments of patriotic enthusiasm, those who wanted Canada to fight because of her imperial duty were careful to demonstrate that Britain was a blameless victim of the perfidious aggression of Germany, and that she had been reluctantly forced into war. In its resolution of support for the war, the City Council of Winnipeg brought together the themes of Canada's imperial duty and Britain's high moral purpose. Canada was going to fight, said the Council, because she was "an integral part of the British Empire...bound by the closest ties of blood and tradition to the Mother Country" which had been "reluctantly forced into war in defence of her most sacred treaty obligations."[3]

It was equally important to distinguish between this war and other British wars, which might perhaps have been less worthy of Canada's support. "There may have been wars in the history of the British Empire that have not been justifiable," admitted the Reverend Canon Murray to the Winnipeg Canadian Club, "but this is a war into which everyone can go with a clean conscience." After an examination of the various explanations of the war's beginnings, Saskatchewan's Premier, Walter Scott, concluded that it should be "a great satisfaction to every Britisher to be able to feel complete assurance of the fact that we are not the aggressors, and that we could not have kept free from the war and retained our self respect."[4]

But many Canadians, particularly those in the West, found this interpretation of Canada as a junior Britain an unsatisfactory explanation for a war effort which required the almost total commitment of Canadian resources. This did not imply any lack of affection for Britain or for Empire, but a different conception of Canada, and a Canadian nationalism different from the surrogate nationalism of British imperialism. The people who held this conception argued that Canada was fighting for herself and for "civilization" in the Great War, since the Central Powers, in particular Germany, represented a threat to Canada's "most cherished institutions and [to] our dearest principles." This phrase was part of an editorial written by the editor of the University of Saskatchewan's newspaper *The Sheaf*, shortly after he enlisted.[5] Another Westerner to voice this view was novelist and minister C.W. Gordon. As "Ralph Connor" he used his war-time novels to propagate this vision of Canada's role in the war. In *The Sky Pilot in No Man's Land*, an English naval officer suggests to the soldiers of a Canadian battalion *en route* to France that their enlistment represented an answer to "the call of the blood." The battalion's medical officer, significantly identified as an Albertan, replies quickly that "there is something more."

> Frankly, my opinion is that the biggest thing, sir, with some of us in Canada is not that the motherland is in need of help, though, of course, we all feel that, but that the freedom of the world is threatened, and that Canada, as one of the free nations of the world, must do her part in its defence.[6]

This was the "cherished institution" of which the editor of *The Sheaf* spoke, described sometimes as "the freedom of the world," sometimes as "liberty and justice," but most often by the single word "democracy." Three years before President Wilson told Americans that they were entering the war to "make the world safe for democracy," the word was used to explain Canada's role in the Great War. "Democracy" was a word into which the people of the West could sink their teeth, teeth cut on direct legislation, the initiative, referendum, and recall. "Democracy" was what the farm organizations were going to use to confront the "big vested interests," and the prohibitionists to crush liquor. It was a concept used to explain the need to assimilate the immigrant, and to justify the need for unilingual education.[7] What better reason to fight a war?

A few voices observed hesitantly that Russia, Canada's ally, was less democratic than Germany, or that "no people has yet been clubbed into democracy."[8] But press, platform, and pulpit rang with the assurance that the war, far from being "the effervescence of jingoism," was "for the maintenance of [the] principles of liberty, fraternity, and equality. The mailed fist of Germany symbolizes the autocratic power wielded by its war lord, which brooks no interference from the common people. Government of the people, by the people, for the people will receive such a staggering blow should the Kaiser's legions triumph, that it will take at least a century to bind up its limbs and set it on its feet again." It was this image of the Great War that captured the imagination of the West and rallied it behind the war effort under the banner of democracy. As Calgary's *Alberta Non Partisan* concluded at war's end, Westerners "would not have responded to fight an aggressive war, but they did respond for a great ideal–democracy."[9]

This theme of a war for democracy was elastic enough to encompass minorities like Scandinavians, Icelanders, and Americans, who felt no affection for Britain, and sometimes expressed actual hostility to the Empire while supporting Canadian participation in the war. One American, an Alberta cattle dealer, wrote Clifford Sifton praising Canada's war effort and hoping that it would have the effect of "consigning all crowns to the junkheap." The hero of an Icelandic-Canadian novel written during the war decides that because "this is a war to stay the tyrant nations, a war to make the world, to make Canada, safe for democracy,...We must do more than be loyal. I am going to enlist."[10]

As the war entered its second year, the argument that democracy was Canada's war aim superseded and eventually absorbed the idea that Canada fought as a dutiful daughter of Empire. "The British Empire is not an Empire," said the Reverend Salem Bland to the People's Forum in Winnipeg. "The British Empire is a federation, a sisterhood of nations, every one of them standing upon exactly the same plane as the mother nation herself." Even if it were an Empire it was compatible with the ideals of democracy, since "Empire to Britain means a system that gives to peoples of the most diverse race, color and civilization peace, unity, freedom. The watchword of the British Empire...is liberty." "It is because England is a great democracy that she became the mother of such countries as Canada," explained the *Western School Journal* on its children's page. "Now these countries have become the grown up children of the great mother they are each little democracies themselves....All our allies hope that when the war is over Germany will become a democracy, so that the people may rule themselves, instead of being ruled by a wicked Emperor."[11]

This view of the Great War as a struggle for democracy, when combined with an understanding of the British Empire as a voluntary association of independent democracies, had an important corollary which was eventually to become the source of domestic turmoil between French and English. John W. Dafoe, who accepted both these premises, put this corollary into words: "Canada is in the war as a principal, not as a colony," he wrote in August 1917. To those who accepted this point of view, it meant a total commitment of Canadian resources, both material and human, to the goal of victory. "Canada has as much right to use every resource in her power to prosecute this war to a successful conclusion as has any other power engaged in it," said D.B. Neely, Liberal MP for Humboldt, Saskatchewan. R.C. Henders, President of the Manitoba Grain Growers, told that Association's 1917 convention that the duty of Canadians "was plain. We must put into the war men and money until we see the triumph of the principles we so highly prize." C.W. Gordon gave this sentiment its classic expression. "Canada is committed to this world conflict," he said in his speeches, "to her last man and her last dollar."[12]

This "last man, last dollar" argument became the intellectual justification for conscription and the income tax, and was repeated again and again in different ways. However it was phrased, it signified a resolution from which few English Canadians could be shaken. As casualties mounted and the list of Canadian battle honours grew longer, it was a determination which grew more intense. The heroism of Canada's soldiers obscured the strategic paralysis of the Allied high command, and in the triumphs of Vimy Ridge and Hill 70, English Canadians drew together emotionally as their young nation reached its fiftieth birthday. The achievement of the Canadian Expeditionary Force provided English Canadians with both an international identity and a collective national tradition which made them "feel inches bigger around the chest," and they were at first oblivious to and later furious at the fact that French Canada was unable to share their vision.[13]

The analogy of a lion and her pride was overworked to describe Canada's new maturity. "Canada may have been one of the cubs of the old lion," wrote an Albertan to Walter Scott, "but it looks to me as though she [is] now very much of a lion herself." Clifford Sifton was one of many to describe the war as baptism "into nationhood with the blood of our sons...shed in the greatest struggle the world has ever seen and in the noblest cause for which men have ever fought."[14] Robert Stead put Canada's "coming of age" into verse.

Youth must lean on the mother's arm
   and obey the mother's will.
But manhood faces the world alone,
And bends its ways till they fit his own.
Yet manhood honors his mother's name
   and loves his mother still.[15]

In whatever terms it was described, English Canada was becoming a nation, welded together by her struggle with the enemy.

The remarks quoted above to illustrate the conception which English Canadians–particularly Westerners–had of the Great War were public and private statements selected from speeches, sermons, letters, newspaper editorials, magazines, novels, poems, and even from a popular song. But what did other residents of the West think when they heard such statements? Did they consider them reflective of their own thoughts? How often and from whom did they hear such words, and were they made by people most Westerners were likely to respect or to agree with?

The first question is difficult, perhaps impossible, to answer in any definite way. The concept of a "climate of opinion" can be valid if carefully qualified, and the illustrations chosen from popular culture probably allow the historian to come as close as he can to the elusive public mind. Russel B. Nye argues that "popular art has been an unusually sensitive and accurate reflector of the attitude and concerns of the society for which it is produced," and the comments of editors, poets, and novelists substantially agree with those of the politicians and churchmen.[16] The second question can be answered with more precision. It is possible to examine the way in which the war effort was officially publicized, and from such an examination draw conclusions about support for the war effort itself.

The Great War was *total* war, in the sense that it involved the efforts of entire populations as well as fleets and armies, to a degree which had never before been experienced. As such, it would have been difficult to conduct the war without some considerable degree of enthusiasm even in those countries lacking representative institutions. In Canada, it would have been impossible. The Great War, argues English historian J.M. Roberts, was "the most popular war in history when it started," and most governments took full advantage of this situation. But to maintain this public support, governments had to nurture it carefully, and fertilize it when it showed signs of languishing. For this reason, the Great War was the first war to be fought extensively with words as weapons, and the first in which propaganda was generally employed.[17]

Propaganda is "the management of opinions and attitudes by the direct manipulation of social suggestion," and the Great War became a propagandist's paradise.[18] Mass literacy was the rule in most of the combatant nations, but civilian populations were unprepared to deal skeptically with propaganda. The means available to spread information were efficient, yet sufficiently limited to permit reasonably effective control if such a thing were attempted. A successful propaganda machine has two functions. The first is the negative one of censorship, of ensuring that the flow of information to the public is regulated in such a way as to prevent the dissemination of information which might contradict official statements or lower public morale. The second function is the circulation of favourable information, either real or fabricated. In Great Britain and the United States, these functions of wartime propaganda were skilfully carried out.[19] In Canada, however, government attempts at publicizing the war effort were badly organized and unco-ordinated, and no sophisticated techniques were adopted to achieve "direct manipulation of social suggestion."

Following Britain's lead, Canada divided the work of censorship and propaganda creation. As Press Censor the government chose an old militia man with a background in journalism, Col. Ernest J. Chambers. Also following the British pattern, Canadian press censorship was voluntary. An order-in-council issued under the power of the War Measures Act gave Chambers authority to prosecute violations of his censorship code, but he could take no action until the damaging material had been printed, then submitted to him for examination. Not surprisingly, this system was ineffective. Editors were eager to let their readers know what local battalions were doing, and published such information when they could obtain it, despite Chambers' protests that these were "clear contraventions of the Censorship Regulations."[20] A more important form of censorship on Canadian news of the war was that imposed by British authorities, through whose hands all Canadian war news passed, but before the United States entered the war, American newspapers were able to publish uncensored articles which sometimes contradicted the official British reports. For this reason, the Borden government banned the circulation of some American papers in Canada, notably those of the Hearst chain.

As inefficient as the censorship arm of Canadian propaganda was, its second part, the machinery for creating and distributing propaganda, was even more haphazard. Until the office of Director of Public Information was created in November, 1917, there was no co-ordinated, officially sponsored attempt to create and distribute either favourable information about Canada and her allies, or to create and distribute information intended to arouse Canadians against the enemy. Despite criticism, during the first three years of war the Borden government hesitated to involve itself in programs designed to mobilize public opinion. In February, 1915, for example, H.B. Ames proposed that a "Speakers Patriotic League" be organized on a nation-wide basis to promote the war and recruiting. Patterned after the Parliamentary Recruiting Committee in Great Britain, the proposed League would use volunteers to deliver short prepared speeches in movie theatres and concert halls. The only government participation requested was a small budget for reproduction of posters. Borden dealt with the request personally, and declined even this small commitment. In a similar fashion, the government refused to take advantage of an opportunity to present official speakers at the showing of war newsreels.[21]

This reluctance to inflame public opinion was perhaps the result of the government's feeling that its problem in 1915 and 1916 was keeping public enthusiasm within bounds. But when attempts were made to influence the public, the government was fortunate to have virtually at its disposal both a ready-made supply of propaganda and an enthusiastic, though informal, collection of propagandists. The propagandists were private citizens who had permanent contact with the public: clergymen, newspaper editors, and school and university teachers. The propaganda was created in Britain. The Canadian government acted as a clearing house for information, purchasing British pamphlets in volume and then distributing them to churches, to newspapers, and to provincial departments of education.

The best example of this system in operation is the circulation of the *Report of the Committee on Alleged German Outrages*, usually referred to as the Bryce Report. It was prepared by a committee chaired by Viscount Bryce, chosen deliberately for his popularity in the United States, and including among its six members historians Sir Frederick Pollock and H.A.L. Fisher. It is a brilliant work of propaganda, written in a reserved, scholarly fashion that makes the accounts of the "atrocities" it discusses seem all the more horrible. After sixty pages of them the *Report* solemnly concludes that the committee members,

> Sensible as they are of the gravity of these conclusions,...conceive that they would be doing less than their duty if they failed to record them as fully established by the evidence. Murder, lust, and pillage prevailed over many parts of Belgium on a scale unparalleled in any war between civilized nations in the last three centuries.

The committee went further. "Our function is ended when we have stated what the evidence establishes" they wrote, "but we may be permitted to express our belief that these disclosures will not have been made in vain if they touch and rouse the conscience of mankind...."[22]

The investigation which resulted in the Bryce Report was begun at the initiative of the British propaganda office at Wellington House, and most of its conclusions came from depositions which subsequently disappeared before they could be made available to inquiring scholars. These facts were unknown to both the Canadian public and its government, however. Released the week after the Lusitania was torpedoed, the report was "one of the triumphs of the war" for British propaganda. Its conclusions made a dramatic impact in Britain and Canada, and helped turn American sympathy toward the Allies. "Wrists of Wounded Slashed with Bayonets," "Tetanus in German Shells," "Robbed the Dead Belgians," "Germans' Wanton Disregard for Life," were the headlines editors chose for their excerpts from the Bryce Report.[23]

By the autumn of 1915, these "atrocity stories" had faded from page one, but their potential usefulness was as great as ever. In March 1916 a suggestion that the Bryce Report be revived came from Thomas Mulvey, Canadian undersecretary of state. In a memo to Secretary of State P.E. Blondin, Mulvey pointed out the report was no longer known to "the bulk of the community," and that "no document...so clearly shows the necessity of straining every resource to win in the war." Blondin agreed, and recommended to the cabinet that the report be purchased in volume and "widely circulated...through the Education Departments of the Provinces, going to schools and teachers, to the universities and colleges, and generally to the press." Cabinet decided unanimously to accept this advice. The result was a second wave of "atrocity stories" based on the Report, some papers gratefully acknowledging the government's assistance in making the material available.[24]

The effect of the "atrocities" on English Canada's view of the War cannot be overestimated. In the words of a contemporary observer, these macabre tales "had a direct influence upon the action of Canada. They put fire into the articles and speeches and sermons; they became part of the material used by the recruiting officers." As well they changed Western Canada's attitude to its German minority. Most important, they helped bring about the redefinition of Canada's role in the war as that of a "principal," since they demonstrated that the CEF in Flanders was "defending civilization from this ghastly thing which threatened her."[25]

II

The limited nature of the Borden government's propaganda efforts during the first three years of war is a comment on the inability of Canadian government to change to meet the wartime situation. But it also demonstrated that public support for the Great War needed little formal stimulation. One reason for this was the unofficial stimulation it received from the agencies the government used to publicize the Bryce Report, particularly the schools and the Protestant churches. Both made a valuable contribution to the arousal and maintenance of public enthusiasm and aided recruiting.

The enthusiastic support of churches for the Great War was common to all participating nations. In the West as in the rest of Canada, the most vigorous work on behalf of the war effort came from the three largest Protestant denominations, the Anglicans, the Methodists, and the Presbyterians. The Church of England's position on the war was determined by its imperial inheritance, but Methodism and Presbyterianism had a background of rhetorical pacifism. This pacifist rhetoric, however, was tempered by a record of continuous support of British wars. More significant, the Great War came at a time when both these churches were becoming increasingly influenced by the theology of the Social Gospel. The Social Gospel's objective was the creation of God's Kingdom on earth, and it was certainly difficult to accomplish this without first defeating Germany and the Central Powers. "In essentials," writes Richard Allen, "the war seemed an extension of the Social Service Congress." Michael Bliss argues that the Methodist reaction to war was not a function of the influence of the Social Gospel, but rather a continuation of traditional Methodist social concern in combination with emerging English-Canadian nationalism. Whatever the reason, Methodists, Anglicans, and Presbyterians came to regard the war as "pre-eminently a religious one" in which Canadians were "fighting for Christ."[26]

The most spectacular of the contributions made by these churches was to the search for soldiers for the CEF. In some cases, clergymen were employed directly by the government as recruiting officers. More widespread, however, was the tendency of individual ministers to take it upon themselves to help out. In

December, 1914, for example, the *Dauphin Herald*'s "Church Chimes" column announced that "Recruiting in Dauphin" would be the topic of the Methodist minister's Sunday sermon. "This will suggest," observed the *Herald*, "the contribution of the Protestant Churches." C.W. Gordon, himself a Presbyterian minister, has provided us with an example of what such a sermon might have been like. In *The Sky Pilot in No Man's Land*, Rev. Barry Dunbar tells the men of an Edmonton congregation that "it is a war of souls, but the method of settlement is not that of reason but of force – a force that finds expression through your bodies. Offer your bodies – these living bodies – these sacred bodies – offer them in sacrifice to God." In addition to this support for recruiting, the churches co-operated with the dominion government in propagandizing food and fuel conservation, urged their members to purchase Victory Bonds, and in 1918 provided speakers for the War Lecture Series created by the Director of Public Information.[27]

There was little internal dissension within the Protestant churches with regard to their positions on the Great War. The attitude of J.S. Woodsworth, and his resignation from the ministry, have received considerable attention, but Woodsworth and William Ivens were the only Western clergymen of note to break with their churches during the war. Salem Bland, Western Canada's most popular and outspoken exponent of the Social Gospel, was an enthusiastic supporter of the Great War, of conscription, and of Union Government.[28]

Interestingly, support for Canadian participation in the war induced Salem Bland on one occasion to make peace with a bitter antagonist within the Methodist Church, J.E. Hughson. In October, 1915, the two set aside their differences long enough to co-sign a letter to Prime Minister Robert Borden. The letter strongly demanded that the "military efforts of Canada should be very greatly increased and a much more extensive and vigorous recruiting propaganda should be instituted."[29]

The Roman Catholic Church never opposed Canada's participation in the war but withheld the unequivocal support tendered by Canadian Protestantism. This attitude is not difficult to understand since many of its communicants were French Canadians or, particularly in the West, non-English-speaking immigrants. Roman Catholicism found itself under criticism for this comparative lack of enthusiasm and Protestant editorialists noted that Catholic Quebec had contributed less than her "share" to the army and accused the Knights of Columbus of being "peacock feather patriots" when compared with the Masonic Lodge.[30] This antagonism, aroused early in the war, would play an important part in the West's response to the question of conscription.

Second in importance only to the Protestant churches as cornerstones of Canada's war effort were the schools and universities. In each Western province, the department of education provided a medium through which three hundred thousand students and their parents could be reminded of their duty to Canada. The provincial governments co-operated with Ottawa in the distribution of the Bryce Report, and purchased and distributed other literature on their own initiative "to enable students and their parents to form a clear judgement on the issues involved."[31] Since the pamphlets distributed were such works as Sir Edward Cook's *Why Britain is at War*, which concluded with the statement that war had been caused "by the determination of Austria to apply brute force against the independence of a small state in South-eastern Europe" and "by the determination of Germany to ride rough-shod over the neutrality of a small state in North-western Europe," it is doubtful if much discussion was required before the desired "clear judgements" were made.

In 1917 the Saskatchewan Department of Education produced its own pamphlet. Canada's *Golden Jubilee of Confederation*, by George M. Weir, was presented to every public school student to commemorate the fiftieth anniversary of Confederation. The booklet was prefaced with messages from Lieutenant Governor R.S. Lake and Premier W.M. Martin reminding the school children that they had "great national duties" because "it is in the defence of the weak and oppressed that the people of Canada are today fighting." But the role of the departments did not stop with the distribution of literature. Weir's pamphlet was accompanied by a letter to each teacher from the deputy minister of education, emphasizing that "at this time of stress in our national life too much prominence cannot be given in your teaching to the event that made it possible for us to take our place as a united Canada...in this great world struggle." In Manitoba the Department of Education's Grade XI English Composition examination for 1917 had as a compulsory question the framing of two paragraphs on the subject "Canada and the War." To provide guidance for teachers, the Department supplied them with this suggested answer: "The Great War is being fought in the cause of liberty. On the one side the War may be called a war for conquest or plunder and on the other a war for freedom or liberty. It is not

Interior of a rural school, Milo, Alberta, 1914.
Glenbow-Alberta Institute, Calgary, Alberta.

the safety of one state or nation that is at stake, it is the freedom of the world."[32]

Most teachers did not need such departmental prodding, and some created their own techniques to make children and the community aware of wartime issues. A Manitoba teacher wrote and produced a musical playlet which enabled her class to act out for their parents and relatives an impression of Canada's role in the Great War. In the finale, nine boys with wooden rifles, each representing one of the provinces, stepped out from offstage to salute "Canada," played, the stage directions suggested, by "a taller girl." The line of boys then marched forward singing:

Ye sons of Canada awake
The Star of morn has left the sky
Your father's flag of Liberty,
That glorious banner floats on high.
But see, the foeman draweth nigh,
To steal the rights your sires have won
Awake! my sons, drive back the Hun...

The war even found its way into arithmetic class, when students were asked to calculate the returns on Victory Bonds. One patriotic pedagogue invented an "Arithmetic War," in which "the children's names are entered and are ranked as privates. Every arithmetic problem solved correctly is a German prisoner captured. When thirty prisoners are taken, the private is given a promotion, thus being promoted until he has reached the highest position." Provincial departments of education supported the initiative of teachers who were especially patriotic. When parents of Blaine Lake, Saskatchewan School Division, complained that their children were being forced to learn patriotic songs, the deputy minister of education informed them that "the singing of Patriotic Songs in our Public Schools is not approved but *encouraged* by the Department."[33]

Few voices were raised in protest against this use of the public school to disseminate propaganda. The children themselves seem to have enjoyed fighting the war in the classroom. In memoirs of childhoods in Manitoba, Saskatchewan, and Alberta, James H. Gray, Wallace Stegner, and J.G. MacGregor all speak of their school years during the Great War with nostalgic affection. Children participated in essay contests with topics like "Canada in the Present War," "Why the Empire is at War," and "Soldiers at the Front." Samples of wartime work reflect the contemporary arguments for Canadian participation. Canada was fighting because "the Germans are too greedy in this war and forgot to keep their word to the Belgians." Britain fought "not only for defence of her provinces, but also for freedom, honour, and justice." Thus spoke the prize-winning essays published in the *Western School Journal.*[34]

It was not only the public school which devoted its resources to creating national feeling during wartime. Provincial universities did their best to mobilize their own students and the population of the West. Unlike public school students, many university students were of military age and, like the churches, the universities acted as recruiting officers. Despite the fact that wholesale enlistments denuded Prairie classrooms of both teachers and students, the universities urged their students to enrol in the CEF. Those who remained behind, many of them freshmen below the required age, took the compulsory military training program which replaced athletic programs. Then, as Rev. Eber Crummy of Wesley College told Clifford Sifton, "at the end of the first year the young men reach an age at which they can enlist so that we have scarcely a young man...of sufficient age and physically fit who has not joined the forces." Eventually through the co-operation of the presidents of the three prairie public universities, volunteers were channelled into a specially created "Western Universities Battalion," the 196th. Pressure on students to enlist, both from peers and professors, was intense. One mother wrote President Walter C. Murray of the University of Saskatchewan complaining that she found it impossible to persuade her son to remain at school. The son, an agriculture student had told her that "they make you feel like two cents at the U. if you don't enlist." At the University of Manitoba the Board of Governors went so far as to withhold permission to register from any unmarried male student who could not show "satisfactory reasons why he has not enlisted for military service."[35]

Universities also provided speakers for patriotic rallies, both on an informal basis and through their departments of extension. W.A.R. Kerr of the University of Alberta informed H.B. Ames that the extension services had "largely assumed the task of providing the Patriotic Fund and Red Cross Society with lecturers and speakers designed to arouse public interest in the war." President Tory's summary of the University of Alberta's contribution, contained in a letter to a faculty member at the front, can be applied to all Western Universities.

The University assisted in recruiting and in patriotic organizations in every possible way, most of our staff spending their spare time in connection with various patriotic organizations....Some of us were out lecturing throughout the country on conditions that brought about the war and I think we did our part in bringing about the state of mind which exists in the province.[36]

Why were English-Canadian Westerners so willing to have their schools used in this manner? One reason is that most of them accepted these premises about the war. More important, however, is the fact that they wanted their public schools to become training grounds for citizenship which could be used to assimilate the children of immigrants. With this conception of the role of the school, the wartime transition to propaganda agent was accepted as nothing less than the natural function of the public school in the face of a national emergency. President Murray of the University of Saskatchewan told the graduating class of Manitoba teachers in 1917 that before the war began "the problem of racial assimilation quickened our interest in the schools as agencies for teaching patriotism and the adoption of a common language. Today the war has intensified our interest in education as a factor in nationalization." This "intensified interest" led eventually to the imposition of compulsory, unilingual education.[37]

III

Thus in the first three years of war, Western Canadians did not have to be persuaded to support the Great War by a sophisticated propaganda ministry. Pro-war propagandists emerged spontaneously at the community level, and had little convincing to do. When a Westerner heard about the issues involved in Canada's participation it was from a member of his own community, in a speech or a sermon, in a newspaper, or a novel, or even in a song. As we saw, most English Canadians in the West accepted the view of the Great War as a struggle for democracy in which Canada fought at Britain's side on a voluntary basis.

This acceptance did not mean that there was no criticism of Canada's war effort. But when it came, such criticism was aimed at strengthening the vigour of Canada's contribution, not at reducing it. For the first two years of the war the Borden government was unable to meet the demands of Westerners for places in the CEF, and Western editors, ministers, and public men demanded to know when the army would be expanded to accommodate all who wished to volunteer. A Winnipeg resident wrote that there were thousands in "the Great West who are clamouring to join the colours...but many of those eager to go, though physically fit, cannot find a place."[38] The government found itself in the position of having to restrain such enthusiasm temporarily. Borden's answer to requests that Canada's contingent overseas be greatly increased in size was that "it is much easier to propose the organization, arming, and equipment of a force of 300,000 men than to accomplish it." But requests did not stop at 300,000. As late as November, 1915, Premier T.C. Norris could tell a meeting in Winnipeg that "the easiest thing in connection with a contingent is to raise the men. Getting sufficient means to support them and those they leave behind is the big question." Not until Borden announced early in 1916 that Canada would maintain an army of 500,000 did the Western complaints stop, and Westerners pronounce the war effort in keeping with their enthusiasm for the conflict.[39]

What produced this enthusiasm among English Canadians in the West? In The Historian's Craft, Marc Bloch makes a comment which can assist in finding an explanation. Describing the way in which ideas have suddenly appeared to become forces which move men to action, Bloch uses the analogy of an infectious disease, and notes that "a contagion supposes two things: microbe multiplication, and at the moment when the disease strikes, a favourable breeding ground." In the case of Western Canada, the "microbe" was the interpretation of the Great War as a struggle for justice, liberty, and, above all, democracy. The "favourable breeding ground" was the West's own belief in the sanctity of majoritarian democracy. The resulting "contagion" was a consensus that Canada should participate actively in the war to the utmost of her abilities.

CHAPTER THREE

The War and the Prairie Economy

I

A cynical explanation of Canadian enthusiasm for the Great War would point to the fact that August 1914 found the country in the second year of a severe recession. Particularly in Western Canada, 1913 and 1914 had been difficult years marked by high unemployment in the industrial sector of the economy and drought and low prices for agriculture. Canadians were hopeful that the war would end this recession, and that Europe's calamity would be North America's economic opportunity, since the special needs of Canada's allies would stimulate a demand for Canadian products, especially wheat, and the effect of war would severely handicap some of Canada's competitors.

By 1916 it seemed to most Canadians that these hopes had been fulfilled. In a paper presented to the Royal Society, Adam Shortt reviewed the effects of previous wars upon the Canadian economy and concluded that, as in the past, the Great War meant for Canada

> ...a time of actual prosperity. The urgent demand for volunteers for overseas service has relieved the country of the threatened problem of unemployment in many urban centres, while the revival of industry in connection with the great variety of army supplies has given ample employment to all the efficient labour remaining in the country. Canada is once more profiting from a share of the thousands of millions being expended by Britain and her allies in the present struggle.[1]

Shortt's judgment has been amplified and repeated, but not substantially altered, by subsequent scholarship. Viewed from a national perspective, the stimulus provided to the economy by the Great War was remarkable. The war was responsible for "sharply rising prices of agricultural products" which encouraged an expansion of production and "lifted Canadian exports of wheat and flour, coarse grains, and cattle and meat to record highs." The war had a similar effect on the extraction of forest products and minerals. More significant, however, is the fact that "by the end of the war Canada was launched as a significant industrial nation."[2]

Although from this national perspective it is not difficult to demonstrate that the Great War brought about an acceleration of Canada's economic development, several important qualifications are necessary when the matter is viewed from a regional standpoint. While the price of all agricultural commodities soared during the war years, not all of this increase could be translated into concrete gains for the Western farmer. Because of his own cupidity and forces often beyond his control, the temporary prosperity of wartime sometimes became a cruel trick, which placed the farmer on a treadmill from which he could not escape. In the non-agricultural sector of the Prairie economy, the benefits of war were of questionable value. The assertion that "the war rapidly transformed Canada from an agricultural into an industrial nation"[3] describes the change that took place in Central Canada, but would have drawn an angry denial if it had been presented to the Board of Trade or the Trades and Labour Council of any Western city in 1919. A detailed examination of the effects of the Great War upon the economic development of Western Canada demonstrates that they were less positive than might be supposed.

What the war created in Manitoba, Saskatchewan, and Alberta—or what it intensified—was an economic development based almost exclusively on the production of one staple crop for export to an overseas market.

II

For Western Canada the Great War resulted neither in industrialization nor its concomitant, urbanization. The national statistics, heavily weighted by Ontario and Quebec, point in the direction of an urban and industrial economy, but no such change took place in the Prairie Provinces. Manitoba, Saskatchewan, and Alberta remained as rural as they had been in 1914, and actually became more agricultural. Manufacturing increased slightly in the West in the census period between 1911 and 1921, but as an employer of labour lost ground to agriculture in relative terms.[4] For Western cities, the exuberant "new Chicagos and St. Pauls" of the Laurier boom, the years of the war were almost as desperate as those of the recession which preceded it.

The pre-war recession had crippled the entire Prairie economy but its most visible manifestation was the mass of unemployed labourers who congregated in all of the Western cities. What made this high unemployment particularly frightening was the fact that, unlike what had happened after previous winters, the return of the fair weather made no appreciable reduction in the number of jobless. In May, long after spring should have removed from the streets most of those laid off for the winter, a group of the unemployed rioted in Winnipeg and were subdued by the police. The condition persisted into July, when the *Grain Grower's Guide* turned its attention from dry weather and poor wheat prices to comment on the situation in the cities. It was indeed unusual for the West to have an unemployment problem during the summer, said the *Guide*.

> It is, however, the natural result of a cause, and we have only to go back a year or two to find it. Then we had three large railway companies stretching their branches at a rapid rate....Thousands upon thousands of unskilled labourers were engaged upon this work. Today construction work of this nature is almost nil, and so these men rush to the cities.[5]

The *Guide* had pointed its editorial finger squarely at the West's problem. The prosperity of Western cities and towns before 1913 had been brought about by the creation of the infrastructure of the wheat economy, and the most important component of this infrastructure was the transportation system. Sober critics had warned that two new transcontinental railways were unnecessary, but building these roads created new towns and cities and provided existing ones with a rationale and a means for expansion. When railway construction slowed down in 1912 the effect on Western cities was sudden and serious. The new railroads were not yet completed but after years of easy borrowing the Canadian Northern and the Grand Trunk Pacific found investors unwilling to purchase their securities at any discount. The declaration of war produced conditions in the financial world that made a difficult situation an impossible one for both railways. Blaming "the war and its effect upon finance," both the CNR and the GTP were forced to borrow heavily from the government in 1915 and 1916.[6]

Little of the money thus obtained could go towards completing construction of Western branch lines; the companies needed capital to maintain existing lines and to purchase rolling stock, and could not afford to begin projected extensions or to finish lines already surveyed and graded. Railway mileage under construction in the West decreased from 3,672 miles in 1913 to 1,253 in 1914, and to 1,003 miles in 1915. Most of this mileage was "under construction" only in the sense that a contract had been let. Only 363.4 miles of track was actually laid in 1915. After a decade and a half of rapid growth, railway mileage in operation increased slightly in 1916, then declined between 1917 and 1919. The result was a reduction both in the operational work force of the railways and in the number of labourers employed by construction companies engaged in contract work. The total number of railroad employees in Canada declined from 178,652 in 1913 to 124,142 in 1915, and did not reach pre-war levels again until 1920. These layoffs were concentrated in the West, where even the lordly Canadian Pacific introduced wholesale reductions in its labour force.[7]

The resulting unemployment rebounded through the Prairie economy, and the failure to complete branch lines dashed the hopes of several smaller cities for important roles as distributing centres. Prince Albert had awaited the completion of a GTP line through Watrous, Saskatchewan, which would have provided overnight communication with Winnipeg. When the wartime shortage of capital made it a casualty, city businessmen were panic-stricken. "The completion of this line is of tremendous importance to this city" wrote a local Conservative to Prime Minister Borden. "[It] will serve thousands of settlers, and make for the opening up of large tracts of first class agricultural lands." The line was not built. Borden's reply blamed "war conditions" for the postponement of extensions on the part of the railways. After August, 1917, when the government began to assume control of the bankrupt railways, its attitude to extensions became even more cautious than that of the private companies had been.[8]

The collapse of railway construction before and during the war years was paralleled by a similar decline in the construction industry in general. Construction is an industry which experiences periodic downturns and seasonal fluctuations, and so the first reaction to the reduced activity of 1913 and 1914 was that the slowdown was temporary. During the war, however, construction activity in both the public and private sectors remained at a standstill even by comparison with the recession. The annual value of building permits issued in Brandon, Winnipeg, Moose Jaw, Regina, Saskatoon, Calgary, and Edmonton plummeted from $23 million to less than $3 million between 1914 and 1915, and remained below $6 million in each of the war years. In smaller Western centres the decline was so precipitous that the *Canada Yearbook* ceased to compile their annual totals after 1914. Prince Albert provides a startling, though not exaggerated, example. In 1912 the city issued 376 building permits with a value of $2,041,850, while four years later the 34 permits issued had a total value of only $66,855. Construction companies and suppliers of construction materials reduced staff or went out of business entirely. Charles W. Dill, Chief Engineer of the National Paving and Contracting Company, expressed the dimensions of the collapse of this industry. Writing to beg Clifford Sifton for help in obtaining government work, he accused the war of having "completely wiped out the class of work we were engaged in" and saw "no prospects of a return to good conditions" in the immediate future.[9]

III

In other parts of Canada, most notably in Ontario, the effects of the recession of 1913-14 had not been as severe as in Western Canada, but all regions of the country looked to the war as an economic stimulant which could mitigate these effects. There were four ways in which the war effort could stimulate the economy of an urban centre. First and most obvious, the city might benefit from agricultural prosperity through its role as a distributing centre for the surrounding rural area. Second, a city might be selected as a training centre for a battalion before it was sent overseas, and third, the needs of the Canadian Expeditionary Force might necessitate purchases which would stimulate production in industries which already existed in a town or city. Finally, and in the long term most important, new industrial plants might be created in response to the demand of Canada, Britain, and the Allies for munitions. For some urban centres in Ontario all of these factors operated in their favour. In the West, however, only the first two became a significant source of new economic activity.

The location of a military base in a community obviously can have a favourable effect on that community's economy. The concentration of soldiers in or near a city usually necessitates construction of facilities to house them, creates some demand for local products to feed and care for them, and results in a military payroll which will be spent with local merchants. It was inevitable that the West would become an important centre for mobilization, since one-fifth of the Canadian Army was recruited in Manitoba, Saskatchewan, and Alberta. Once recruiting started, Western towns and cities set up an undignified clamour to be chosen as training centres, a clamour which reflected their economic despair. The Winnipeg City Council wired the Minister of Militia and Defence that "Western troops should be mobilized in Winnipeg or in other towns in the West." Moose Jaw was equally direct in its request, stating simply that "considerable distress prevails in Western Canada and our merchants and citizens need all the assistance possible to pass through it." Medicine Hat demanded "special consideration" because of "drought and serious labour conditions." Edmonton offered the free use of its exhibition buildings in hopes of becoming a mobilization centre.[10]

Minister of Militia Sam Hughes found himself embroiled in an argument with Western civic officials when he thundered to the Mayor of Winnipeg in an open letter that the City Council should watch "the firing line in Europe" and ignore "the local business establishment." But despite this controversy, Western cities were treated reasonably well by Hughes' department, particularly during the winters of 1914 and 1915. When possible, troops were allowed to train in the area in which they had been recruited. The department even divided a battalion between Moose Jaw and Swift Current at the request of the local boards of trade. The department spent about $70,000 refitting buildings to accommodate troops in the Western provinces but more important was the monthly payroll spent by the soldiers themselves. The *Calgary Daily Herald* reported that in November, 1914, this amounted to $18,000 at Victoria Barracks in Calgary, and was sufficiently impressed by this figure to applaud the "untiring efforts of R.B. Bennett, K.C., M.P." in persuading the authorities to train a battalion in Calgary.[11]

With regard to the location of training facilities, Western Canada was the beneficiary of a conscious policy "to equalize the distribution of such funds and benefits throughout the whole of Canada," and Western businessmen acknowledged that "the money spent by the Department of Militia has been of great benefit commercially." But as far as the other expenditures necessary to maintain the Canadian Army were concerned, the West did poorly at the pork barrel. During the early stages of the war, contracts for clothing and equipment were let to civilian manufacturers without tender, with the emphasis being placed on rapid delivery. Western cities suffered under the double disadvantage of a poorly developed industrial capacity and a paucity of political friends in the high councils of the Militia Department. Even allowing for the latter difficulty, the minuscule amount of purchasing done in the West is a startling reminder that Canadian industry was concentrated in the Central Provinces. Between August, 1914, and February, 1915, for example, the Militia Department spent $4,755,902.62 to outfit the Expeditionary Force. Of this total only $25,158.33 were spent in Manitoba, and nothing in Alberta or Saskatchewan. The two lucky manufacturers were both in Winnipeg–Christie, Grant and Company, which received an order for shirts, and Finnie and Murray Ltd., which made tents. With these exceptions, the Canadians who went to war were outfitted by the industry of the East. From the metal flasks used to collect a recruit's urine sample to the handcuffs used to restrain military prisoners, the myriad items needed to outfit a modern army were largely products of Central Canada, and their purchase did not stimulate the tiny manufacturing sector of the Western Provinces.[12]

More important to Canada's industrial development than supplying the CEF was the manufacture of shells and other munitions for the British government. Canada sought and received millions of dollars worth of munitions contracts between 1914 and 1919, and the industrial expansion necessary to undertake this work provided a permanent addition to Canadian industrial capacity. Foundries, machine shops, steel plants and shipyards developed in response to the demands of the Great War. Little of this expansion took place outside the provinces of Ontario and Quebec, however, and virtually none at all took place in the Prairie West.

Orders for munitions production were channelled to individual firms by two official bodies. During 1914 and most of 1915, the dispensing of contracts was the responsibility of the "Shell Committee" under the chairmanship of General Alex Bertram. This committee was dissolved in November, 1915, and replaced by the Imperial Munitions Board under the direction of Sir Joseph Flavelle. The IMB, an agency of the British government, coordinated production in Canada until the end of the war.

Neither the Shell Committee nor the IMB was enthusiastic about the potential for munitions manufacturing in the West, but it was the Shell Committee that was the most blatantly discriminatory in its distribution of contracts. Despite the creation of a "Western Shell Committee" under the chairmanship of Winnipeg manufacturer T. Russ Deacon, and despite the fact that a capacity existed to do such work on a limited basis, few orders for munitions were placed in Western Canada. The small number of shell orders received by Western firms made the committee a target for a barrage of abuse from the West. The Shell Committee answered these complaints alternately by denying their validity and by arguing that sending shell-manufacturing west would cause intolerable delays in production schedules.[13]

When Western companies did obtain shell contracts, they had the same problem that would-be Western manufacturers faced in peace time. There was no source of steel within Manitoba, Saskatchewan, and Alberta. The Shell Committee's specifications insisted that Canadian-produced basic steel be used, so attempts to import steel from the United States were blocked both by the American steel's high acidic content and by the Canadian tariff structure. Western manufacturers were prepared to purchase steel in Ontario and to pay to ship it west, but found that steel companies were unable to fill their orders without long delays and reduced volumes. "The result," complained Winnipeg Mayor R.D. Waugh, was that in the few Western shell factories "the mechanics are losing more than half their time and the manufacturers are suffering the loss of their plants through lack of material."[14]

The case of the Canadian Brakeshoe Company, which proposed to solve this problem by producing steel billets in Calgary for shell-making in Winnipeg, provides a useful example of the sort of relationship which existed between Western manufacturers and the Shell Committee. Canadian Brakeshoe calculated that it could produce these billets in Calgary and deliver them in Winnipeg at a price of four cents a pound. Once there they could be used by those Winnipeg firms which had obtained shell contracts but had difficulty obtaining steel. The Shell Committee gave Canadian Brakeshoe a contract at four cents a pound, but insisted that the billets be delivered in Montreal. The extra transportation costs eliminated the Calgary company's profit margin, and the contract had to be refused. R.B. Bennett, Conservative MP for Calgary, tried to get the Shell Committee to reconsider its terms. In letters to General Bertram he demanded "justice for the West" and accused the Shell Committee of allowing "financial interests of Eastern Canada" to influence its decision to impose contract terms which it knew to be impossible. The committee's reply gave Bennett little satisfaction, but came close to admitting the truth of his charges. "We do not consider it is in the interest of the Empire" it wrote, "to encourage the erection of plants for forging shells in Calgary when there are sufficient plants already in the Dominion."[15]

The Imperial Munitions Board was instructed to attempt to improve relations with the West when it assumed control of munitions production. The IMB's secretary, Lt. Col. David Carnegie, looked over outstanding "problem cases" from the West, and assured the region's manufacturers that the board was "anxious to see the establishment and development of industries in the West" despite the attitude which had been displayed by the Shell Committee. The board had an opportunity to prove its good faith when a change in British ammunition requirements threatened to wipe out the minuscule Western shell production entirely. Western shops had been producing the eighteen-pounder high explosive shell, a type of artillery ammunition that proved to be of little use on the Western Front and which was soon in oversupply. Sir Joseph Flavelle, chairman of the IMB, and Lt. Col. Carnegie personally persuaded British authorities to order an additional 100,000 of these shells, arguing that the beneficial effects for Canadian unity would be worth far more than the costs of the superfluous munitions.[16] Flavelle also reserved orders for 150,000 4.5-inch shells to give Western shops work when the eighteen-pounders were finished. As far as the IMB was concerned, it was bending over backwards to meet Western needs. In his *History of the Imperial Munitions Board*, David Carnegie wrote that

...contracts were distributed from the Atlantic to the Pacific. And if it be questioned why shells could be forged in Ontario and shipped to Edmonton to be machined, it can confidently be stated that the psychological value of the shells in visualizing for the people of Edmonton the physical evidence of the contest in which their sons were engaged was something far beyond the cost of transportation. The war was at their very door.

But neither Western manufacturers nor Western workmen were ever to be convinced that the West was being treated fairly, and bitter complaints continued throughout the war. Western representatives in the Federal cabinet exchanged angry correspondence with Flavelle about the small amount of munitions work provided for Manitoba, Saskatchewan, and Alberta. Flavelle, who regarded any contracts let in the West as charity designed "primarily to give employment to labour," found these complaints annoying. When Arthur Meighen asked for a further contract in Saskatchewan, Flavelle's temper flashed. Pointing out that not all deliveries had been made on the company's first contract, Flavelle replied that "this seems to be a characteristic of the Western men; they storm for further orders before previous orders are anything near completion." When Meighen reminded him that deliveries had been delayed because an Ontario factory had failed to ship components, Flavelle exploded:

> The Board objects to manufacturers drilling for the first operation so far ahead of the completed shells. In this respect the West have [sic] been particularly at fault. Delayed on their finishing operations, they press on with the first operations, and having finished operations, they call out for fresh orders.

This attitude to Western entrepreneurs was shared by Mark H. Irish, the board's director of labour. After an inspection tour of Western plants on IMB contracts, Irish concluded that only one of the seven factories which he visited was efficient enough "to give one the impression of an Eastern plant."[17]

Like its employers, the Western working class was considered unreliable for munitions work by the Shell Committee and the IMB. When called upon for an opinion, F.P. Jones of Canada Cement Ltd. told the Shell Committee that "...the cost of manufacture in the West would be about 100% higher than in Eastern Canada, that the West could not compete industrially with the East. Owing to the great fertility of the soil, the population had become lazy and incapable of doing industrial work at high pressure." More serious, however, was the West's tradition of unstable relations between labour and management. Mark H. Irish was particularly concerned about the situation in Manitoba. He thought that the provincial government's Bureau of Labour was being run by a man who was "little more than a Hyde Park agitator," and feared the possibility of a "socialist disturbance among the work-people." The IMB did have disproportionately more lost time due to work stoppages in its few Western factories. This occurred, in part at least, because unemployment made it possible for Western capitalists to attract workers at rates below the fair wage scales set by the Board.[18]

Partly because of such attitudes, and always in the name of efficiency, the Imperial Munitions Board continued the pattern established by the Shell Committee. Existing Western machine shops, like the now underemployed shops of the railways, were given small orders but few new plants were created to handle munitions-making. Thus the IMB made its predictions about Western shell production a self-fulfilling prophecy. Any attempt to overcome transportation costs by granting special railway rates for munitions was refused by the minister of finance, who feared it would create "a dangerous precedent." Nor were tariff barriers reduced to permit the use of American steel, even when Canadian steel was in short supply.[19]

When the final report of the IMB is examined, the regional bias of its operations becomes clearly visible. Excluding shipbuilding, the IMB distributed contracts for more than $1 billion worth of munitions. Only $6,978,854.70 of this sum was let in Manitoba, Saskatchewan, and Alberta, and some of this money was spent to purchase material produced elsewhere. This amounts to less than one per cent of total munitions production, again excluding shipbuilding. The exact figure is .67 per cent. The total value of contracts let to Western firms was smaller than that of those given to Orillia, Peterborough, Renfrew, Sault Ste. Marie, or St. Catharines, Ontario. The West was convinced that it was facing the same National Policy that denied it industrial development in peace time. For once, the West's disappointed capitalists would have agreed with the contention of Winnipeg's working-class newspaper, *The Voice*, that

> ...there has been the usual determination among the manufacturing forces and others in the East to shut the West out. Just as soon as British orders were to hand in this country, every machine shop and foundry of any importance whatever in the East got something to go on with. They were not equipped for the job; get equipped but do your best anyway was the order. But with the West it was different. The Manufacturer's Association have the belief that Western Canada is destined to grow rich with the one purpose of being exploited by it [sic]. The idea that manufacturing shall be carried on there in competition to them is not to be tolerated.[20]

It is impossible to escape the conclusion that the decision to deny munitions contracts in any meaningful volume to the Western Provinces was a conscious one. Whatever the problems of Western cities, Canada's national interests and those of the Allies were served most effectively by turning the economy of the West towards wheat production, and the urban unemployed became an important source of harvest labour in 1915 and 1916. The arguments used by the IMB about "efficiency" sound reasonable until one considers the fact that British Columbia received contracts totalling $58 million, ten times the amount given to Manitoba, Saskatchewan, and Alberta. The Prairie West was never given a real opportunity to participate in munitions-manufacturing. Whether it could have responded must remain an unanswered question.

IV

Denied the largess of the Imperial Munitions Board, Western cities were left face to face with their pre-war economic problems. Until 1917 unemployment continued, despite the large number of enlistments. Harvest work temporarily reduced this number in the autumns of 1915 and 1916 but winter saw the total unemployed increase again. Many who had jobs were put on "short time" and fell into the category we now describe as "underemployed." As late in the war as March, 1917, Mark H. Irish observed that unemployment in Winnipeg was high enough to make staffing the few shell factories very easy, and to eliminate "the slightest chance of a shortage of employees."[21]

Because of the nature of the economic collapse, unemployment was high among skilled English-speaking workers as well as among unskilled immigrant labourers. J.B. Walker, commissioner of immigration at Winnipeg, conducted a survey in the spring of 1915 and found "about two thousand unemployed British born mechanics in the City of Winnipeg...engineers, fitters, boiler makers, rivetters, machine men, electricians, brass workers, iron moulders." These men had been employed in the construction industry and the railway shops, and many had been without work or on "short-time" since 1913. When the war failed to bring new opportunity to Western cities, few of these workers were prepared to homestead and abandon their trades for agriculture. Opportunity existed for them elsewhere, and there was always the alternative of enlistment. Both avenues were popular, and both led away from the West. Early in 1915 skilled tradesmen began an exodus from Western cities to opportunities in Eastern Canada, in the United States, and in Britain. The *Labour Gazette* reported that more than 100 machinists had departed from Winnipeg for British munitions factories, while unemployed machinists from Moose Jaw followed suit. A similar migration of ironworkers was reported to Duluth, Minnesota, and of machinists to Ontario. This movement continued throughout 1916, as the few Western plants with munitions contracts confronted delays and were forced to put men on reduced hours or to lay them off. As the manager of Saskatchewan Bridge and Iron Works complained when a shipment of steel billets failed to arrive as expected, "Every time we have these delays we lose valuable machinists either leaving the country for the States or enlisting in the overseas battalions. These men are extremely difficult to obtain and are getting more scarce every day."[22]

Smaller cities in particular suffered during recession and war, and some saw population, by which all civic "boosters" measured growth, actually decline. There were only eighteen cities in the Western Provinces in 1914, and three of them, Regina, Wetaskawin, and Portage la Prairie, showed absolute declines in population between the censuses of 1911 and 1916. Four of the other smaller cities, Brandon, Prince Albert, Lethbridge, and Red Deer, showed only slight population gains. A comparison of the figures for 1911 and 1916 does not tell the full story of the stagnation of these cities, as the former do not demonstrate population at its pre-war height. When later population information is available, the effects of the war years appear in proper perspective. Edmonton and Prince Albert both make slight gains when Dominion Census data are used. But when these figures are compared with their own municipal statistics, Edmonton is seen to suffer a loss of 18,000 between 1914 and 1916 and Prince Albert a loss of almost 6,000 between 1912 and 1916. Half of Manitoba's thirty towns actually lost population between 1911 and 1921.[23]

The spin-off from high agricultural prices, in combination with the need for men in the CEF, was all that carried the West's urban areas through the difficult war years. One Winnipegger, an enthusiastic booster for his city and region, was forced to admit that "business is dull compared to former times" and that "Eastern Canada is best now." The only thing that kept his civic pride alive was his contention that Winnipeg "is still probably the best city in the West" since it had "no 'bread line' as in Vancouver, Calgary, Moose Jaw, etc." A bumper crop in 1915 started activity again in the service, transportation, and merchandising sectors of the Western economy, and cities began "to feel the effects of more money in the country." But the total number of business units in the West showed a decline in 1915; and, despite the opening of new agricultural areas, in 1920 there were only 180 more business units than there had been in 1914. Stores in smaller towns could not compete with national mail-order houses, which sold everything from yard goods to lumber, and many merchants were driven out of business despite the relative prosperity of the Western farmer. Others remained in operation only because the owner could find no buyers. "I wish someone would be foolish enough to come along and buy me out" wrote a Saskatoon grocer as he pleaded with an aunt for a loan to keep his business solvent.[24]

Like their businessmen, the cities and towns themselves were in financial trouble. Prairie cities had fallen victim to delusions of grandeur during the first decade of the century. Visions of the success of Winnipeg danced in the imaginations of city councillors, and municipalities floated bonds to equip themselves with waterworks, paved streets, sewage systems, and large high schools. The recession of 1913-14 saw this confidence shaken and finally shattered, as assessments on real property plummeted with a decline in real estate values, and cities found it impossible to collect those taxes they levied. The slump in business activity reduced municipal income from fees and licences, and the condition of money markets made further borrowing out of the question.[25]

Several Prairie urban municipalities were forced to suspend the interest payments on their bonds during the war. The most spectacular examples of such defaults were Battleford and Prince Albert, which suspended in 1915 and 1918 respectively, provoking angry reactions from American and British bond-holders and threats that unless the municipalities were forced to make good, default would "cause uneasiness about other similar Canadian Securities, especially in the West." Provincial governments washed their hands of such matters, and municipalities facing financial crises were forced to deal with them by drastically reducing expenses. The easiest place to effect economies was by slashing the salaries of municipal employees and policemen, and many towns and cities adopted this course. It was a course that was to have serious repercussions in 1918 and 1919, as disgruntled municipal civil servants joined construction workers as the spearhead of Western labour discontent.[26]

Although the war temporarily relieved some problems of the Western urban economy by putting agriculture back on its feet, it did not solve any of them. Dr. Costello, Calgary's city manager, made this clear when he addressed a conference of municipal officers in July, 1918. He admitted that the side effects of agricultural prosperity had in some cases "saved the day for both individuals and municipalities," but warned his audience that "most of our financial difficulties have for their tap root the pre-war conditions...and to a very large extent the day of reckoning has been merely postponed and threatens when it comes to be just so much more dire."[27]

For some smaller cities this day of reckoning had passed and the hopes of spectacular growth had passed with it. The larger cities retained their functions as transportation and distributing centres but were not allowed to partake in the industrial expansion of wartime.

V

It is deceptively easy to dismiss the years of the Great War as a period of prosperous expansion for Western agriculture and to enquire no further. Commenting on the high farm incomes of the early years of the war, an outraged Stephen Leacock described the Canadian farmer as a "war drone" able to use the profits of inflated grain prices for "pianos, victrolas, trotting buggies, books, moving pictures, pleasure cars and so on."[28] Leacock could no doubt have pointed to agricultural statistics as proof of the war's beneficial effects for the Prairie farmer. Wheat, the West's staple crop, was absorbed by Britain in whatever quantities it could be produced and the harvest of 1915 was the largest in the short history of the three Prairie Provinces. Acreage seeded and total amounts of wheat exported doubled between 1914 and 1919, and in 1917 its price was fixed at $2.21 a bushel, three times its pre-war level. The Dominion Census illustrates the agricultural expansion which occurred during the decade dominated by the Great War. Between 1911 and 1921 the rural population of Manitoba, Saskatchewan, and Alberta increased from 858,000 to 1.25 million, keeping pace with the population increase in urban areas. The total number of farms increased by 28 per cent, total farm acreage by 52.5 per cent and total improved farm acreage by an astounding 95.3 per cent. The high prices of wartime and of the immediate post-war years were an important cause of this expansion. Coming as it did after two years of drought and recession, it is not difficult to understand why one Manitoban referred to the war as "a God send and a Blessing to this Western Country."[29]

But the war years had deeper implications for the long-term development of Western Canadian agriculture, and to appreciate these fully, it is necessary to consider briefly the nature of Western agriculture before the Great War began. Unlike farming in most of Central Canada and the Maritime Provinces, Prairie agriculture was of the type described by agricultural economists as "monoculture of cereals" or more simply, "cash grain farming." In many parts of the Prairies, farmers devoted their land almost exclusively to the cultivation of wheat. In a typical year about 55 per cent of all land seeded to field crops was planted to wheat. Another 30 per cent of acreage in Manitoba, Saskatchewan, and Alberta was seeded to oats, which were grown to provide feed for the horsepower needed to produce the wheat crop. Barley, flax, and hay grasses covered all but a tiny percentage of remaining field crop acreage.[30]

The market for the Western wheat crop was thousands of miles to the east, in Central Canada or in Britain. Wheat had become the fourth in the succession of staple products which so heavily influenced Canadian economic development. It had the disadvantages of any other staple product, in that it created an economy in Western Canada that was highly specialized, unable to convert to any other form of production, and at the mercy of the vagaries of an international market. Unlike Canada's other great staples of fur, fish, and timber, wheat production depended on variable climatic conditions. For a Prairie farmer, the differences between a good crop, a poor crop, or no crop at all could be determined by a few inches of rainfall.

The recession of 1913-14 provides an example of what could happen to the Prairie wheat economy when unfavourable circumstances worked in combination. In those years, as during the depression of the 1930s, low international prices for wheat coincided with drought in southern Alberta and southwestern Saskatchewan and the farmer was caught in the jaws of a vise of reduced yields and prices lower than the cost of production. By the summer of 1914, some quarter-section farmers faced starvation.[31]

Obviously not every Prairie farm family faced this situation, but the two consecutive disastrous years underscored a point which provincial ministries of agriculture had been trying to make clear for several years, that escape from the over-reliance on staple wheat production could come only by diversification into mixed farming and livestock raising. There is considerable evidence that in 1914, the year in which the Great War began, Prairie farmers were at last beginning to listen to this argument. Most apparent was the reduction in acreage sown to wheat of 7 per cent, over 700,000 acres, and a similar reduction in oats acreage. The acreage devoted to fodder corn, alfalfa, turnips, and potatoes showed slight increases, and the numbers of milch cows, beef cattle, sheep, and particularly hogs on Western farms increased. The Saskatchewan Department of Agriculture joyously intrepreted this as the sign that "farmers now realize that it is economically essential to have something more than grain to depend upon." Dean W.J. Rutherford of the Saskatchewan College of Agriculture confidently predicted that "extensive wheat farming is only a passing stage...wheat growing, like the bison, in the course of a few years will have to be protected and safeguarded in order to prevent its becoming extinct."[32]

The Great War quickly made a mockery of Rutherford's prediction. The demand of the Allies was primarily for wheat, and the Western farmer rushed to meet this demand. Grain farming was the path of least resistance for a Prairie farmer, and an expansion of grain acreage could be accomplished more quickly and more easily than a similar expansion of livestock production. Wheat acreage in Manitoba, Saskatchewan, and Alberta increased from 9.3 million acres in 1914 to 16.1 million in 1918. In 1916 wheat and oats, its support crop, covered 90.3 per cent of Prairie field crop acreage. Even before the price of wheat was fixed at $2.21 in 1917, the urge to expand production was irresistible. Farmers' sons established their own farms, city-dwellers moved on to the land. Almost 40,000 new farms were created in the West between 1916 and 1921. Agriculture students at the University of Saskatchewan laughed at "the number of former real estate men that were in attendance at the Short Course [in Agriculture]," and the editor of the university newspaper predicted correctly that "high grain prices will give a greater impulse to the back to the land movement than any propaganda could." Despite the fact that immigration was ended by the war, there were 92,465 homestead entries during the war years.[33]

Farmers who were already established improved more acreage, purchased more land, or rented land from those who enlisted. The percentage of improved acreage on Prairie farms increased from 40 per cent in 1911 to 46.8 per cent in 1916 and 51 per cent in 1921. The "land sales barometer" revealed an increase in sales of available railway land grants. The Canadian Pacific sold almost 600,000 acres of farmland in 1918, as compared with less than 160,000 in 1915. Those who could not afford to buy, or who could not find land available which was suitably located, rented from farmers who went to war. Rented land increased between 1911 and 1921 from 11.1 per cent to 19.1 per cent of all land farmed. Most of this rented land was farmed by an "owner-tenant," who had a farm of his own in addition to the land he rented. Herbert Warren, whose farming experiences have been described in *Seventy South Alberta Years*, is typical of many farmers during the Great War. A quarter-section farmer when the war began, he purchased his second quarter after harvesting the bumper crop of 1915. In 1916 Warren planted 90 additional acres "on shares," and then purchased a third quarter-section in 1918.[34]

The expansion of 1915 to 1919 took place during a period in which the price of land increased along with the price of wheat. The same land which brought the CPR an average of $13.55 per acre in 1915 was worth $21.53 in 1917. In a study based on the Vulcan and Lomond districts of Alberta, southeast of Calgary, John Proskie similarly concludes that the price of land declined slightly between 1910 and 1914, and then peaked in both areas between 1915 and 1919.[35]

As with land, the cost of other factors of production increased during the Great War. The wages of agricultural labourers more than doubled between the beginning and the end of the war, and the problem of an adequate labour supply remained a difficult one for the Prairie farmer. In cereal monoculture more so than in other types of farming, labour needs are concentrated at certain periods, particularly in August and September during harvesting. The Prairie farmer whose operation was large enough to require hired help solved this problem by importing harvest labour from Eastern Canada or by hiring a smaller farmer who needed to supplement his income, thus eliminating the need to pay a full season's wages to a man who was needed for only a few weeks of work. The wartime demand for both soldiers and factory workers gradually shut off the West's first source of cheap labour, while high wheat prices kept small farmers home to run their own farms.

During 1915 and 1916 high unemployment in Western cities and the granting of sowing and harvest leave to soldiers training in the West prevented serious labour shortages, but by 1917 labour was expensive and in short supply. Monthly wages paid to male farm workers increased by 50 per cent between 1916 and 1917 and a further 35 per cent the following year. There was also a deterioration in the quality of help available and farmers complained bitterly about paying "top dollar" to "a Bohonk or a teenboy [sic]." It became impossible to get help for short periods, and labour costs were further increased by the necessity of keeping a hand all summer to be sure of having him available for the harvest.[36] The labour shortage of 1917 and 1918 did not prevent Prairie farmers from increasing the total acreage of field crops during each of the war years, despite their vocal protests about the unavailability of agricultural workers. But the increased cost of farm labour raised the cost of production and eroded the benefits of increased prices. More important in the long run, the shortage of cheap labour meant that the land was less intensively cultivated and that important farm tasks were left undone.

If labour and land costs failed to absorb a farmer's profit margin, the cost of investment in machinery remained to consume it. At the implement dealer's, farmers were called upon to pay a price inflated both by war and by the protective tariff. As one farmer complained to C.A. Dunning in 1918, "a disc harrow that cost 110.00 last Spring is now 156.00, a plough that was 80.00 last Spring is now 148.00." But despite such complaints, high prices did not deter a wave of wartime purchases. Massey Harris, Canada's largest implement company, increased its domestic sales by 55 per cent in 1915, and in 1917 sales reached record heights. In November, 1917, the *Swift Current Sun* reported that "farm machinery companies in Saskatchewan are now experiencing the biggest boom for farm machinery recorded in this province for many years," and that "the increased prices for the machinery does [sic] not deter [the farmers] from buying the stock." These purchases did not involve adoption of particularly significant technological advances but usually meant the replacement of old equipment with new, or the supplementing of a drag harrow with a disc. Although some innovative farmers used the war period to try new machinery, cultivators and packers do not seem to have been adopted in large numbers.[37]

Despite the labour shortage and the high cost of feed, only a few Prairie farmers replaced their horses with the gasoline tractors which were available. The Canada Food Board and the dominion Department of Agriculture tried to promote the adoption of tractor power, but power farming did not begin seriously until the mid 1920s and was not general until after the Second World War. Despite the removal of the tariff on tractors valued at less than $1,400.00 in 1918, tractors sold very slowly. In 1926, with 119,451 farms, Saskatchewan had only 26,700 tractors, some of which were large outfits belonging to professional threshers and breakers. The insignificant impact of the tractor on the Prairie farmer during this period is demonstrated by the doubling of the number of farm horses in Manitoba, Saskatchewan, and Alberta between 1911 and 1921. The ratio between acres cultivated and the number of farm horses is almost identical for the years 1913 and 1919.[38]

Tractor tests at the Manitoba Agricultural College, 1915.
Foote Collection, Manitoba Archives.

The reluctance to abandon the horse was not because farmers lacked interest in tractors, nor was it because they did not recognize the potential applications of tractor power to grain farming. There simply were no suitable light tractors available at prices farmers were willing to pay. An abundance of competing designs, from the Bates Steel Mule to the Waterloo Boy Kerosene tractor, clamoured for the farmer's dollar, but most of them were not far past the experimental stage. Prices ranged from $800 to $1,200, for which the farmer could purchase five to seven work horses, while a tractor could do the work of only four. Horses could be fed by home-grown oats and did not consume gasoline, then rapidly rising in price. Farmers knew how to care for horses but little about the care and feeding of a traction engine, and hiring a man to operate a tractor, if such a man were available, made little economic sense. Western farmers recognized that power farming was the way of the future but also that the future had not yet arrived. "It is all very well to experiment with gasoline tractors," wrote a Manitoba farmer in 1918, "but we know from experience what horse teams can do."[39]

Twentieth-century technology did make an impact on the rural West during the Great War but it was in the form of the automobile, not of the tractor. Farmers who ignored the Fordson lined up to buy the Ford Model T, the Chevrolet 490, and the Maxwell Roadster. An open touring car cost between $500 and $700, and wartime increases could not dissuade many farmers from purchasing a machine that could so dramatically improve the quality of their lives. "The day you buy an automobile it will pick your farm right up and drop it two-thirds nearer the religious, social and market centres," was the *Farm and Ranch Review*'s opinion. The auto could be used to improve net profits and "no qualms of conscience will be felt because the horses ought to be resting in stable or pasture, instead of being out on the road." A large number of Western farmers agreed. The number of automobiles registered in Manitoba, Saskatchewan, and Alberta increased fivefold between 1914 and 1918. Between 1916 and 1917 alone there was an increase of 85 per cent in the number of autos in the West, an increase greater than that in any other region.[40]

These automobiles, like the new land and the new equipment with which to farm, were purchased during a period of inflation and at a time when the cost of the credit on which most of these purchases were made was also increasing. Most of the profits from high wartime prices were used to finance further expansion rather than to reduce the existing burden of debt. Western farmers trying to establish themselves had always had difficulty obtaining bank credit. During wartime, agriculture had to compete with the financial needs of the concurrent industrial expansion and the results were higher interest rates for those farmers who could obtain money through bank loans. Many could not and therefore financed auto and machinery purchases through implement dealers at still higher rates of interest. The *Farmer's Advocate* looked with alarm at the number of men who were mortgaging small farms to gain capital for expansion and warned that chances were one in two that these farms would be sold to pay those mortgages. "There is a difference," warned the *Advocate*, "between speculation and progressiveness." Many farmers ignored such advice and the result was "a mountainous burden of debt" which had to be paid after wheat prices had returned to normal levels.[41]

VI

This increased level of debt was not the only unwanted legacy of the Great War for the agriculture of the Prairie West. In their scramble to take advantage of sudden high prices, farmers traded the long-term productivity of their land for short-term profits. No area of Western Canada can count on more than twenty-five inches of annual rainfall; some areas must produce crops with only fifteen inches. To make this possible, every drop of precious moisture must be conserved. To that end, two techniques were generally adopted, summerfallowing and fall plowing.

In Western Canadian dry farming, summerfallowing is more than simple crop rotation as employed elsewhere. Wheat and oats are exhaustive crops and land sown to them must be occasionally "rested" to prevent loss of its productive capacity. But on the Prairies summerfallowing is also an important means of utilizing the limited moisture available, and of bringing weeds under control. In 1914, proper dry farming practice recommended that one-third of all improved acreage be left as summerfallow. This fallow was not planted to a restorative "trash crop" such as clover or alfalfa, but was left to weeds which were plowed down and harrowed before they could consume much moisture. This technique allowed the farmer to "store" an extra year's moisture in his summerfallow, and to use it to produce two grain crops, before again leaving the field fallow.[42]

The large increases in field crop acreage between 1915 and 1919 were accomplished in part by neglect of the proper techniques of summerfallowing. The editors of agricultural weeklies all warned that "When you get around to that field that should be summerfallowed *quit seeding*. Get out the cultivator and give it a loose top."[43] These warnings were largely ignored and hundreds of thousands of acres were seeded which should have been left fallow. Equally serious was the fact that because of the shortage of labour and the increased attention paid to grain crops, those acres that were left fallow were not tilled as thoroughly as they should have been.

The second dry farming technique abandoned by farmers in a hurry to make profits was fall plowing. By plowing under stubble in the fall, the land was better able to absorb moisture from the winter snowfall, and thus better prepared for seeding in the spring. To save time, labour costs, and exhausting work for themselves and their horses after the gruelling harvest period, farmers avoided fall plowing by sprinkling kerosene in their fields and simply burning off the stubble. This not only robbed the land of needed moisture but also destroyed necessary organic matter and nitrogen, thus contributing to depletion of the soil and to soil drifting.

Two additional factors which militated against proper agricultural technique became more pronounced during wartime. The first – a direct result of enlistments – was the increased amount of land farmed by tenants, who, agricultural economists contend, seldom have sufficient interest in their land to employ tillage methods which are most productive in the long term. The second was the increase in average farm size, from 289.4 acres in 1911 to 335.4 in 1921. Half-section farms became the norm, and three-quarter-section farms were no longer unusual. The large farm complicated many of the problems caused by monoculture of wheat. As the *Farmer's Advocate* complained, larger farms did not necessarily mean better farms because

> ...they require too much hired labour, too large a proportion of the farm sown to grain crops, and what is perhaps of most importance, they put farm homes too far apart....By this system of large farms we have developed weeds to the extent that they are a very important factor....We have cultivated our land in such a manner that soil drifting has become a very serious problem.

But the trend toward larger and larger holdings could not be held back by editorials.[44]

Nor could the warnings of farm weeklies and provincial departments of agriculture force farmers to give up techniques like
stubble-burning, which were "immediately profitable but permanently wasteful." Farmers were urged to "play safe," and to
"increase our production not by more farming but by better
farming", but these admonitions were largely unheeded. One
reason for this was that the warnings of the provinces were
undermined by the bulletins and advertisements of the dominion
Department of Agriculture, which encouraged the Prairie farmer
to follow the lead of his own cupidity, suggesting that "every
effort should be made to produce wheat" and officially discourag-
ing beef cattle production and the raising of breeding stock. The
department's "production and thrift" campaign of 1916 actually
suggested planting fallow and stubble-burning as methods of rapidly increasing production to meet the wartime emergency. This
brought an angry rejoinder from W.R. Motherwell, minister of
agriculture of Saskatchewan, who described the suggestions as
"little short of madness." Motherwell was forced to admit sadly
that because the advice came from "so eminent a source," thousands of Western farmers were accepting it.[45]

For whatever reasons, Western farmers neglected proper agricultural techniques during the Great War–and quickly paid the
price. Failure to summerfallow and insufficient tillage contributed to an outbreak of stem rust which damaged Western crops
in 1916, the first such outbreak since 1904. Starting in 1916,
there began a steady reduction in yields per acre for wheat, oats,
and barley. After a spectacular crop in 1915, yields dropped until
1919 when the yield was 9.7 bushels per acre, the lowest in Western Canada's history and 5.7 bushels per acre less that of 1914.
This downward movement of yields reduced the profit that the
Western farmer would have been able to get from high prices.
The huge crop of 1915, when the average wheat yield was 29.3
bushels per acre, was sold at prices averaging 80 cents a bushel.
In 1917 and 1918 when prices had been fixed at $2.21 a bushel,
average yields were less than half those of 1915. Thus the huge
1915 crop was worth only $325 million, while the much smaller
crop of 1917 was worth $405.7 million. Dry weather in 1918
made the results of the neglect of proper dry-farming techniques
more serious than they might have been otherwise, but as Seager
Wheeler warned Western farmers at the conclusion of the war,
low yields were caused not simply by weather, but by "the abuse
and ill treatment of the soil by the many slack methods in force
today."[46]

The wartime situation induced Prairie farmers to expand at high cost and made them poorer grain farmers. But it also retarded the diversification into stock raising that had seemed well underway in 1914. Although hog and cattle prices increased as rapidly as the price of wheat, Western farmers were no more attracted to animal husbandry than they had been in the years before the recession of 1913-14. It took three years to raise cattle to market weight using the techniques general in 1914, while an increase in grain production could show a profit in three months. Livestock raising required special skills, and large amounts of labour. As the Western Canada Livestock Union pointed out, it was possible to make use of inexperienced help in harvesting grain, "but when it comes to the breeding and feeding of livestock, some experience is necessary," and little such labour was available at any price. Not only was labour more expensive, but the price of barley and other feed grains doubled between 1914 and 1917. These high prices did not match the increase in the price of wheat, however, and farmers concentrated on wheat rather than feed grains. A shortage of feed caused stock to be sold prematurely and deterred other farmers from attempting to raise hogs or cattle. Some farmers sold grain they should have retained for feed, hoping to keep stock alive on pasturage in November and April. Only in 1916 did this work, as the West enjoyed a mild winter. In the other war years stock had to be slaughtered–often necessary breeding stock.[47]

Another impediment to diversification away from grain farming was the situation with regard to farm credit. Credit for stock raising was more difficult to obtain than credit for expansion of grain production. Stock raising meant that fences and sheds had to be constructed, feed grown or purchased, and feeder and breeding stock obtained; this large initial outlay would not show returns for a year in the case of hogs, three years in the case of cattle. The dominion government made two half-hearted attempts to make credit more easily available to farmers by amending the Bank Act in 1915 and again in 1916 to permit loans against stored unsold grain and against stock already on the farm. Neither change meant much to the Prairie farmer's ability to venture into stock-raising, and both were described by the agricultural press as "just so much more armchair bunk." Even if local bank managers were prepared to back attempts to change from grain to livestock, they found themselves "fettered by head office red tape" and by a wartime policy even more negative to long-term loans than that of peacetime. The *Farmer's Advocate* felt that the greatest single contribution the government could make toward Prairie diversification into stock would be the creation of a system of "rural credit banks, government or co-operative," but the dominion government was unwilling to undertake such an experiment.[48]

Those farmers who surmounted credit difficulties and labour and feed shortages to raise hogs or cattle found that poorly developed marketing facilities made it difficult or impossible for them to sell their stock at a profit. In a report presented in 1916, a Saskatchewan Livestock Commission denounced the "absurdly illogical system" by which the Western stock raiser was "compelled to lose the just reward of his labour," and nothing which happened later in the war years improved that system. Western Canada lacked the extensive cold storage facilities which would have permitted the shipment of refrigerated carcasses. The West's livestock producer had to pay high transportation charges to ship live animals to Calgary, Winnipeg, or the United States. The railway rates, already regarded as high by producers, were supplemented by a "car cleaning charge" imposed on all stock shipments. Producers were paid for their stock according to its "off car" weight, before the animals, after spending days in boxcars, had been fed or watered.

For all these reasons the Prairie farmer remained a "wheat miner," and was more committed to growing grain for export in 1919 than he had been in 1914. As early as January, 1915, the *Farm and Ranch Review* expressed shock at "the disregard with which many men are letting go of their breeding hogs and cattle" and at the decline in an already weak Western dairy industry. Farmers sold beef cattle for veal to invest in new land. The *Farmer's Advocate*'s correspondents reported that on farms throughout the West "the livestock have gone and all is staked on a couple of crops of wheat." Even the Western Section of the Canadian Bankers' Association, despite the reluctance of the banks to lend money to support stock raising, moved to protest the casual sale of valuable breeding stock which it felt had "assumed serious proportions." The total number of dairy cattle, beef cattle, sheep, and hogs on Prairie farms increased between 1914 and 1919, but the rate of increase did not match that of field crop acreage. Between the census years of 1916 and 1921, the average value of livestock on a Prairie farm declined from $1,864 to $1,602, although the average value of land, buildings, and machinery all increased over this period.[49]

VII

The war's high prices brought temporary prosperity to Prairie agriculture, but the scramble for short-term profits led to increased levels of debt, costly damage to the land, and continued overdependence on wheat to the detriment of a more balanced agricultural development. Western Canada's urban areas did not share the full measure of the temporary prosperity, and, as we saw the wartime demand for munitions provided them with little opportunity to industrialize. While Central Canada became more and more urban and industrial, the West remained both rural and agricultural. Despite growth in absolute terms the urban population of the West did not increase proportionately between 1911 and 1921, and in fact the rural-urban balance remained stable until the 1940s. More significantly, the percentage of the work force engaged in industrial activities–transportation, construction, and manufacturing–declined during the decade marked by the Great War, while the percentage engaged in agriculture increased. Western agriculture became concentrated even more heavily on the production of one staple crop for export to an unstable world market. In 1919 Western farmers were further from self-sufficiency than they had been in 1914. The three Prairie Provinces grew enough wheat to feed the British Isles, but they did not grow enough potatoes to feed their own populations.[50]

Westerners blamed their problems on the development policies of the dominion government, dominated by the malevolent greed of Central Canada's "big interests," and to an extent their accusations were justified. The Department of Agriculture encouraged the Prairie farmer in his reckless course toward self-destruction between 1915 and 1919, and its transportation and tariff policies were not altered in any meaningful way to ease his spiralling costs of production. As farmers bitterly observed, they were the only producers to have the price of their product fixed in a period of rampant inflation. A comparison of the "Farmers' Platforms" endorsed by the Grain Growers and the United Farmers of Alberta reveals the same complaints about the tariff, credit difficulties, and transportation problems in 1910, 1916, and 1921. As John W. Dafoe noted in October, 1916, "at present they are obscured by the war, but they will re-emerge when peace returns." Similarly, Western cities could indict the Shell Committee, the Purchasing Commission, and the Imperial Munitions Board for failing to give them an opportunity to become more than service centres for the surrounding agricultural areas. The radical rhetoric heard before and during the Winnipeg General Strike was in part the voice of Western working class expressing its discontent at being denied its share of the spoils of war.[51]

The years of the Great War were the apogee of the transcontinental economy the National Policy had been intended to create. With their British competitors distracted by the war, Central-Canadian manufacturers expanded behind the wall of the protective tariff, and Western farmers produced their staple crop, wheat, and shipped it to markets in Europe along the east-west axis of the Canadian transcontinental railways. It was a modern version of the short-lived achievement of the North West Company, a second "commercial empire of the St. Lawrence." And like the North West Company, the "wintering partners"—the residents of the West—were not always satisfied that the direction of the company came from two thousand miles to the east. It has become a commonplace for Westerners to blame the direction of their region's development and its lack of industrialization upon the National Policy, but at no time has the charge had more validity than during the Great War.

CHAPTER FOUR

English Canadians
and Ethnic Minorities

I

The most popular metaphor for Canadian society is that of the mosaic. In contrast with the American "melting pot," a tolerant, pluralistic Canada is supposed to have allowed her cultural minorities to retain their distinctiveness within "a unity admitting of a thousand diversities." Because of "the principles of British fairplay" ingrained in the Canadian character immigrants were never subjected to "any methods of forced assimilation, such as those to which...the United States resorted." One period of Canada's history is regarded as an exception to this general harmony. During the Great War, most historians tell us, English Canadians did not behave in a manner befitting a "mosaic." Because of the strains of war, discrimination against immigrant groups–both of enemy and non-enemy origin–became the rule rather than the exception.[1] A passage from Vera Lysenko's *Men in Sheepskin Coats* refers specifically to Ukrainians, but is similar to the comments of other authors. "One repressive measure followed another, directed against bewildered Ukrainians," she writes. "Thousands of harmless 'Galicians' were rounded up by the police and herded into concentration camps....The slightest criticism on the part of a Ukrainian and he was dragged from home, factory or hotel and placed in an internment camp." The scene of most of this repression was Western Canada, for the obvious reason that Manitoba, Saskatchewan, and Alberta contained the largest concentrations of non-English-speaking immigrants. There the prejudices of a war-inflamed public opinion led to discriminatory educational legislation to supplement the internment and disfranchisement imposed by the dominion government.[2]

This chapter contains a rather different interpretation of the effects of the Great War upon the relationship between minority groups and the majority English-Canadian culture of Western Canada, an interpretation which is based on three arguments. The first is that the attitudes of English-Canadian Westerners toward minority cultures before the war were not as tolerant or as uniformly favourable as is sometimes implied. The second is that the war did not, with one notable exception, change these attitudes very much. The third is that despite the discrimination directed against minority groups in the political and educational spheres, and despite the inflammatory rhetoric of English-Canadian "patriots," the war's economic side effect was to produce a significant economic gain for the immigrant farmer.

One further introductory remark is required. In this discussion I have included one minority group which is of course not an "immigrant" group in the usual sense of the word, Western Canada's French Canadians. This is done in part for convenience, since the problems with regard to education which beset other minorities directly involved French Canadians. But including French Canadians among those regarded by English-Canadian Westerners as "foreigners" also seems to illustrate the prevailing opinion that the French, far from "partners" in Confederation, were simply another ethnic group speaking another foreign language.

II

The minority groups which suffered most in the emotional atmosphere of wartime were, naturally enough, those of enemy alien nationality who had not yet been naturalized. This group included such exotic species as Turks and Bulgarians but, in terms realistic for Western Canada, meant Germans and subjects of the Austro-Hungarian Empire. This latter group, largely composed of Ukrainians from the provinces of Galicia and Bukovina, numbered about 95,000 in 1914. The number of German nationals was much smaller, less than 20,000, but the fury unleashed by the public upon each group was inversely proportional to its size.[3]

In their wartime reaction to the German immigrant, Western Canadians took part in what in the United States has been described as "the most spectacular reversal of judgement in the history of American nativism." In both Canada and the United States, Germans had been exempted from the hostile nativism directed at non-English-speaking immigrants. Those who subscribed to the pseudoscientific racism then current concluded that the Germans, as a Teutonic people, were only slightly less desirable as immigrants than Englishmen. Such "experts" as J.S.

Woodsworth, J.P. McConnell, and Frank Oliver described them as "among our best immigrants"; "thrifty, honest and intelligent...enterprising and public spirited"; "of the highest character," far superior to "the stiletto carrying dago [or] the degenerate Central European." Not only was the German as an individual praised, the society from which he came was held up as a model to the world in such diverse fields as industry, music, medicine, and education. Western-Canadian temperance groups, for example, noted with satisfaction the progress of prohibition in Germany, praised German doctors for their research on alcohol, and applauded Kaiser Wilhelm for his "openly declared total abstinence principles." As to the danger of war with Germany, a Winnipeg minister pointed out that "the Germans are a peaceful people, interested in education and commerce and science," with a "better record for peace for the past generation than Great Britain herself."[4]

When war began, Canadians were at first reluctant to give up these preconceptions. Prime Minister Borden reminded Parliament and the public that Canada had "absolutely no quarrel with the German people." War had occurred only because the Germans had "unfortunately" fallen under the domination of "a warlike autocracy." A Prairie minister told his congregation the same thing, and added that the Germans were "not savages, but Christians like ourselves. Some of them, most of them, are Protestants [who] worship the same Father, and pray to Him for victory." *The Voice*, a Winnipeg labour weekly, argued that the German people, led by the socialist party, would soon rebel against the Kaiser and bring the war to an end.[5]

This careful differentiation between the German people and their leaders did not last very long. The much publicized reports of German "atrocities" in Belgium and the torpedoing of the Lusitania started the transition in public attitudes. Casualty lists, which brought the realities of war to sorrowing families, completed it. The *Swift Current Sun*, for example, had been particularly responsible in its comments on Germany and the "enemy alien" question. In June, 1915, however, its editor S.R. Moore concluded that although some of the atrocities "may have been exaggerated," "the report of the Bryce Commission...proves beyond question the Belgian charges." "Up to the present we have not joined in the general abuse of Germany" was the sad comment of *The Voice*:

We have not done so because we thought the prevailing British estimate of Germany must necessarily be heavily biased. But there is no evading the Lusitania horror. It was the act of blood-crazed madmen, seemingly bent on earning the detestation of mankind. Germany has proved herself an outlaw.

By 1918, Canadians were ready to blame the war on every German, "from Bertha Krupp to the lowest peasant," as the Calgary city council phrased it.[6]

The result of this new willingness to blame the war and its horror on the German people was a new stereotype of the German, as unflattering as the old picture had been laudatory. Self-appointed racial theorists demonstrated that English Canadians and Germans had no racial affinity; a writer in the *Winnipeg Telegram* redefined "Anglo-Saxon" as "Anglo-Celtic," with the admonition that "all Scottish, Irish, and Welsh people and most English folk would do well to remember that they are not the descendants of an insignificant German tribe." Once prized above all other non-English immigrants, the German now "did not know the values in truth and love and virtue, in honour and manhood, and morality and character," and was "absolutely impossible to assimilate as a Canadian citizen."[7]

Several good examples of this "new German" appear in *The Major*, the first of Ralph Connor's (C.W. Gordon) two wartime novels to be set in the West. The villain of *The Major* is Ernest Switzer, a naturalized citizen of American birth but of German descent. When an Englishman argues that "there is no such thing as a German loyal to Canada," Switzer's neighbours defend him from this criticism. Gradually, however, Switzer's character is revealed to all. Ernest is an arrogant militarist who has neither a sense of humour nor a sense of fair play. He is cruel to women and determined to satisfy his passions at any cost. Switzer's ultimate treachery occurs after the war begins, when he attempts with the aid of German labourers to sabotage a vital Alberta coal mine. To make certain that the reader realizes that Switzer is representative of all Germans, Gordon includes two minor characters. Holtzman, a "German social democrat," undermines the war effort by heckling at a patriotic meeting and Professor Schaefer, a German-American scientist, returns to Germany in 1917 to lend his brain to the war machine.[8]

Germans, both in the West and elsewhere, felt the disapproval accompanying this new image and responded in the only way available to them: they informally "changed" their nationality. Frederick Philip Grove, then principal of a Manitoba school, became a Swede, one of the most popular alternative identities. Thousands of others verbally crossed the Baltic to join him or became Norwegian or Dutch, the other possible countries of refuge. The census reports of 1911 and 1921 provide some interesting figures to demonstrate this. In 1911, 18,696 residents of Manitoba, Saskatchewan, and Alberta gave their place of birth as Germany. In 1921, with little in or out migration, the figure had declined to 13,242. The 1911 figure for those born in Sweden, Norway, and Holland is 33,826. In 1921, again with little migration, it is 38,925. The difference between this increase and the German decrease is only 355. Since the statistic refers to *place of birth*, natural increase does not change these figures. Towns with German names responded as well. The most famous Canadian change-over was Berlin, Ontario, which became Kitchener, but Dusseldorf and Carlstadt, Alberta, also were rechristened, as Freedom and Alderson.

The largest group of enemy aliens, however, were not Germans but Ukrainian subjects of Austria. The Western-Canadian public did not know them by this term until the war was over and variously described them as Galicians, Ruthenians, or simply as foreigners. The Ukrainians were not the victims of any sort of public re-evaluation, for they had never enjoyed public favour in the first place. Those on the land as homesteaders were safe from the public eye, but those who worked in construction camps or as agricultural labourers were "scarcely citizens" even if they became naturalized. An English visitor to Western Canada in 1914 suggested that to a Westerner, a Galician workman was little better than the despised Chinaman.[9] As peasants without political consciousness, certainly without a sense of Austria as any sort of "fatherland," the Ukrainians posed exactly the same problem after the war that they had before it. Because of the recession many of them were without work and, because of structural deficiencies in provincial educational systems, neither the Ukrainian nor the German children were learning English fast enough to satisfy most English-speaking Western Canadians.

Unfortunately for the Ukrainians, their situation was complicated by the Austro-Hungarian desire to promote unity within their diverse Empire. To encourage Ukrainians to participate in the war, Austria-Hungary promised to create a separate Ukrainian state once a victory had been won. As a result, one of the few articulate voices among Canadian Ukrainians, the Ukrainian Catholic Church, which controlled part of the Ukrainian-language press, declared its sympathy with Austria rather than with Britain's ally Russia. The church was not "pro-German," nor was it "anti-British," but did speak out against Russian policy in the Ukraine. These were the circumstances surrounding the decision of Bishop Nicholas Budka, Ukrainian Catholicism's Canadian prelate, to issue a pastoral letter which spoke of Austria as "the threatened fatherland," and urged all male Ukrainians to "immediately report to the consulate and leave for the old country."

Budka's pastoral has received far more attention than it probably deserves. It was issued eight days before Britain entered the war, and retracted at once when Budka recognized its political implications. The sentiments expressed were denounced by gatherings of Ukrainians and officially rejected by the Ukrainian Orthodox Church. Although it did get Western Canada's Ukrainian minority "off on the wrong foot," most English-Canadian Westerners accepted the retraction. In an editorial entitled "As to Slav Loyalty," John W. Dafoe made it clear that "there never has at any time been any question as to the loyalty of the majority of Slav settlers. They will be faithful sons of their adopted country."[10]

Dafoe's prediction proved absolutely correct. As one writer observed, pointedly singling out the French Canadians for comparison, Ukrainians "displayed a substantial and credible degree of loyalty...certainly more than that displayed by certain other elements who have resided in our country much longer." It is estimated that as many as ten thousand naturalized Ukrainians enlisted during the war, and rural Ukrainian communities were regularly and successfully canvassed on behalf of the Patriotic Fund and the Red Cross. This participation in the war effort perhaps spared some Ukrainians from the public hostility directed generally at those considered alien enemies, and service in the army saved a naturalized citizen his franchise.[11]

Those of enemy alien nationality, of whatever background, faced two types of discrimination during the war: "unofficial" discrimination, which came from the public, and the official disabilities imposed upon them by the dominion government. For the enemy alien, unofficial discrimination took the form of loss of employment (during the early years of war), or verbal and sometimes physical abuse at the hands of aggressive patriots or returned soldiers. It might also mean the antagonism of his neighbours, who perhaps suspected him of espionage. "We have a great many foreigners in the West and they are everywhere," wrote one worried Saskatchewan resident to Premier Scott. "No doubt a great many of them are spys.[sic]...They no doubt have the whole country mapped out so that in case of a reverse of arms in Europe and they should be advised that the old Kaiser was going to win out there no doubt would be an uprising and they would know just where to strike [sic]." Scott, to his credit, counselled "quiet vigilance." Public hostility increased as the costs of war became greater and as the number of returned soldiers in Western communities grew. As veterans' groups came into existence, they joined civilian nativists in demanding that disabilities be imposed on enemy aliens.[12]

Government policy towards enemy aliens was determined as much by public pressure as it was by any perception of these groups as a threat to Canada's security. Despite public fear, the danger of espionage or sabotage in the West was slight, and disturbances created by enemy aliens during the war were "not any more serious than a cowboy's round-up celebration or the spending of a year's treaty money by a band of Indians." Still the Western press demanded stern measures, suggesting that "if the authorities do not cope with this nuisance...the people will be constrained to take the matter into their own hands, with regrettable results to all concerned."[13]

The dominion government's enemy alien program had as its basic component a system of checks on the mobility of aliens. Each enemy alien was required to register with a local magistrate, to report on a monthly basis, and to turn in all firearms. To make this program effective, a means of detaining those thought dangerous was necessary and a system of internment camps was created on the authorization of an Order in Council issued in October, 1914. These camps, almost all of which were located in the Prairie Provinces, British Columbia, or northwestern Ontario, seem to have been prompted more by the high unemployment rate among immigrant workmen than by fear of subversive activity. Over eight thousand aliens were eventually interned, only three thousand of whom were actually enemy reservists. Once manpower came to be in short supply in 1916, all but a few of the internees were parolled.[14]

More far-reaching in its effects than internment was the gradual suppression of periodicals published in enemy alien languages. During the first years of war only those journals published outside Canada were prohibited, and those originating within Canada were subject only to the censorship imposed on all the press. Even so, loss of advertising revenue forced *Der Deutsch Kanadier* (Calgary) and the *Alberta Herald* to suspend operations in 1915. Heavy restrictions, however, were placed on the enemy alien language press in September, 1918, when the war was almost over. These restrictions, which first required English translations in parallel columns and then forbade publication altogether, illustrate the way in which action against enemy aliens was taken both because it was politically popular and to forestall "vigilante" action by veteran's groups.

In August, 1918, J.A. Calder, minister of immigration and colonization in the Union cabinet, wrote Attorney General Turgeon of Saskatchewan, expressing the fear that unless papers publishing in German shut down, "some incident will turn a mob loose with the usual results." The Order in Council which accomplished this was preceded by a wire from Turgeon's cabinet colleague, C.A. Dunning, warning that "immediate action necessary foreign papers along lines discussed" since "Veterans here likely to cause trouble shortly."[15]

The most openly discrimnatory dominion enactment of the Great War was the War-time Elections Act of 1917. It differed from internment and registration in that it applied to naturalized citizens of enemy origin as well as to enemy aliens, and deprived uncounted thousands of their right to vote. Although designed to ensure either a Conservative victory in the election of 1917 or Liberal agreement to a Union government, it too was undertaken only because the Borden government had received considerable assurance of its popularity as well as its possible necessity. The prime minister and members of his cabinet received many letters advocating such a disfranchisement. Some were from Conservatives, who feared with justification that all naturalized enemy aliens would vote Liberal, but most were from concerned English-Canadian Westerners without political affiliation. "The Canadian population will not stand for these foreigners having a vote and undermining Canadian National Affairs" was one correspondent's way of summarizing what was a general sentiment. Proposals to deny the franchise to European immigrants had been commonplace before 1914 and, to an extent, wartime demands were just an extension of this sentiment. The War-time Elections Act when introduced was well received in the West. One Manitoban even assured Borden that it was an example of "Lincoln's system, government by the people and for the people!"[16]

Also significant is the almost total absence of protest from those disfranchised under the Act, which included every enemy alien naturalized since 1902 and all conscientious objectors.

Some protests were engineered by the opposition but, since loss of the franchise guaranteed exemption from conscription into the army, it was hard for politicians to create much feeling against it. In the Mennonite and Doukhobor communities the Act was actually welcomed, since few exercised their franchise in any event and both groups feared cancellation of their exemption from military service. As J.A. Boudreau notes, "the immigrants who lost their votes were occasionally used as a [political] issue by both sides, but were themselves passive observers."[17]

III

The other minority groups in the Canadian West fell officially outside the "enemy alien" category. The reaction of each of these groups to the Great War, and the subsequent reaction of the English-Canadian majority to each minority ethnic group, varied considerably. Pacifist religious sects–Mennonites and Doukhobors–were clearly identified as a "problem" during wartime. Mennonites were in an especially sensitive position because of their use of the German language. Their response to this situation was to maintain a low profile, avoid political activity, and keep out of the public eye. To demonstrate loyalty and to improve their public image, Mennonite communities made substantial contributions to the Red Cross, the Patriotic Fund, Belgian Relief, and bought large amounts of Victory Bonds. For the first three years of war this strategy worked, and brought the sect favourable publicity. Under the headline "Mennonites Give $761.00 for Red Cross Work," the *Swift Current Sun* praised local Mennonites and castigated "anyone who doubts that the heart of the Mennonites is with the country in this war, even though their religion prevents them from using the sword."[18]

As the war became more bitter, however, particularly after the wholesale cancellation of exemptions from conscription in April, 1918, English-Canadian tolerance of pacifist sects became more grudging. Most Mennonites and Doukhobors had been guaranteed exemption from military service and that guarantee was respected, despite demands that males of military age be conscripted for the army or for farm work. Local Military Service Act tribunals sometimes attempted to draft these men, particularly if they had left their own communities to take jobs elsewhere. All such attempts were overturned in the courts, however. As with Germans and Ukrainians, the amount of verbal abuse directed toward pacifist religious groups increased as more veterans were demobilized because of wounds. "If this country is not good enough to fight for," wrote one returned soldier, "it is not good enough to live in," expressing a sentiment which was almost unanimous among veterans and more prevalent among the civilian population by 1918.[19]

The best demonstration of increased hostility to pacifist groups, particularly the Mennonites, came during the migration of the Hutterian Brethren to Manitoba and Alberta in 1918. The Hutterites had originally settled in the Dakotas, Nebraska, and Kansas but emigrated after the United States entered the war. They referred to themselves as Mennonites in the hope of obtaining official exemption from conscription and, although the dominion government saw through this stratagem, the English-Canadian Westerners were unable to notice a difference between the two groups. Resistance to this migration, although extremely vocal, was completely ineffective. The dominion government was denounced by the Great War Veterans Association for "a gross breach of faith in allowing valuable and selected lands to be sold to this class of settlers." In Alberta, however, municipalities actually made special attempts to attract Hutterite colonies to their neighbourhoods, since it was felt that they would stimulate trade. The Hutterite migration demonstrates that potential profits spoke more loudly than prejudice as far as most Westerners were concerned.[20]

Some minorities accepted the Great War with surprising enthusiasm. Long-established groups like the Icelanders behaved very much as did the English-Canadian community. By 1914 the Icelanders had become sufficiently assimilated to be almost "honorary Anglo-Saxons." Over one thousand enlisted in the Canadian Expeditionary Force and Icelandic historians proudly claim that the Icelanders did not take "second place to any national group." During the war an Icelandic chapter of the Imperial Order of Daughters of the Empire was founded and Icelandic women joined in the frenzy of knitting, bandage-making, and fund-raising. As an observer commented in an assessment of the degree of "Canadianization" of various immigrant groups, "the Icelanders have merged into our Canadian civilization very quickly" with the result that "they were very loyal to our cause during the war and made great sacrifices."[21]

No less loyal, though for different reasons, was Western Canada's Polish minority. One of the promises of the Allies was a Poland free of external domination, and the Poles in Canada worked fervently for the Allied cause. Twenty thousand of Canada's thirty thousand Poles lived in Manitoba. The Winnipeg Polish Gymnastic Association became a recruiting centre for the Polish Army in France and Polish Canadians requested without success that a special battalion be created for them in the Canadian Expeditionary Force. The provincial government of Manitoba contributed $2,500.00 to aid Polish recruiting and urged Saskatchewan and Alberta to do likewise. As Howard Palmer has pointed out, once a minority could demonstrate its patriotism to English-Canadians, it was "accepted to an unprecedented degree." In wartime charities like the Red Cross, Polish women found themselves working with the IODE, the social lionesses of Prairie cities, and in Patriotic parades the Polish float added a touch of ethnic diversity to the demonstrations of enthusiasm.[22]

On an individual basis, however, the Pole was simply another "foreigner," indistinguishable from the mass of Eastern European immigrants. The proposal to create a distinct battalion of Canadian Poles for overseas service was rejected on the grounds that it would be "infiltrated by the disloyal," since "Germans, Austrians and Poles all fraternize in Western Canada." This incorrect opinion held by Canada's generals was shared by the man in the street and angered the Polish community, which resented being identified with "age long enemies" like the Germans and Austrians. When the war ended their resentment combined with the attraction of a new Polish Republic to induce several thousand Poles to return to Europe.[23]

The largest single group of unnaturalized residents in the Canadian West were the American farmers who had begun to pour north of the border after the turn of the century. At one point so many Americans were entering Alberta and Saskatchewan that Parliament was warned that a virtual American state was being established in the West. Although a few reports can be found of American immigrants who criticized Canada's participation in the war, most seem to have accepted the notion that the Great War was a "struggle for democracy" even if they felt no sentimental connection to the Empire. It was in fact an enthusiastic American resident of Alberta, seemingly unaware that Canada was a constitutional monarchy, who cheered Canada's military participation as a step toward eliminating monarchy from the world. After the United States entered the war in April, 1917, the notion of a just war to "make the world safe for democracy" was further confirmed among the West's American population.[24]

The dislocations of war did play a role, however, in ending large-scale American immigration to the Canadian West. Ameri-

Polish community float for a patriotic parade, Winnipeg, 1916.
Manitoba Archives.

can settlers had concentrated in southwestern Saskatchewan and southern Alberta, the driest parts of the two provinces. Drought and depressed prices started a return to the United States in 1913 and 1914, and the war prevented a new movement from beginning. The agricultural boom of 1915 provided opportunity for farmers and farm labourers without the necessity of migration to Canada, and the wartime cost increases made it harder for newcomers to enter farming as a vocation. During the first two years of war the most incredible rumours of crops being seized in Canada for war purposes and greatly increased taxes circulated in northern states to further dissuade would-be immigrants. As the Canadian Department of the Interior concluded in its 1916 *Annual Report*, Americans felt a "reasonable timidity in leaving a peaceful home for a country they felt was in the midst of war," but the American interest in Canadian farmland was never renewed and the northward movement did not recommence after the Great War ended.[25]

IV

Marked as they were by rhetorical and concrete expressions of nativism, the years from 1914 to 1919 were in this sense difficult ones for members of "foreign" minority groups whether they were naturalized citizens or enemy aliens. The nativism which these groups encountered did not begin suddenly with the Great War, however, and in one important respect, the Great War provided these same minorities with an opportunity to establish themselves in an economic sense. The first winter of war followed two years of recession, and immigrant workers and farmers felt its hardship. Crops were bad, prices low. Unemployment was widespread enough to become the inspiration for the system of internment camps.

In 1915, this began to change. Most members of minority groups were engaged in agriculture, whether in the communal agriculture of the religious colonies, as homesteaders, or as farm labourers. Few of these people ever knew the rigours of an internment camp, and the fulminations of nativists, the censorship of the press, and the loss of the ballot made little impact on their daily life. What did affect them was the coincidence of high prices for agricultural products with a shortage of available labour.

As for the immigrant with his own homestead, his economic position improved relative to that of the English-Canadian farmer. In general, his was a small operation. The farmer and his family provided most of the labour required; his sons did not usually enlist, nor were many conscripted for military service. These conditions removed the effects of the labour shortage which was driving up the price of production. While many English-Canadian farmers found profits offset by increased costs, the smaller immigrant farmer received a significantly higher return. The immigrant farmer, Ukrainian, German, Mennonite, or Doukhobor, was able to turn his profit toward expansion, either by improving more of the land he owned or acquiring more land. Another advantage enjoyed by the immigrant farmer was his peasant's conservatism in crop selection. He tended to balance his crops, and was not manipulated by the speculative frenzies that drove English-Canadian farmers, often at a loss, into such things as flax in 1917 and 1918. Thus the immigrant farmer avoided paying an inflated price for seed or for transportation to market to take advantage of upward price fluctuations. The average farm size of the minority group farmer remained smaller than that of his English-Canadian counterpart, and smaller than the Prairie average, but in terms of total growth minority group farms showed greater increases in size, improved acreage, and field crop acreage betwen 1916 and 1921.[26]

For those who did not own farms at the war's beginning, the economic benefit of war came in the form of high wages paid to farm labour. The large number of Westerners overseas reduced the number of workers available in the West itself, and the competition of wartime industry prevented the customary importation of help from Central Canada. Wages for agricultural labour had been considered abnormally high in 1912 when they reached levels above $40.00 per month. By 1916 monthly wages in all three Western Provinces were over $50.00 monthly, and in 1917, with American entry into the war, began the jump that was to take them to $100.00 a month by 1920.[27]

It was this prosperity which increased English-Canadian hostility during 1917 and 1918, and led to demands for conscription of enemy aliens and pacifists for farm labour. "These foreigners have us where the hair is short as regards wages," wrote Mrs. Irene Parlby to Violet McNaughton with an uncharacteristically salty turn of phrase. What made it worse, she continued, was that "their people over there are mangling and killing off our men." Another of Alberta's well-known women expressed the same feeling in public. Roberta MacAdams, elected to a soldier seat in the Alberta Legislature in 1917, told the *Toronto Telegram* that "it makes one feel sad to visit the West now. You see the country being cleared of our fine Anglo-Saxon stock, and the alien left to fatten on war prosperity." Farmers' groups joined veterans' organizations to demand "another form of conscription," the "rounding up of all aliens...to help shoulder the brunt of food production. Have them placed on farms and ranches at a remuneration not to exceed that paid to our brave boys." Thus the *Farm and Ranch Review* outlined its version of the proposal. This was one public demand to which the government refused to acquiesce, however. The legislative response to the prosperity and expansion of non-English minorities came from the provincial governments of Manitoba and Saskatchewan, and affected educational rights rather than economic expansion.[28]

V

Internment, the War-time Elections Act, and the suppression of the foreign-language press were direct results of the wartime situation. The effects of these measures were limited to those minorities which could be connected with the Central Powers, and those effects ended with the Armistice or shortly thereafter. More serious in the long term to Western minorities were the amendments introduced by the provincial governments of Manitoba and Saskatchewan to their educational statutes, since these amendments touched all linguistic minorities and were meant to be permanent. The new schools' legislation was introduced in Manitoba in 1916, and in Saskatchewan in December, 1918. For this reason, some authors have attributed to the war the agitation leading to the suppression of non-English educational rights. Because it is difficult to establish a precise connection, this argument emphasizes the "climate of opinion engendered by the war," which "increased the opposition to languages other than English."[29]

The war did have this sort of effect and was undoubtedly a factor in the timing of the legislation, particularly in Saskatchewan. But it is important to understand that the agitation for compulsory unilingual education was not simply the product of Anglo-Saxon bigotry inflamed by wartime xenophobia. It was instead the culmination of a lengthy campaign to secure educational reform so that the public school could serve as a method of assimilating the non-English-speaking immigrant.

The public school had always been regarded by Westerners as the primary element in that imprecise process which they described as "Canadianization." The Protestant churches had made attempts to proselytize with missionaries, with much the same approach as that used among native peoples, but even churchmen realized that this was unlikely to have much success. Rev. E.H. Oliver, an educator as well as a minister, pointed out that the churches had made "no contribution towards Canadianization." Nor was there "hope of Canadianizing these people through the newspapers which they read. *The hope of Canadianizing these people lies in the public school.*" The exponents of assimilation recognized that the immigrant generation itself would not adapt other than superficially. Their hope lay instead with the children, in whom a dedicated teacher could instil the values and ideals which would enable them to take their proper place in Canadian society. The school system was thus to be "the melting pot from which the *second generation* may emerge Canadian to the core."[30]

But to varying degrees, each provincial educational system had "leaks" which prevented the "melting pot" from turning out a satisfactory product. Manitoba faced the most difficult legislative tangle. The right to bilingual education in English and a second language had been established in 1897 by the Laurier-Greenway compromise and extended in 1912, when an amendment introduced by Conservative Minister of Education G.R. Coldwell granted full financial support to separate schools of minority religious and linguistic groups. By 1914 almost 17,000 students were attending schools which taught in two languages—or claimed to. Many English-speaking Manitobans were convinced that, particularly in the "Ruthenian" school districts, little English was actually being taught. Teachers for those districts came from the province's Ruthenian Normal School and many had limited ability in the English language. With the war and resulting prosperity, more Ruthenians were able to establish themselves on farms and become ratepayers, and the situation threatened to worsen, rather than improve. John W. Dafoe gave voice to this English-Canadian fear:

The Ruthenians invade a settlement occupied by English. Farming small areas, they grow in numbers until they soon constitute a majority of the ratepayers, though in aggregate they may present only a small percentage of the property holdings. Once the majority is assured the agitator—usually a priest—appears in the background; and there follows the putting in office of a board of Ruthenian school trustees, the dismissal of the English teacher, the engaging of a Ruthenian teacher and the conversion of an English school into a so-called bilingual school. The exodus of the English then begins and keeps up until the settlement is almost solidly non-English.[31]

On paper, the Saskatchewan school system should have eliminated this problem, since its bilingual provisions were much more limited. Confessional schools received the support of taxpayers of their own faith. French was permitted in the primary grades, and in advanced years French or another language other than English was permitted to be used for one hour at the conclusion of the school day. This loophole was turned into a window by the fact that Saskatchewan also permitted "private schools" which could teach in any language, and by the fact that the province had no real means of restricting teaching in a second language to one hour in areas where it was legally permitted. In 1918, 214 schools taught in French or another language; and there were 82 private schools in most of which the instruction was in German.[32]

Alberta's educational legislation made no more extensive official concessions to linguistic minorities than did Saskatchewan's but it too was more flexible in practice. Alberta's Ukrainian minority, concentrated in close-knit communities because of dominion land-granting practices, was easily able to circumvent the law. These communities founded and dominated their own school districts, more than 100 of the province's 1,610. The trustees, duly elected, simply hired their own teacher on the basis of his ability to instruct in the Ukrainian language, often from the Ruthenian Normal School in Manitoba. Alberta's overworked school inspectors, fifteen in number in 1913, were unable to enforce the law.

Thus, although the situation was different in each province, all English-Canadian Westerners had reason to be concerned about the future. And there were other reasons for their alarm common to the three provinces. In some rural areas with immigrant majorities, students did not attend school at all, or went for only part of the official school year. Many students left to work on their family's farm before they had completed the primary grades. The result was an educational system that could not complete the task of assimilation with which English-Canadian Westerners were eager to charge it.

The obvious inadequacies produced demands for educational reform before the war appeared to complicate the situation. Alberta used the most straightforward solution at its disposal in dealing with the problem of making its schools into a cultural common denominator. In 1913 Deputy Minister of Education

Robert Fletcher simply began to enforce existing school laws. He refused to grant even temporary permits to teachers without sufficient ability in English, assumed direct control of those school districts which refused to dismiss now unqualified teachers, and replaced these teachers with his own appointees. The test of strength which established provincial authority came, appropriately enough, in the Bukovina School District during the term of 1913-14. The department's appointee was physically assaulted by the mothers of his students, who reportedly "struck him on the head with a pot and proceeded to maul him generally, using their teeth upon him very firmly." But the new teacher, a man named Armstrong, stuck it out. The inspection staff was increased, and attendance legislation introduced and effectively enforced. Alberta's school attendance increased from 60 per cent of those eligible in 1911 to 69 per cent in 1916, and to 76 per cent in 1921.[33]

The West now had its example, for Alberta's success was seen as such by English-Canadians in Manitoba and Saskatchewan. In Manitoba, however, the situation could not be changed as quickly or as easily. In that province the demand for compulsory, unilingual education came from a more general reform movement which had as one of its basic objectives the assimilation of the immigrant. This movement rallied behind the provincial Liberal Party and helped it crush the scandal-weakened Conservatives in August, 1915.

The sense in which unilingual education was seen as a reform measure is reflected in its companions on the legislative order paper, namely, prohibition, woman's suffrage, and direct legislation. In his speech introducing unilingualism, Minister of Education R.S. Thornton described the supporters of bilingualism as "reactionary forces," unable to see that "this question must be dealt with looking *forward* not backward....We are building today for the Canada of tomorrow, and our common school is one of the most important factors in the work." Significant as well is the breadth of English-Canadian support for the measure. Even Winnipeg's labour newspaper, *The Voice*, which rejected wartime jingoism, praised the Liberal government for "doing the people of the country one of the greatest services it is possible to by removing the standing menace of national friction and replacing it by a common tongue and a united people."[34]

The Saskatchewan Liberal government of Premiers Scott and Martin proceeded much more deliberately in its attempts to restructure the school system. Both men showed a commendable and practical determination to keep the question from becoming a partisan issue. Scott took the lead in placing the language question securely within the framework of educational reform. In a speech to the legislature in June, 1915, he called for the formation of a "Better Schools" movement to answer it. The result was the Saskatchewan Public Education League which studied the language problem in conjunction with School District Consolidation and agricultural and vocational education, and produced a pamphlet entitled *Saskatchewan's Great Campaign for Better Schools*, distributed throughout the province in 1916.

The Saskatchewan school legislation problem took on more serious overtones in March, 1916, at the same time as the Manitoba house debated its newly introduced unilingual system. A group of English-speaking trustees tried to have the Saskatchewan School Trustees Association pass a resolution in favour of unilingualism. The resolution failed, and in fact failed again in 1917, but it underlined the fact that a demand for change was there. The provincial government appointed H.W. Foght, an American education specialist, to investigate the situation. Foght's report, tabled in June 1917, clearly outlined the situation created by existing legislation.

Foght discovered that more than half of Saskatchewan's students were in the first grade. Most stayed only a short time in school, and left "without getting the training in citizenship that is so essential in a democratic nation." Although he avoided making the point directly, Foght implied through a series of six "case studies" that a poor school district and a non-English district were synonymous. A district with an English-speaking population had "the best type of community school," one which could "solve the problems of Saskatchewan." A French School District, on the other hand, did "very little in community building." Worst of all was a Ruthenian district, which was "wholly unsanitary," its school building "very crowded and ill smelling with unkempt children," without a "class in the government and history of the British Empire and Saskatchewan." More serious was the teacher's ability in English, which was "very limited" and led to the "children repeating grammatical errors made by teacher." These districts existed, said Foght, because of loopholes in the law, and because "the schools of Saskatchewan are inspected, not supervised."[35]

The Saskatchewan government dealt with these criticisms in two parts. The School Attendance Act of 1917 made attendance at a public school compulsory for children between the ages of seven and fourteen. The legislation imposing unilingualism was put off until December, 1918. French was given some special status, being allowed in the first grade. School trustees were officially required to take an oath of allegiance.

Thus by 1919 each Western province had taken steps toward fashioning a school system capable of performing the function of "Canadianization." Although, as Premier Martin of Saskatchewan commented, "undoubtedly the war has emphasized certain conditions that would not have called for comment in times of peace," educational change was also made "inevitable because of the nature of our immigrant and settlement." The educational systems of Manitoba and Saskatchewan were changed *during* the Great War, not by it. What caused the imposition of compulsory unilingual education was the determination of English-Canadian Westerners to use the school as the primary tool of assimilation, a determination that originated before 1914. The movement for unilingual education contained an element of pure Anglo-Saxon Protestant bigotry, but the roots of the movement extended back into the first decade of the century. Unilingual education was seen as a reform and the movement drew its strength from the English-Canadian population of the West, which, as Harold Foght put it, "is dominated by people of *progressive* type...who have shown a striking determination to escape the hindering influence of back-eastern conservatism by taking action before the educational institutions become afflicted with inertness, resulting in failure to respond to the changing life of their *democratic* civilization."[36]

"Democracy" was the ultimate justification for unilingualism and, in suppressing the educational rights of their minorities, the Western Provinces demonstrated a conception of democracy more American than British. Defenders of bilingualism protested that the new language provisions were against "the best traditions of our Empire," and that they revealed "total ignorance of our history and of the spirit that the liberty-loving Fathers of the Confederation have breathed into our laws." Some unilingualists tried to answer these arguments. "British fairplay means the virtue of tolerance," wrote George Weir in a pamphlet distributed by the Saskatchewan Department of Education. Then using the example of Nova Scotia's attitude to Confederation, he continued: "...but perhaps there may also be a juncture where intolerance becomes a virtue. Majority rule is a maxim of British justice; at least in the presence of a national crisis minorities should yield. Without majority rule our parliamentary institutions would prove unworkable." But most Westerners did not concern themselves with such sophistry. John W. Dafoe summed up their justification of unilingualism. "It is all very well to inveigh against majority rule," he wrote, "but there is no escaping the fact that the majority has the power to rule."[37]

One important question remains to be answered. Why was Western Canada's French-speaking minority not excepted from this legislation? Here the war, or more specifically the attitude of French Canada to it, played a more critical part. Quebec's reaction to the Great War, particularly to the policy of conscription, is well documented. French Canadians in the West followed Quebec's lead, although they spoke more softly in doing so. French Canada never accepted the argument that the war was for freedom or democracy, and argued legalistically from the beginning that "le Canada est en guerre chaque fois que la Grande-Bretagne, sa mère patrie, est aussi en guerre." Western Canada's French-language press treated the war as a European problem and watched instead the encroachments on the teaching of French in Ontario, arguing that "tous les Boches ne se trouvent pas seulement en Allemagne." When conscription was announced, it cried "C'est assez" in its headlines and denounced the Military Service Act as "une loi unique et stupide," designed only to fulfil "la rêve de Joseph Chamberlain et de son école."[38]

Particularly in Saskatchewan this stance helped to determine the outcome of the schools issue, for it gave Protestant zealots like the Rev. Murdock MacKinnon a lever to use on the French language. "French must go [since] Quebec failed us during the war," he exhorted a Regina audience. "Let all enlightened citizens speak, write, and wire until French goes with German." Western Canada's French Canadians recognized that part of the hostility toward French as a language of education stemmed from "l'attitude de Québec vis-à-vis de la guerre, et plus spécialement de la loi conscription."[39]

But Manitoba extinguished French rights in 1916, before conscription even seemed a threat. There was another factor involved in the inclusion of French with foreign languages, simply that Westerners did not see any difference between French Canadians and other minority groups. One reason for this, which has been insufficiently considered by historians, is the attempt of the French-Canadian hierarchy of the Roman Catholic Church to create a sort of pan-Catholic bulwark against the loss of separate schools. Archbishop Langevin of St. Boniface made himself the spokesman for Poles, Ukrainians, and Germans on matters of linguistic rights. As John W. Dafoe told a French-Canadian friend, "the French, the Polish, and the Ruthenians, having made a common cause, invited and received identical treatment." P.A. Talbot, a French-speaking MLA from Manitoba, recognized the determination of his English colleagues. In a letter to Sir Wilfrid Laurier on the schools question, he commented that "il est assez difficile de blâmer les Anglais" for wanting to eliminate Polish, German, and Ukrainian as languages of instruction. The problem, he concluded, was "comment le faire sans affecter les canadiens français?" "Comment le faire?" As he and his fellow French Canadians were to find out, there was not any way acceptable to English-Canadian Westerners.[40]

VI

The Great War made a contribution to the vigour and intensity of Western-Canadian nativism but nativistic behaviour had been evident in the West throughout the years preceding 1914. Before the war began, English-Canadian Westerners were actively concerned about the apparent inability of their society to digest the large numbers of European immigrants it was receiving, and were giving active consideration to a more effective program of assimilation. What the war did was make more obvious a situation which had long existed and create a public demand for an immediate solution. "This has been brewing for a long time," said the *Swift Current Sun*, "but the war has brought it to a head, and brought the Anglo-Saxons to their senses." Applying the analogous American "melting pot" to Western Canada, a Winnipeg minister concluded that "the war has lifted the lid and shown us how many of these elements have failed to fuse."[41]

But despite public determination to increase the effectiveness of attempts to "Canadianize" the immigrant, the war brought few real changes in Canada's overall immigration policy as defined by the dominion government. The British Nationality and Status Act of 1913 had increased the residence requirement for naturalization from three to five years, and required an "adequate knowledge of English or French" and "good moral character" of prospective citizens. The years of war temporarily shut off the flow from Europe but there was no restrictive legislation at war's end to parallel that introduced in the United States in the 1920s. Immigration and the cheap labour it provided were still regarded as essential to Canadian economic growth and this consideration superseded the demand of social reformers that Canada "stand guard at the gates." But if the war failed to convince Canadians of the necessity of a more selective immigration policy, it did cause them to lend their support to two other reform causes, prohibition and woman's suffrage.

CHAPTER FIVE

War and Social Reform

I

A broad-based Western Canadian reform movement existed before the Great War began, and associations advocating prohibition of beverage alcohol, woman's suffrage, or economic reform existed in Manitoba and the North West Territories before the turn of the century. After 1900, the problems of immigration, urban growth, and an expanding wheat economy gave the political, social, and economic dimensions of reformism increasing relevance. In the decade before the war, reform causes won new supporters and became an important theme in Western Canadian life. The "reform movement" which espoused this theme was not a monolith. It was composed of a variety of pressure groups, dedicated to such diverse objectives as tariff reform, the single tax, direct legislation, prohibition, and woman's suffrage. The movement's members belonged to no particular political party and only in Manitoba did they find it necessary to enter party politics to gain their ends. The movement's common philosophical denominator was the Social Gospel, which swept North American Protestantism at the close of the nineteenth century.[1]

By 1914, Western reformers felt that they had made considerable progress toward their goals. Each Prairie Province had an active Social Service Council, committed to the eradication of the liquor traffic and prostitution, and to the amelioration of social conditions in Western cities. The Woman's Christian Temperance Union also spoke for prohibition, and was the leading force in demands for woman's suffrage. Direct Legislation Leagues promised to purify political life by using the initiative, referendum, and recall to make governments more responsive to their electorates. Grain Growers' Associations used their voice, the

Grain Growers' Guide, to support these reforms and to promote tariff and tax reform as well.

But by August, 1914, none of these causes had enjoyed significant success. No Western province had enfranchised its women or introduced prohibition. Direct legislation had been partially implemented in Saskatchewan in 1912 and Alberta in 1913, but Saskatchewan's electorate had failed to endorse the Direct Legislation Act in a referendum. In January, 1914, the *bête noire* of Western reformers, Premier R.P. Roblin of Manitoba, observed sanctimoniously to his attorney general that "seemingly crime does not decrease, seemingly the world is getting no better, seemingly the efforts of social and moral reformers is [sic] not as effective as we would like."[2]

It was on Premier Roblin that reform eyes were fixed in July, 1914. The Manitoba Liberal Party, in the grip of the provincial reform movement, was challenging Roblin's fifteen-year-old Conservative government. The Liberal platform was a reformer's banquet, with direct legislation as an appetizer, woman's suffrage as the entrée, and a promised referendum on prohibition to conclude the meal. Roblin opposed each of these items, and, for the first time, reform and the status quo were presented to a Western electorate as clear-cut alternatives. C.W. Gordon of the Social Service Council described the significance of the confrontation for Western reformers:

> On the one side are the Christian Churches, various [reform] organizations, social workers, and all the decent citizens, on the other the Roblin Government, the Liquor traffic, and every form of organized vice and crime.

But "decent citizens" were apparently not a majority in Manitoba, for the Roblin government was returned for a fifth consecutive term.[3]

The defeat in Manitoba did not mean that reformers throughout the West faced a hopeless situation. The Liberals made significant gains in seats and in their percentage of the popular vote. But the defeat did suggest that in a head-to-head confrontation with "the forces of reaction" (as Nellie McClung described those who opposed reform), reform ideas did not enjoy the support of a clear majority of the electorate. Although the reform movement had increased both in size and vigour, it had not succeeded in winning the enthusiastic endorsement of the general public. This endorsement was necessary if such reform objectives as prohibition and woman's suffrage were to be effectively implemented. It was in their quest for this broad public support that reformers were aided by the Great War.

If Canadian soldiers were giving their lives for "Liberty and Justice" in Flanders, was it not the duty of those who remained behind to see to it that these same things prevailed in Canada? Reformers argued that the Great War was an opportunity to accomplish this very thing, a sign given to Canada in order that "the national sins which are responsible for this awful carnage may be eradicated so righteousness and peace may be established." As Mrs. Nellie McClung told her many readers, the war was necessary for national regeneration, for "without the shedding of blood, there is no remission of sin." If the sacrifice was not to be wasted, the reform program had to be implemented. Even Clifford Sifton, hardly an ardent reformer, recognized that the Great War made it necessary for both Eastern and Western Canada to "cast out everything that threatens its moral health." The war produced a transformation in public attitudes to reformism, changing them to the point that "men who scoffed a few years ago are the foremost now to demand reform." The transformation was particularly pronounced in Western Canada. As Mrs. Irene Parlby told the Saskatchewan Grain Growers, "before the war the real spirit of the West had been smothered in materialism" and public action had been difficult. Because of the common goal of victory, "the big broad free spirit is beginning to emerge again."[4]

In addition to changing public attitudes to the idea of reform, the wartime experience modified attitudes to the role of the state as the enforcer of reform measures. Many reform objectives, most notably prohibition and changes in the system of taxation, called for a previously unacceptable degree of state intervention in the lives of its citizens. The expansion of governmental power necessary to meet the wartime emergency gave government intervention a sanction which it had not had before 1914. The state became "more than a mere tax-collector or polling clerk," it became an organization capable of vigorous, positive activities. An Alberta prohibitionist noted that "the European War has taught us that the State has a right to take such action as will best conserve its forces for the national good." Because of the demands of war, no truly patriotic citizen could react to such action with "resentment or resistance"; the correct course was "a new and affectionate loyalty." This new willingness to grant a more active role to government combined with the wartime ideal of redeeming Canadian society to produce a climate of opinion favourable to reform. It was this climate that the reform movement exploited to gain its ends, in some facets of the movement more successfully than in others.[5]

II

The reform objective which received the greatest impetus from the wartime atmosphere was the prohibition of alcoholic liquors. Despite the social problems which liquor created in the rapidly expanding West, prohibitionists had been unable to convince the Western public or their provincial governments that prohibition was the necessary cure. The events of August, 1914, introduced a new factor into the equation. The Great War provided the necessary catalyst in the public reaction which brought about prohibitory liquor legislation, not only in Western Canada but throughout North America. More than any other reform group, prohibitionists were able to use the exigencies of the wartime situation to lend new credence to their arguments and to exploit the desire to purify society which emerged as part of the domestic side of the war effort.

Prohibitionists had long been fond of military metaphors to describe their struggle. The cause itself was "*warfare* waged against ignorance, selfishness, darkness, prejudice and cruelty," while a successful referendum campaign might be compared to Wellington's victory at Waterloo. Sara Rowell Wright of the WCTU liked to speak of her years as "a private in the rear ranks of the movement," and a book of temperance poems and songs was called *The Gatling*, in reference to the way its contents were to be deployed against the liquor traffic. The war made these rhetorical flourishes a mainstay of temperance propaganda. The liquor traffic was clearly identified with the Kaiser and his brutal hordes as a force blocking the way to a more perfect society. Since a Westerner would "despise the Kaiser for dropping bombs on defenseless people, and shooting down innocent people," he should also despise the liquor traffic, since it had "waged war on women and children all down the centuries." The techniques to be employed in the eradication of both the Kaiser and the liquor traffic were made to seem exactly the same. The Rev. J.E. Hughson of Winnipeg urged Westerners to "use ballots for bullets and shoot straight and strong in order that the demon of drink might be driven from the haunts of men." A cartoon in the *Grain Growers' Guide* carried on the analogy pictorially, depicting a "war" on the entrenched liquor interests, with "votes" being loaded into a field piece by the forces under the banner of "Temperance and Righteousness."[6]

It was not only the tone of prohibitionist rhetoric that was adapted to suit the Great War, its content was modified as well. The war provided the temperance movement with two important new arguments, with which to influence public opinion. The first concerned the moral and physical health of the thousands of young Westerners who had entered the army, many of whom were leaving home for the first time. What would happen to the decent boys from Prairie farms when, befuddled by unfamiliar liquor, they fell victim to the prostitutes who haunted military camps in Canada and overseas? Blighted by horrible unnamed diseases, "thousands of clean-minded innocent young boys who would otherwise have been decent upright citizens will now be nothing but a scourge to their country when they return."[7]

One way to avoid such a result was to keep liquor out of the hands of soldiers. As the Medical Officer of Ralph Connor's *Sky Pilot in No Man's Land* pointed out, "Cut out the damned beer. Cut out the beer and ninety percent of the venereal disease goes...[Soldiers'] mothers have given them up, to death, if need be, but not to this rotten damnable disease." To "cut out the beer," women's groups and WCTUs bombarded legislators and commanding officers with resolutions demanding that bars and "wet" canteens be closed "for the sake of our soldiers." It was not enough to restrict such protection to the period when they were in uniform, only to allow them to become victims of the liquor traffic once they were civilians again. It was the responsibility of every Westerner to see that the veterans found "a clean pure Province for them when they return to us, in which they may rest their shattered nerves and poor wounded bodies." This could only be guaranteed if prohibition became a reality.[8]

No one thought to ask the "clean minded innocent young boys" if they wanted to be rescued from the clutches of temptation. Evidence about the soldiers' opinion on the prohibition question is contradictory. During referenda on the prohibition in Manitoba, Saskatchewan, and Alberta polls in military camps returned "dry" majorities, but no attempt was made to poll the vote of the young men serving overseas. After prohibition was in force, a Calgary private wrote A.E. Cross of the Calgary Brewing and Malting Company that his comrades "would be solid for to have it back to the good old days again" on their return, and soldier poets poked rude fun at both "dry" canteens and prohibitionists. One particularly piquant rhyme entitled "From the

Trenches," derisively celebrated the

> Preachers over in Canada
> Who rave about Kingdom Come
> Ain't pleased with our ability
> And wanted to stop our rum.

> Water they say would be better
> Water! Great Scott! Out here
> We're up to our knees in water
> Do they think we're standing in beer?

Thus it would seem that soldiers were as divided in their opinions of prohibition as most Westerners had been before 1914. But among the public as a whole, the prohibitionist movement was rapidly making converts, and producing a consensus in favour of prohibition.[9]

An important factor in producing this consensus was a second new temperance argument, again one peculiar to the wartime situation. Canadians were told constantly by their governments that efficiency was a prerequisite for victory over Germany. Prohibitionists quickly capitalized on this theme, pointing to the production and consumption of liquor as a drain on Canada's ability to wage war. Not only did drunkenness squander the nation's human resources, it wasted its physical resources as well. A drunken soldier was unfit to fight, an alcoholic worker was unable to produce, and grain distilled into whiskey could not be used to feed starving Allies. Newspapers sympathetic to the war effort put this argument forcefully before the public, asserting that "the bar must be closed because the national existence is at stake. The ship must be stripped for action. All dead weight must go by the boards if we are to win."[10]

As well as providing prohibitionists with two new important arguments, the situation created by the Great War gave them new answers to the most effective defence of the liquor traffic. With thousands of Westerners dying in France to serve their country, criticism of prohibition as a violation of individual liberty lost most of its impact. *Manitoba Free Press* editor John W. Dafoe reflected the popular mood when he pointed out that "the propriety of subordinating individual desires to the general good need not be elaborated at this moment, when millions of men, representing the cream of British citizenship have put aside all their individual inclinations and ambitions." Nellie McClung was even more blunt. "We have before us," she wrote, "a perfect example of a man who is exercising personal liberty to the full...a man by the name of William Hohenzollern."[11]

With their own rhetoric refurbished to suit the wartime situation, and with their opponents' most effective weapons temporarily silent, prohibitionist organizations intensified their efforts to put their case to the public and to the provincial governments. The traditional mainstays of the movement, the WCTU and the Social Service Councils, were joined in their campaign by groups which had not formerly been associated with prohibition. The Orange lodge, the IODE, the Anglican Church, the Winnipeg Canadian Club–all came to the conclusion that prohibition was "the best way of dealing with the liquor traffic *at the present time.*" These new allies meant that prohibitionists could apply increased pressure on Western governments, and the movement began to gain concessions rapidly.[12]

In Manitoba, for example, the anti-prohibitionist Roblin government raised the legal drinking age from sixteen to eighteen and suspended the licences of seventy-two establishments found to be flouting the liquor laws. The Liberal government of Saskatchewan engaged in the same sort of short-term measures, but Premier Scott and his colleagues began to realize that the public was demanding more and that "the time [was] high ripe for action." The step on which they decided fell short of prohibition. In March, 1915, the government announced that the liquor trade in Saskatchewan was to become a state monopoly. Liquor was to be available only in provincially operated dispensaries; all bars, saloons, and stores were to be closed. Scott viewed the decision as a frank concession to wartime public opinion and confided to Senator James H. Ross that this opinion was so strong that "to stand still any longer meant suicide for this government." Scott and his cabinet regarded their dispensary system as a radical step in the direction of prohibition. J.A. Calder thought it amounted to "having decided to go the limit," and expressed "very grave doubts" as to whether a referendum on prohibition could ever be successful in Saskatchewan. The events of the next two years were to show how rapidly the war could change public attitudes to prohibition, and make a mockery of the prediction of as astute a politician as Calder.[13]

In July, 1915, with the Saskatchewan dispensary system scarcely in operation, the voters of Alberta gave a solid endorsement to prohibition in a referendum. All but sixteen of the fifty-eight provincial constituencies returned prohibitionist majorities, with "wet" victories coming only in the northern part of the province and in the areas in which a majority of the voters were class-conscious coal miners, beyond the reach of prohibitionist propaganda. Manitobans followed suit seven months later, with an even larger majority. Only three constituencies remained "wet" in a prohibitionist landslide. Saskatchewan, which has been so proud of its system of government control, suddenly found itself to the rear of temperance sentiment on the Prairies. The government responded once more to public demands and Saskatchewan became the third Western province to endorse prohibition by referendum, in December, 1916. The Saskatchewan majority was the largest of the three, demonstrating again that as the war against Germany became longer and more bitter, the war against booze enlisted more and more recruits. [14]

There are several revealing similarities among the three referenda, in addition to the fact that all were resounding prohibitionist victories. In each campaign the Great War played an important rhetorical role, and temperance workers succeeded completely in convincing the Western public that prohibition and patriotism were synonymous. The referenda themselves were treated as an opportunity for those truly in support of the war effort to stand up and be counted. As the Cypress River *Western Prairie* warned on the eve of the Manitoba balloting, "anyone who will vote in favor of liquor might as well enlist under the Kaiser as far as patriotism goes."

This identification helped prohibitionists overcome opposition among a traditionally hostile group, the Catholic immigrants from Central and Eastern Europe. It had been "this very heavy foreign population" which J.A. Calder had thought would prevent a "dry" Saskatchewan, and much of the opposition faced by prohibitionists during the war did in fact come from this quarter. But many of these people saw the prohibition referendum as a kind of loyalty test, through which they could prove that they were good Canadian citizens, even during this time of crisis. Prohibitionists encouraged this belief, and actively sought non-Anglo-Saxon votes. For the first time, their efforts were rewarded. In Manitoba, the Ruthenian Catholic Political Club and the Slavonic Independent Society "spoke fervently in favor of temperance," while *The Canadian Farmer*, a Western Ukrainian weekly, urged its Saskatchewan readers to "get organized and vote against the [liquor] stores!" Not all non-Anglo-Saxons were converted, but enough voted for prohibition in each of the three provinces largely to neutralize the ballots of their wet countrymen. After the Alberta referendum, the WCTU's Superintendent of Work among Foreigners "knelt in thanksgiving to our Heavenly Father that not all foreign-speaking people voted wet, but that right prevailed and carried the day, even in several of their own district communities." North Winnipeg, perhaps the most aggressively "foreign" community in the West, rejected prohibition by only sixty-five votes. The *Manitoba Free Press* made an observation which applied throughout the West when it noted with satisfaction that "the greatest disappointment of all to the wets was the foreign vote."[15]

The only group completely unmoved by wartime arguments on behalf of prohibition was Western Canada's French Canadians. French Canadians and prohibitionists had never enjoyed cordial relations, partly because of the movement's Protestant character and partly because of its wholehearted support for unilingual education. Since most French Canadians had a lengthy North American ancestry, the idea that they needed to prove their loyalty by accepting prohibition did not occur to them. As the French-language *Le Manitoba* was careful to point out, this did not mean that French Canadians were "plus intempérant que les autres," simply that they resented the totalitarian techniques of prohibition and prohibitionists. In each Western province, Francophones rejected prohibition in the referenda of 1915-16. The comparative effectiveness of patriotic arguments for prohibition on French Canadians and non-Anglo-Saxon immigrants can be demonstrated by an examination of the results of the provincial referenda. The Alberta constituencies of Victoria, Whitford, St. Albert, and Beaver River all rejected the "dry" arguments. Victoria and Whitford, with predominantly Ukrainian electorates, did so by the relatively narrow margin of 1,392 to 1,022 while St. Albert and Beaver River, with largely French-Canadian populations, recorded a combined majority of 889 against prohibition, 1,484 votes to 595.

The second important similarity between the referenda campaigns in Manitoba, Saskatchewan, and Alberta was the demoralization of the opponents of prohibition who had a vested interest to defend. The Great War not only defused the arguments used by the defenders of liquor, it sapped the strength of the defenders themselves. In Alberta, liquor dealers had "very little success" in raising funds to oppose prohibition during wartime. In both Manitoba and Alberta the licensed Victuallers' Association had to turn to the United States for anti-prohibitionist speakers. The Manitoba Association co-operated with the Bartenders Union to obtain Clarence Darrow, who received an enthusiastic reception from "wet" faithful, but an icy one from the general public. The Alberta Victuallers did no better with A.C. Windle, an anti-war editor from Chicago. Windle's outspoken opposition to the Great War allowed prohibitionists to re-emphasize their argument that "wet" sympathy meant a lack of patriotism, and that booze and Kaiserism were inextricably inter-twined. In Saskatchewan's referendum campaign of 1916, there simply was no opposition to the prohibitionists. The Government Dispensary system, in effect for more than a year, had decimated the ranks of hotel keepers, who generally provided the "anti" leadership.[16]

Because of a combination of new factors, all of them attribu-table to the Great War, the Prairie Provinces adopted prohibitory liquor legislation during the first two full years of the war. Provin-cial prohibition was not total prohibition, however. The right to restrict interprovincial trade belonged to the dominion govern-ment and for this reason provincial temperance acts could not prevent individuals from importing liquor from another province for home consumption. A thriving interprovincial export busi-ness rapidly developed. Liquor dealers like William Ferguson of Brandon informed customers in the neighbouring province that "having decided to remain in business, and having still a large stock of draught Brandies, Scotch and Irish Whiskies, Rum, Hol-land Gin, Port and Sherries, [I] will continue to fill orders for *Saskatchewan.*" So much liquor came into Alberta across the British Columbia border that Bob Edwards' *Calgary Eye Opener* included the satirical "Society Note" that "Percy M. Winslow, one of our most popular and dissipated young men, left Monday morning for Field, B.C., where he has accepted a lucrative posi-tion as shipping clerk in one of the wholesale liquor houses. We predict a bright future for Percy."[17]

Western prohibitionists were determined not to stop short of the ultimate goal. To plug the loopholes in provincial legislation, they turned to Ottawa. Petitions, letters, and resolutions re-minded members of Parliament of the gravity of the situation and urged them to introduce measures to abolish the sale and manufacture of alcoholic liquors during wartime. Prohibitionists gave enthusiastic support to Unionist candidates throughout the West during the election of 1917. Dominion prohibition was one of the many reforms which they expected to emanate from Unionism, and the Union Government's bipartisan character and crusading style appealed to the prohibitionist mind. Many influential prohibitionists campaigned on behalf of Union government, among them Dr. Salem Bland, Rev. C.W. Gordon, and Mrs. Nellie McClung. Their work was rewarded, for shortly after they took office the Unionists introduced federal prohibition as an Order in Council under the War Measures Act, to come into effect April 1, 1918.

This made the prohibitionist victory in theory complete. All that remained was the task of making certain that the hard-won legislation was enforced. The war aided prohibitionists in this respect as well, and 1917-18 became the most effective years of the prohibition experiment. Even before the dominion government put an end to importation, Manitoba could report that "drunkenness had been reduced 87% for the first seven months of the operation of the [Prohibition] Act...all other crime has been reduced by 32%" and that "the support accorded the Act has surpassed the most sanguine expectations of its friends." A jubilant Saskatchewan farm wife wrote to Premier Martin that "our little town, which was formerly a drunkard's paradise, since the banishment of the bars and dispensaries has assumed an air of thrift and sobriety." Alberta's Chief Inspector under the Temperance Act claimed that as a result of prohibition arrests of drunks were reduced by 90 per cent, and drinking, crime, and drunkenness decreased in each Prairie province during the last two years of the war. Once the war ended, however, the prohibitionist solution to society's problems became increasingly less effective. The assault on prohibition began almost as soon as the war ended, and prohibitionists no longer had the wartime situation to stimulate public interest in their program. By 1924 all three Western provinces had replaced prohibition with government-operated liquor stores.[18]

How much of the prohibitionists' fleeting success can be attributed to the Great War? To describe the imposition of prohibition as a purely wartime phenomenon would unduly discount the work done before 1914 to convince Westerners of the need for liquor restriction. But it was the emotional atmosphere of wartime which completed the prohibitionists' work, and which allowed prohibition to operate reasonably effectively for two short years. It was the Great War's accompanying national reappraisal which made once indifferent citizens listen to temperance arguments for the first time. Once this was accomplished, the majoritarian zeal which marked the domestic war effort ensured the right "psychological moment to strike the blow." The *Saskatoon Phoenix* understood this process completely. "The temperance party," said an editorial, "has the war to thank for bringing public opinion *to a focus* on the matter of temperance reform."[19]

III

The second reformist campaign aided significantly by the Great War was the movement for woman's suffrage. The prohibition and suffrage movements were so closely intertwined in both program and personnel that what advanced one cause almost automatically had the same effect on the other. In the three Western provinces, the WCTU played a leading role in both and an ardent prohibitionist was usually an ardent suffragette as well. In many parts of the Prairies, the heart of the pre-war suffrage movement was the Equal Franchise Department of the local WCTU.

The war's favourable effect on the achievement of woman's suffrage is ironic, for prior to 1914 the woman's movement had thought of itself as pacifistic and regarded war as one of woman's greatest enemies. War was part of the scheme of masculine domination which denied women an effective voice in society. "History, romance, legend, and tradition," wrote Nellie McClung, "have shown the masculine aspect of war and have surrounded it with a false glory and have sought to throw the veil of glamour over its hideous face." It was for the "false glory" that men went to war, abandoning women to face alone the true responsibilities of life.[20]

The Great War challenged these pacifist assumptions. The wars which women had so roundly condemned had been those with which they themselves were familiar: the South African War, the Spanish American War, and colonial wars in Africa or the Far East. This new war was something very different. Germany was not the tiny Transvaal Republic, but an aggressive modern industrial power. Canada was not fighting for colonial conquest, but for "liberty," "justice," her very survival. Had it not been "the Kaiser and his brutal warlords" who had decided to "plunge all Europe into bloodshed?" And what about Belgium, gallant little Belgium, where "the German soldiers made a shield of Belgian women and children in front of their Army; no child was too young, no woman too old, to escape their cruelty; no mother's prayers, no child's appeal could stay their fury!" Surely such inhumanity had to be checked lest it dominate first Europe, then the world.[21]

It was not only the Great War's causes and nature that made it justifiable. There were its anticipated results as well. There was no reason for Canada's war aims to stop with the defeat of Germany; the same spirit which could accomplish this first purpose could accomplish another as well, the purification of Western-Canadian society, a sort of "spiritual and mental housecleaning." By 1915 Nellie McClung was prepared to concede that the war would be justified if it did no more than bring about prohibition, and was sufficiently reconciled to the conflict to suggest that "it would almost seem as if there is a plan in it after all." Most Western suffragists shared her opinion and ardently threw themselves into Red Cross work, Belgian relief, or other activities auxiliary to the war effort. E. Cora Hind, *Manitoba Free Press* commercial editor, announced that she "would have gone herself if women were accepted." Suffragist enthusiasm was to prove justified, for the war was to play a major role in providing their long-sought victory.[22]

As with the prohibitionist movement, the Great War's first effect on the suffrage movement was on its rhetoric. As Aileen S. Kraditor has pointed out, pre-war suffrage arguments can be divided into two categories, those based on justice and those based on expediency. The older, justice-oriented theme contended that women had a natural right to vote, as did all citizens. Arguments which emphasized expediency stressed instead the good effects that women's vote could accomplish in society. Both types of argument were eminently adaptable to the wartime atmosphere.[23]

The new significance which the Great War gave to arguments based on justice is obvious. If the war were really "the greatest fight for liberty since the Dutch and English broke the power of Spain in the 16th Century," why, women asked, could they not enjoy in Canada the same liberty for which their sons were fighting and dying? Since the war was to be the "vindication of democracy," should not the democratic rights of millions of Canadian women be vindicated at the same time? Men who indulged in such descriptions of the war found themselves caught on the hook of their own eloquence. As W.L. Morton has succinctly put it, "those who would carry democracy abroad must see that it is without reproach at home." Clifford Sifton provides an example of a pre-war opponent of woman's suffrage trapped by his enthusiastic interpretation of the Great War as a struggle for democracy and liberty. His suffragist cousin Ida A. Sifton pointed out the inconsistency of his arguments, and Sifton changed his position on the suffrage question.[24]

Arguments based on expediency gained more force in wartime as well. The public came to accept the idea that the war could be used to redeem Western Canada from her pre-war materialism.

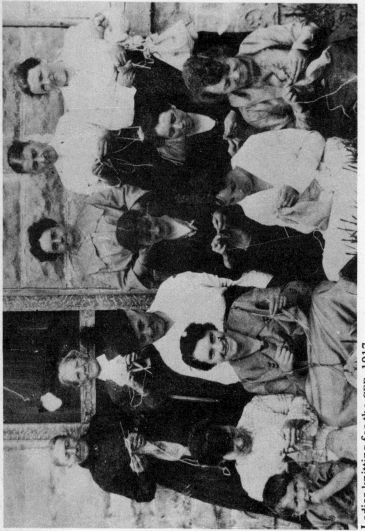

Ladies knitting for the CEF, 1917.
Manitoba Archives.

This might be accomplished without women's votes, but what would happen when the war ended, and reforming zeal dissipated? Women's votes were necessary to prevent backsliding and a return to evil in the post-war era. If this should happen, all the sacrifice, all the bloodshed, would be in vain. As a "war widow" told R.J.G. Stead:

> We women, we women of the war—we have nothing left to be selfish for. But we have the whole world to be unselfish for. It's all different, and it can never to back. *We won't let it go back. We've paid too much to let it go back.*

To prevent this "going back," women demanded the vote. The predominantly English-Canadian and Protestant suffragists of the Prairie West also found another reason why their votes were necessary: to submerge the "unCanadian influence" of naturalized enemy aliens. This created the paradox of groups like the Provincial Equal Franchise Board of Saskatchewan demanding "the disfranchisement of any person...detrimental to the nation's welfare on account of pro-German principles" at the same time as they asked for an extension of the vote as an affirmation of the democratic principle![25]

Not only the rhetoric, but the organizational strength of the woman's movement was profoundly improved by the war. Initially suffragists thought that the war would postpone the achievement of their goal, and war work did force them to devote less time to activities directly concerned with winning the vote. As an organizational aid, however, woman's war work proved to be a stimulus to membership for such groups as the United Farm Women of Alberta and Manitoba. The number of Saskatchewan Homemakers Clubs expanded from ninety to one hundred and ninety between 1914 and 1918, a growth attributed to "demands arising from the war." These clubs had other objectives besides suffrage, but once they became members, women who had formerly been indifferent or apathetic were suddenly exposed to suffragists, and to their ideas.[26]

Women's organizations often co-operated with one another on Red Cross or Patriotic Fund campaigns or in "bees" to knit and sew for the troops at the front. Groups not formerly concerned with suffrage were brought into contact with their more activist sisters in associations like the WCTU. As these women gathered to produce incredible quantities of towels and toques, socks and shirts, balaclavas and bandages, they did not sit mute. Quiet housewives conversed with ardent advocates of equal suffrage, and while

...the nimble fingers of the knitting women are transforming balls of wool into socks and comforters, even a greater change is being wrought in their own hearts. Into their gentle souls have come bitter thoughts of rebellion....They realize now something of what is back of all the opposition to the woman's advancement into all lines of activity and a share in government.

In their Annual Report of 1918, the United Farm Women at Manitoba credited "war relief and patriotic work" with the formative role in the development of "a spirit of national sisterhood."[27]

It was not knitting for the Red Cross alone which produced this new frame of mind. The Census of 1911 had already revealed that increasing numbers of women sought employment outside their homes, a trend which was accentuated by the war. There was no extensive munitions industry in Western Canada to use female labour in manufacturing, but in clerical and minor professional occupations, women took the place of men who left their jobs to enlist. Before the war domestic service had been the occupation of half the working women in Western Canada. After it ended only a third of women workers held such jobs. In the interval between the Census of 1911 and that of 1921 the percentage of the female work force in clerical positions doubled and the same growth was repeated in the professional category, much of this latter increase accounted for by teachers. Alberta alone employed 630 more female teachers in 1916 than in 1914. Wartime also gave women an opportunity in government service and Western provincial governments employed four times as many in 1921 as they had ten years earlier. New opportunities for women did not stop with employment. Women began to infiltrate other areas regarded once as de facto male preserves. At the University of Manitoba, for example, the "two major honours," student presidency and newspaper editorship, went to women in 1917.[28]

In addition to this role as men's replacements, women pointed to the fact that they bore much of the war's real suffering. They were the ones who struggled to keep farms operating and families together in their husbands' absence. As wartime inflation doubled the cost of living the task of caring for a family on the pittance provided by the Patriotic Fund to soldiers' dependents became more and more difficult. Women were also the ones left to "carry on" after husbands, fathers, or sons were killed or maimed in France. Wilson Macdonald caught this sense of sacrifice in verse:

Ah! the battlefield is wider than the cannon's sullen
  roar;
And the women weep o'er battles lost or won.
For the man a cross of honour; but the crepe upon
  the door
for the girl behind the man behind the gun.[29]

Suffragists enjoyed this image of the noble woman, quietly continuing with her duty and bearing her grief in silence. In reality, however, everything done for the war effort by women was given the widest possible publicity and described in the most heroic terms possible. In his study of the domestic impact of the war on Britain, *The Deluge*, Arthur Marwick describes British women as a "gigantic mutual admiration circle" during wartime, and this comment can be applied to their Canadian counterparts. Women's pages of western dailies were filled with stories of patriotic service done by women. The caption accompanying a series of pictures featured in the *Winnipeg Tribune* provides an example:

> It is the men warriors who reap all the material rewards of war; it is the men who have medals pinned upon their breasts; it is the men whom the world lauds as heroes. What of the women who labor and suffer at home in the cause of justice and freedom? In Winnipeg there are thousands of women who are doing as much to win battles as their soldier fathers, brothers, husbands and sons. There are women who are devoting every waking hour to the provision of comforts for boys at the front, and to planning for their care when they return.

Magazine articles publicized the female side of the war effort, making it clear that women "count it an honour to engage in an occupation that strengthens the hands of our Empire." Politicians especially were not allowed to forget women's contributions to the struggle with Germany. Letters reminded them how "truly and nobly our women have shown themselves equal to any emergency," and urged that women be given still greater responsibilities.[30]

Because of this surge of publicity, and partly by direct contact with the new woman, the image men held of women began to change. Some resented the fact that the Red Cross and other activities fell largely into female hands. F.W. Rolt, secretary of the Edmonton Red Cross, found woman's new assertiveness so alarming that he resigned his position, claiming that although "I don't wish to control the ladies, still less do I wish to be controlled by them." But most men, even if they shared Rolt's fears about female domination, were grudgingly forced to concede that women were proving that they deserved equal citizenship. When Parliament debated the question in 1917, for example, R.B. Bennett reversed his former opposition to woman's suffrage. Since women during the war were "discharging their full duties with respect to service," he felt that they must be admitted, "side by side with the male population...to exercise the highest rights and highest functions of citizenship." Two Western members from the other side of the House voiced enthusiasm for Bennett's conversion. W.A. Buchanan stated simply that he was "in favor of women [sic] suffrage...because I believe the women have earned the right to that franchise since the war commenced." Michael Clark added that Bennett's opinion would be well received in the West. since it was "in accordance with the opinions of the vast majority of the people of Western Canada."[31]

It was the provincial governments, however, which acted first on the suffrage question. During the opening months of 1916, each Western province granted its women the provincial franchise. Manitoba came first in January, and in March Alberta and Saskatchewan followed suit. Only one vote was cast against woman's suffrage in all three provinces, that significantly by a French-Canadian member of the Alberta House. Albertans made up for this by returning Louise McKinney and Roberta Mac-Adam to the Legislature in the provincial election of the following year, and by naming Emily Murphy as the first woman magistrate in the British Empire.[32]

The federal franchise was not to come as suddenly or as completely. The dominion government's grant of woman's suffrage came in stages. It was established in principle by the Military Voters Act, which gave the vote to women serving in the armed forces. The controversial War-time Elections Act, enfranchising close female relatives of men serving or who had served overseas, established it further but still not completely. Those women who gained the ballot, especially those in Western Canada, used it to vote for the government which had given it to them. Complete woman's suffrage, like prohibition, was one of the many things reformers hoped for from the newly elected Unionists. Suffragists were not disappointed. Prime Minister Borden personally introduced a franchise bill in April, 1918, and parliamentary assent followed rapidly. On January 1, 1919, less than two months after the war ended, the crusade for woman's suffrage was over, as far as the Prairie Provinces were concerned.

Woman's suffrage would have come eventually without the Great War. There can be little doubt that the women of the Western Provinces would have gained the provincial franchise before too many years had passed, and the federal franchise would have followed after a much longer struggle. But the Great War, with its impact on the suffragists' rationale, organization, and public image, speeded the victory at both levels. Perhaps, however, the war's real importance to the women's movement extends beyond the primary question of the right to vote. The dislocations of war won for some women a foothold in fields formerly reserved for men, and ended the traditional pattern of domestic service as the working-class woman's only occupation. These new opportunities did not bring equality with men for either bourgeois professionals or working-class clerks but did provide a new self-respect. By changing the ordinary woman's image of herself and her position in a world dominated by men, the war advanced the cause of women in ways not simply political.

No other reform group was able to exploit the wartime situation as successfully as were the advocates of woman's suffrage and prohibition. The direct legislation movement enjoyed a brief moment of elation in 1916, when Manitoba's Norris government introduced an Initiative and Referendum Act. The Act was not accompanied by any large-scale campaign based on the mid-war enthusiasm for democracy, but was the fulfilment of a commitment Norris had made while leader of the opposition. The Saskatchewan Conservative Party attempted to resurrect the direct democracy issue during the 1917 provincial election, but were unable to use it to gain any political advantage. This was in part because of the fact that a substantial number of those who had originally supported the initiative and referendum had done so as a means to obtain prohibition, not because of a strong belief in direct legislation for its own sake. By 1917 these people were satisfied, and saw no need to campaign for a tool they no longer needed to use.

The economic reforms sought by Western reformers proved even more difficult to obtain. These had to come from the dominion Parliament, a body not as easily influenced as a provincial government. The war did pave the way for some specific objectives. During 1917 the first Canadian tax on incomes was imposed, and the principle of railway nationalization as exemplified by the case of the Canadian Northern was also well received in the West. Western support for Union government was based on the assumption that more such action would be forthcoming, most particularly a reduction in the tariff. In this respect, and on the question of economic reform in general, Westerners were to be sadly disappointed by the Unionists during the final year of the war.

CHAPTER SIX

1917
Conscription and Coalition

I

For the Allies and for Canada, 1917 was the most critical year of the Great War. It was a year marked by military disasters: mutinies almost destroyed the French Army, revolution took Russia out of the war, Rumania was overrun, and the Italian Army collapsed at Caporetto. At sea, Germany's resumption of unrestricted submarine warfare threatened to sever Britain's North Atlantic lifeline. The infrequent victories that were won were bought at a heavy cost. The capture of Vimy Ridge in April by Canadian troops–the greatest Allied victory to that point in the war–left four thousand Canadians dead. Vimy was just the first part of the tremendous load which was thrust on Canada's soldiers during 1917.

Within Canada, as in Flanders, 1917 became the most critical year since Confederation. Canada's fiftieth birthday was a grim anniversary which began with a national controversy over the Conservative government's manpower policy and ended with the triumph of the newly formed Union government in a bitter midwinter election. For working-class Canadians the "high cost of living" became the most talked about problem, as inflation added 40 per cent to the prices of food, fuel, and shelter. The dominion government took its first halting steps toward regulation of the economy, creating a compulsory wheat marketing board, introducing an income tax, and appointing food and fuel controllers. Over all the other events of the year loomed the Military Service Act–conscription for overseas service–which was to divide Canada along racial lines more completely than at any time in her history.

The people of the Prairie West both reacted to and helped shape the events of the critical year of 1917. The coalition of conscriptionist English-speaking Liberals and Conservatives which called itself the Union government was formed in part to meet Western demands for an end to political partisanship and it gained its parliamentary majority by a virtual sweep of prairie constituencies. To understand why this was possible requires an examination of Western responses to the issues of 1917, to the one overriding issue of conscription and to the Union government which was created to enforce it.

II

The "Conscription Crisis" of 1917-18 is one of the most written-about episodes of Canadian history. It has been interpreted traditionally as a "racial" confrontation pitting French against English, but in recent years the dimensions of the conflict have been extended by historians who have discovered opposition to compulsory military service outside Quebec. This further resistance is attributed to two groups, farmers and organized labour, and centred geographically in Western Canada. Evidence does exist to support the hypothesis that English Canadians in the West and elsewhere were not of uniform mind on the question of conscription, but it is important not to exaggerate the divisions which existed and thus obscure the essential validity of the original interpretation. When faced with the choice at the ballot boxes in the election of December, 1917, English-speaking Westerners chose to vote on the basis of race rather than region or class.[1]

The question of conscription came before the public in two stages. It was introduced in October 1916 when the National Service Board was created to take a national census of the male population between the ages of eighteen and forty-five, with the ostensible purpose of providing information which would permit more effective deployment of Canada's manpower resources. This census, popularly described as "registration," was followed in May, 1917, by the Military Service Act which provided for conscription and which became law three months later after a bitter parliamentary debate. The outline of the emerging national division became perceptible as twenty-five English-speaking Liberals voted with the government in favour of the measure, while only four French-speaking Conservatives did the same. Members of Parliament from Manitoba, Saskatchewan, and Alberta endorsed conscription by a vote of nineteen in favour to only two opposed. The only Western members to vote against the Military Service Act were J.P. Molloy, Liberal representative of the French-Canadian riding of Provencher in Manitoba, and Frank

Oliver, Liberal member for Edmonton.

Were these parliamentarians representative of the opinions of their constituents? Not all Westerners exhibited the same degree of enthusiasm for conscription as did their members of Parliament. French-Canadian Westerners denounced the action of conscriptionist Liberals as "une acte de trahison au Canada et au Laurier" and responded to the Military Service Act with the same anger displayed by French Canadians in Quebec, Ontario, and New Brunswick. Mennonites and Doukhobours, exempt on religious grounds, undoubtedly disliked the law but kept silent. Most ethnic minorities adopted the same approach, no doubt anxious to avoid the attention of those groups more vigorous and vocal in support of conscription.[2]

Historians of the trade union movement contend that organized labour in Western Canada, with its leadership drawn largely from British skilled workers, felt itself subject to no such constraints. Charles Lipton maintains that Canadian labour "held back fervent support from the war," displaying instead a "tacit acquiescence...distinct from the more outspoken pro-war policy of the British and French trade union movements." Martin Robin sees "a strong resistance to the war regimentation, a resistance which culminated in fierce opposition to conscription." Although there was opposition to conscription from trade union leaders, these generalizations are probably overdrawn. Anti-conscriptionists were unable to move beyond speeches and resolutions to concrete action, and did not succeed in creating a working class based opposition to conscription within the West.[3]

The Great War placed Canada's infant labour movement in a difficult position. Organizational progress had been steady though slow, and in August, 1914, 166,000 workers belonged to unions. Labour leaders were justifiably fearful that the exigencies of war would be used as an excuse by employers to "check the remarkable growth of labour movements" and to erode hard-won gains in wages, hours, and working conditions. This realistic fear combined with political ideology to produce in the Canadian trade union movement the same ambivalence toward the war that existed in the British labour movement. While Western labour leaders like R.A. Rigg issued much-quoted statements affirming the principle that "the working men of one country have no quarrel with the working men of another country," one-quarter of Western Canada's union membership was quietly enlisting. In Winnipeg, centre of the Western labour movement, Labour Day 1914 was quiet, "first because of the slackness of the season, then the coming of the war has taken the reservists and many volunteers." To those vocal patriots who pointed to organized labour as a possible hindrance to the Canadian war effort, the *Nutcracker* replied that:

> Canada's army, like all other armies, has been drawn almost exclusively from the wage earning class. So great has been the depletion of Union men owing to enlistment that many unions have had to surrender their charters. In Calgary over 60 percent of the trades unions have enlisted.[4]

The Western Canadian labour movement underwent the same transition that most pre-war pacifists experienced. A.W. Puttee's *The Voice*, the most widely read labour paper in the West, provides an example. In August, 1914, *The Voice* argued that the socialist movement would quickly undermine German militarism and bring the war to a swift conclusion. By the end of October *The Voice* "frankly admitted that the socialists have not lived up to the theories they professed. Evidently then, the theories were unsound." In its New Year's edition an editorial declared that workers would "do well to work for Britain's success in the terrible conflict in which she is now engaged" and warned against the "school of extreme thinkers which holds that to the proletarian it is a matter of indifference which side wins," an opinion which *The Voice* denounced as "a dangerous fallacy." R.A. Rigg sadly concluded that, like *The Voice*, the union movement had been "overwhelmed by the shock of the sudden onslaught, and with the potent appeal of press and public subservient to capitalist interests." He followed this statement by enlisting in a railway battalion, much to the delight of that same capitalist press.[5]

The enlistment of union members and pro-war editorials in labour newspapers suggest more than "tacit acquiescence" to the Great War by the labour movement but not that labour would uncritically accept conscription. The 1915 national convention of the Trades and Labor Congress urged its members to make "a mighty endeavor to secure early and final victory for the cause of freedom and democracy" but the same convention specifically rejected compulsion as a means of securing recruits. *The Voice* and other labour papers watched the progress of conscription in Britain and counselled the British worker to refuse to submit to it.[6]

When the National Service Board introduced registration, the fears of union leaders appeared to be confirmed. J.S. Woodsworth concluded that "this registration is no mere census. It seems to look in the direction of a measure of conscription." Trade union membership had dropped throughout 1915 but was climbing back to its pre-war level because of the stimulus of wartime industrialization in Central Canada. Now conscription, concealed behind the stalking horse of registration, threatened to erode union progress once again. As J.W.S. Eddy of the Regina Trades and Labour Council told Premier Martin of Saskatchewan, the labour movement was

> ...convinced that if these men are allowed to carry out their schemes...all of those protections against abuse which the labor organizations have built up through many years of effort and struggle will be completely swept away and that these men would so firmly fix their control over labor conditions that it would take many years to again remove it.[7]

Most Western Trades and Labor Councils issued resolutions critical of the manpower census, identifying registration with conscription. The Winnipeg Council resolved to block registration by advising its members not to complete their cards and the Regina Council agreed to do the same. Councils in Medicine Hat and Saskatoon refused to go so far but expressed serious misgivings about registration. The most vocal opponents of registration were three Manitobans, R.A. Rigg and F.J. Dixon, who were members of the Legislature, and Winnipeg city councillor S.J. Farmer. They argued that registration was the first step in an attempt of "the privileged classes of the country...to enslave the laboring classes" and urged that questionnaires be returned unanswered. This formidable rhetoric failed to arouse an equally formidable resistance to registration. The report of the National Service Board shows that 86 per cent of the cards distributed were filled out and returned. The *Manitoba Free Press*, fervent in its support of registration, was able to report that in one working-class district only eight of the 500 cards distributed were not returned, and to gloat editorially that "very little opposition is being experienced, even in those parts of the city where it was more or less expected."[8]

When the decision to adopt conscription was announced, Western labour once again became vocal in its opposition and a second series of resolutions and protest rallies began. "If I have to shed my blood," F.J. Dixon told one such rally, "I would prefer to do it here, where I know it would be for freedom." At the annual meeting of the Trades and Labor Congress six anti-conscription resolutions were presented by Western delegates, two from Manitoba and four from Alberta. W.H. Hoop, a Winnipeg delegate, unsuccessfully proposed that a general strike be used to resist conscription.[9]

It took courage for these men to oppose conscription and their stand made them targets of public criticism. Letters to the editor described these labour leaders as "a disgrace to the Empire" and suggested that "men who have no wider vision than to oppose national registration should be interned." There were also proposals to deprive those who objected to conscription of the franchise. The greatest fear of English-speaking Westerners was that by demonstrating a crack in the wall of English-Canadian enthusiasm, these labour opponents of conscription would inspire similar opposition among the West's German and Ukrainian immigrants. The *Winnipeg Tribune* recognized that "the country needs just such fearless, radical, and independent men such as Messrs. Dixon and Rigg" but nonetheless expressed its

> ...abhorrence of any word or act designed to neutralize or impede the great task which lies so close to all true hearts. It is simply intolerable to have any note of discord sounded in our midst at this critical juncture, more especially when that note comes from men who have been elected to positions of trust and responsibility, whose actions and words *cannot fail to have a highly pernicious influence upon the minds of foreign masses of our population whom we are doing our best to assimilate and train up as British citizens.*

Angry editorials were not all that anti-conscriptionists had to face. Returned soldiers heckled their meetings and sometimes carried out physical assaults, and several anti-conscriptionists paid for their principles with the loss of their jobs.[10]

But the spirited opposition of labour leaders to the Military Service Act had no more effect than their opposition to registration. Their dramatic rhetoric struck a responsive chord among the militant United Mine Workers of District 17 in Alberta and British Columbia, but in Western cities union members generally do not seem to have shared the determination of the leadership. Meetings called to oppose conscription sometimes ended by passing resolutions in support of it as returned soldiers crowded in to make the case for compulsory service. Opposition to conscription was an important element in the nomination of seven labour candidates in the dominion election in December but none was able to retain his deposit. The situation was very much as *The*

Voice had described it a year before conscription became an issue in Canada. "There can be no doubt that the government could enforce conscription should it so desire," had been *The Voice's* opinion. "The workers of Canada have no political or economic strength capable of putting up an effective resistance. They might howl, but they would have to submit."[11]

The farmers of Western Canada generally supported both the national registration campaign and the subsequent conscription, insofar as the publicly expressed opinions of the Manitoba and Saskatchewan Grain Growers' Associations and the United Farmers of Alberta may be interpreted as the opinions of the 100,000 members of the three organizations. There could be little question in any English-speaking farmer's mind about the justice of Canada's cause or her responsibility in the Great War. The newly elected president of the Manitoba Grain Growers told the association's annual meeting in January, 1917, that Canada's "honour, our soul, our national liberty are at stake" and that "our duty is plain; we must put into the war of men and money until we see the triumph of those principles which we so highly prize." The logical extension of this understanding of the war was conscription, particularly since the Western provinces had contributed a disproportionate share of the volunteers to the Canadian Expeditionary Force. After a visit to the West, General S.C. Mewburn was able to report that popular sentiment was "more intense for compulsion than in the East" while an Edmontonian could assure Prime Minister Borden that "a great majority of the English-speaking people of the West are favourable" to the Military Service Act.[12]

Many Western farmers, however, were afraid that conscription, a reasonable proposal in principle, was being used by the Conservatives to accomplish political ends as much as military ones. Conscription, with its popularity in English Canada, could be no more than a trick of "the big interests" which would use it "to cover up the bad record of the government" and "to divert attention from economic reform" so important to the West. Because of this fear, some Western farmers gave their support to conscription on two conditions.[13]

The first was one which had been mentioned by some labour groups, the idea that wealth should be conscripted as rigorously as manpower. Thus the Grain Growers endorsed the manpower census of the National Service Board but in their resolution of support urged "that a Census of the wealth of Canada be immediately taken." After the Military Service Act had passed its second reading, the United Farmers of Alberta resolved to "hereby affirm our belief in the principle of selective conscription of men to carry on the war and in *the conscription of wealth* for the same purpose." The farmers' resolutions provided no clear-cut definition of the phrase "conscription of wealth." The term came to encompass demands ranging from an end to wartime profiteering to the nationalization of all of Canada's industries. When uttered by a Western farmer, however, it meant the introduction of an income tax coupled with heavy taxation of the abnormally high profits of Central Canadian manufacturers. This was seen by the West as the first step toward a more equitable basis for federal taxation, since it would supplement the revenue provided to the government from the tariff and perhaps make possible future reductions in duty.[14]

The farmers' second qualification in supporting conscription was that it could only be enforced by "a National Government, in which the interests of the political parties shall be made entirely subservient to the interests of the state." To drive this point home forcefully, an Alberta farmer clipped an Arch Dale cartoon from the *Grain Growers' Guide* and mailed it to the prime minister. It pictured Laurier and Borden, adrift in their "Ship of State" on the turbulent sea of "National Unrest." Both party leaders are rowing vigorously, and beads of sweat dot their foreheads. But since they are pulling in opposite directions, the "Ship of State" is going nowhere. On the jetty "the People" in the person of a Western farmer shouts advice. Waving the banner of "National Welfare," the farmer suggests to Borden and Laurier that "if you really want to make headway, hoist this flag and pull together."[15]

III

The idea that political differences should be set aside in federal politics for the duration of the war was not new, nor was it peculiar to the West. The *Manitoba Free Press* had cried "Let Faction Cease" on the day after war was declared and a sort of political truce had prevailed during the first wartime session of Parliament. Once that session had been concluded, however, both Liberals and Conservatives violated the truce whenever they considered it to their advantage. The Conservatives' chief Western organizer, Minister of Public Works Robert Rogers, tried to persuade his party to go to the people early in the war to turn patriotism to party advantage and gain a larger majority. This proposed election never took place but, if it had, the Liberal organization in the West would have been ready to move quickly to deal with it. The political truce, for the few months that it was observed, was motivated by tactical considerations rather than patriotic convictions on the part of politicians. "The parties have publically declared a truce," editorialized The Nutcracker, "but each is working underhandedly for advantages."[16]

The demand for a "National Government" meant something more than a ceasefire in the battles of party politics. The midwar political crisis over conscription focused public attention on the dominion government's conduct of the war. Businessmen, service clubs, farm organizations, labour unions, and church groups met, discussed Canada's participation in the Great War and resolved that that participation could be directed most effectively by a government without partisan affiliation. Like "conscription of wealth" this vague concept of a "national government" was not always clearly defined in the resolutions that emanated from these meetings. Some simply wanted the Borden government to "reinforce" itself by adding members of the opposition to create a government like that formed in Britain the previous December. Other resolutions were more drastic, demanding the resignation of Borden's Cabinet and its replacement by "a really national government, not merely a coalition of Conservatives and Liberals," a government "in which all classes of the nation would be represented."[17]

But Western resolutions agreed on one thing, that it would not do to replace the Borden Conservatives with the Laurier Liberals. The Grain Grower's Guide felt that to defeat the government and simply replace it with the opposition "would be a catastrophe at the present time." J.W. Dafoe warned Clifford Sifton that "the feeling of discontent is directed towards both parties, and it is by no means certain that the Liberals would profit by it in the event of an election." To Westerners who hoped for an end to party government as a means of achieving political and economic reform, this demand for national government was a hopeful sign. "Never was such a non-partisan spirit abroad," wrote Violet McNaughton, a Saskatchewan grain grower and long an advocate of an end to "partyism."[18]

Before the war began, Western farm organizations had talked of entering politics independently of the two "old" parties. In a 1916 article for Maclean's Magazine, Nellie McClung pointed out that "party lines are not so tightly drawn in the West" and that in the case of social reforms like prohibition "great issues have been decided outside of politics." Wartime made non-partisanship even more necessary, and the 1917 provincial election in Saskatchewan provided concrete evidence that united political action could be effective. In the provincial constituency of Swift Current, D.J. Sykes had been elected as a farmers' candidate after receiving the endorsement of the Grain Growers and the newly formed Non Partisan League. Specifically citing this example, an enthusiastic farmer wrote to the *Manitoba Free Press* to inform politicians that since Canada was "not going to get unity at the top" Western farmers intended to "start at the bottom."[19]

In two Western constituencies independent candidates were nominated in the summer of 1917 to contest the as yet uncalled federal election. In Marquette, Manitoba, 250 farmers met in convention to nominate R.H. Dennison, who pledged himself to the "farmers Platform" of the Canadian Council of Agriculture and coupled this pledge with a commitment to support the rigorous enforcement of conscription. In Moose Jaw the president of the Saskatchewan Grain Growers' Association, J.A. Maharg, was nominated by a similar convention. Prime Minister Borden was urged not to allow him to be opposed by a Conservative, since Maharg promised to be "a tower of strength to you in your fight for conscription" and would swing a great many of the rank and file of western farmers that no other men in Canada could swing." This outbreak of non-partisan activity delighted the *Grain Grower's Guide*, which urged that it continue. "The West was never in a better position to elect independent progressive candidates for the House of Commons than it is today," wrote editor George F. Chipman. "Public opinion is thoroughly aroused and neither of the federal political parties has any firm grip on this country. Both of them are in bad odor."[20]

Party politicians did not take these first steps toward the creation of an independent regional party in the West lightly. Prime Minister Borden, his Western ministers, and members of the Liberal opposition were well aware of the danger that such a grass-roots political movement, based in the farmers' organizations and professing dedication to the war effort, posed to them, and realized that only the creation of a "Unionist war administration" was likely to "prevent the formation of a western political party, now imminent." But putting together such a government proved difficult to accomplish. Attempts to produce a suitable coalition which could cut short a third party movement were unsuccessful during the summer of 1917, foundering on the rocks of interparty distrust and suspicion. Liberal partisans in particular held fast to the hope that their party might win an electoral victory on its own.[21]

The extent to which the "hard boiled practitioners of the political game" were able to frustrate attempts at a coalition government was demonstrated during a regional convention of Western Liberals held in Winnipeg on August 7 and 8. Summoned by Western MPs favourable to conscription in co-operation with the provincial governments, whose premiers also favoured conscription, the convention was expected to produce a definite resolution committing Western Liberals to compulsory service and to Union government. Instead it became "a bomb that went off in the hands of its makers," by failing to endorse conscription and by affirming its "appreciation" of the leadership of Sir Wilfrid Laurier. The explanation of this was that, despite general support throughout the West for both Union government and conscription, it was not the public that was represented at the convention. The selection of delegates was left to the local constituency associations, with the result that those most active in the party "machine" wound up with voting credentials. In Brandon, for example, delegates were chosen by the constituency executive alone. Most Liberal farmers were unable to attend the convention because wet weather had delayed haying into early August. In Alberta, C.W. Cross and Frank Oliver, two ancient enemies, joined forces to hold many Alberta delegates for Laurier. Conscriptionist Liberals howled that the convention had been controlled by "the professional politician, the hide-bound partisan, and the party heeler," but came to the conclusion that despite "the strong sentiment in favour of a Union Government...the idea will never be carried into practice." Laurier was delighted with the result of the Western Liberal Convention, which seemed to doom Union government. With a touch of bilingualism he wrote a Saskatchewan supporter that "à tout événement, all's well that ends well."[22]

But all was not ended, although attempts at union were temporarily halted. The West was not inclined to allow the verdict of the convention to stand as its regional attitude to a national government. The Liberal delegates were reviled by the daily press and by farm and labour journals as "political wire pullers" and "the job hunting crowd who certainly do not represent the people of this Western Country." The convention itself was described as "a party frameup" directed by "machine manipulators" and "seething at all times [with] a spirit of partisanship," and was accused of failing "to grasp the greatest opportunity that has ever been presented to Western Canada," an opportunity to secure "a truly national government." A week after the convention a non-partisan assembly was held in Winnipeg Centre, at which Conservatives, Liberals, and trade unionists were present. The delegates nominated Rev. S.G. Bland, a Social Gospeller well known to social reformers, as the third Western independent "win the war" candidate pledged to support a union government. Arrangements were made to conduct similar nomination meetings in another constituency. In an editorial entitled "People are Restive," the *Swift Current Sun* concluded that "it is plain to us that what the people want is a national administration." A sales representative who had spent the summer touring Manitoba, Saskatchewan, and Alberta confirmed that this was indeed the sentiment of the West. He informed the prime minister that after speaking to "the businessman, the farmers, the traveller, the train man, the school teacher" he had come to the conclusion that "they are sick of past political schemers who place party before everything else."[23]

The danger of independent political action from the West helped convince both Liberals and Conservatives that a coalition government was desirable and the introduction of the War-time Elections Act made such a coalition inevitable. The act, passed by means of closure in September, 1917, disenfranchised all citizens who were of enemy alien birth if they had been naturalized after March 31, 1902, or who habitually spoke an enemy language. Members of pacifist religious groups and other conscientious objectors were also disenfranchised. Exceptions were made for those who had sons, grandsons, or brothers serving overseas in the Canadian forces. At the same time as it removed these former voters from the electoral lists, the War-time Elections Act added a group of new voters, wives, widows, mothers, sisters, and daughters of members of the Canadian forces who had served or were serving overseas. By taking the vote from an important group of Liberal supporters in Saskatchewan and Alberta, the Act had the effect of propelling Western Liberals into a coalition. Liberal MPs battled the War-time Elections Act, since they recognized that its success would be a serious political blow to them. From the majority of English-speaking Westerners, however, there was surprisingly little adverse reaction to the Act. The West had been concerned about the influence of the immigrant in politics before the Great War began. Reformers feared that the immigrant's lack of political knowledge made him the tool of the electoral machine, while conservatives thought that this same naïveté meant that he could be led easily to socialism. To protect the Canadian political system, proposals to control access to the franchise had come from writers at both ends of the political spectrum. The special conditions created by war brought proposals advocating disenfranchisement of enemy aliens from editorialists, veterans' groups, and even from the Provincial Equal Franchise Board of Saskatchewan![24]

Thus that part of the War-time Elections Act which removed the franchise from naturalized immigrants met few serious objections. "If they have no voice in the life and death struggle in which this country is engaged, they are much more fortunate than if they had never left Europe," was the reaction of one Western editor. The aspect of the Act that did attract criticism was its failure to extend the franchise to all "British" women. As one woman suffragist told a reporter from the *Manitoba Free Press*, "the West is very much stirred up. There is much indignation that women born under the Union Jack should be numbered among the aliens." Most women overcame their indignation, however. Mrs. Irene Parlby told Violet McNaughton that Western suffragists "have come to see that it is a war measure and they have realized that it alone would give us conscription."[25]

The loss of an important part of their political base was the final factor in convincing English-speaking Liberals from Western Canada to become part of a Union government, and Liberals in Ontario realized that the party could not survive without its Western strength. This change of heart was so abrupt that Craig Brown and Ramsay Cook have sarcastically observed that "the sound of Liberals rushing to Ottawa could almost be heard across the land." The new Union cabinet, made up of twelve Conservatives and ten Liberals, was announced to the public on October 12, 1917. Five cabinet ministers, two of the former and three of the latter, were chosen from Manitoba, Saskatchewan, and Alberta. As an overt concession to Western farm opinion the president of the farmer-owned Grain Grower's Grain Company, T.A. Crerar, was named as minister of agriculture, but the other four—Arthur Meighen, Sir James Lougheed, J.A. Calder, and Arthur Sifton—were professional politicians with long-standing party connections.[26]

IV

The long-awaited "National Government" now existed, and the West had played a vital role in convincing the politicians that it was necessary to create it. The task the new Union government faced was to convince Westerners, particularly farmers and workers, that it was truly a non-partisan government "in which all the different interests of the national activities and life" were represented. One interest which was clearly not represented was French Canada, and French Canadians in the West denounced the new coalition as a plot of "l'intérêt financier" and suggested that it would collapse within a month. This opposition was expected and was dismissed as without consequence. Leaving aside the French minority, one Unionist supporter expressed the confident belief that "outside of machine politicians of both sides of politics and our foreign population...the West will be behind the new government." To an extent, this prediction proved accurate. The "hard-boiled" Liberal politicians like Frank Oliver who had originally objected to coalition found the new cabinet unacceptable. The "foreign population" probably disliked the new government but kept its opinions to itself, as it had done on most issues since the beginning of the war.[27]

But there was also criticism directed at Union government from those who had been very much in sympathy with the idea of a national government but who refused–not without reason–to consider the Union as true non-partisanship. Most notable among these critics was the Non Partisan League, organized in Alberta and southwestern Saskatchewan during the spring of 1917. This league had originated in the United States and migrated to Canada in time to nominate candidates in the Saskatchewan and Alberta provincial elections. Two of its Alberta candidates, Mrs. Louise McKinney, president of the WCTU, and James Weir, a director of the UFA, were successful. The league's primary ambition, however, was to wrest leadership of the farmers' movement in Alberta from the United Farmers; and it was the progress of this struggle that came to determine its attitude to Union government.[28]

In its newspaper *The Nutcracker* (later the *Alberta Non Partisan*), the league had been vocal in its advocacy of a national coalition government, suggesting that Borden add Michael Clark, A.B. Hudson, Premier Brewster of British Columbia, C.A. Magrath, or Charles Hibbert Tupper as new Western cabinet members. Once negotiations to construct a Union government had commenced, the League's secretary, J.H. Ford, began correspondence with Borden in an attempt to have it represented in any new cabinet. Claiming that league membership "by December may be possibly between ten and twelve thousand," and that this meant control of "the balance of *voting power* in about eight Federal Ridings," Ford suggested that the league was prepared to support a Union government led by Borden which included "representatives chosen by the Non Partisan League." Borden refused to consider this or two subsequent requests for such consultation, and instead hoped to gain support from the numerically superior UFA. [9]

As a result, the Union government announcement on October 12 was subjected to bitter tirades from the *Alberta Non Partisan*, despite the fact that it was similar to the one *The Nutcracker* had proposed four months earlier. "Make no mistake ye farmer electors," intoned the *Non Partisan*'s editor, William Irvine, "the ship of state sails under the same old buccaneer management. There have been a few changes in the crew, but the same incompetent seaman walks the quarterdeck." T.A. Crerar was castigated particularly severely for having "sold out for the mess of pottage," and Frances Beynon, former women's editor of the *Grain Grower's Guide*, accused him of having been "brought over to the side of the enemy."[30]

Organized labour shared the Non Partisan League's hostility to Union government. *The Voice* had also called for an end to political division in wartime but was unhappy with the new coalition, dismissing it as an "advance guard for special privilege." In a prognostication singular in its inaccuracy, it told its readers that Western cities would reject the Unionists and instead be "a labour stronghold" in the upcoming election, and that "the farmers are not taking this 'union' stuff. They believe in farmer representatives to protect the farmers."[31]

To most English-speaking Westerners, however, Union government appeared to be what they had been waiting for. Those who had feared that they would have to support the Conservatives to obtain conscription were relieved. As one of them wrote to T.A. Crerar, "if a U.G. had not been formed many of us would have been compelled to play the game of the Eastern Interests or be associated with those who have not the interests of the Empire at heart." Westerners were also proud "to note the large place which Western men are given in the thought and life of this affair." The inclusion of Crerar was particularly important to a favourable acceptance by the West of the Union cabinet. Although he had been an active Liberal, his position as president of the Grain Growers' Grain Company made him appear to have come from outside the political arena, and convinced some skeptics of the cabinet's non-partisan authenticity. Salem Bland wrote to Crerar that Union gave "the promise of a United Canada" and that he was sure that "the new Government will capture the West." Mrs. R.F. McWilliams, a Manitoba suffragist, congratulated Crerar on his decision to enter the cabinet, and promised the help and sympathy of "the organized women of the West" to the Union government. The *Grain Growers' Guide* summed up this enthusiasm and concluded that

> ...never since Confederation had there been a cabinet at Ottawa containing the brains, force, and executive ability represented in the new Union Government....History will accord a high place to those strong men in both parties whose love for their country has been greater than their love for party.[32]

In October, 1917, the last thing that concerned the members and supporters of the Union government was the verdict history was likely to return upon them. They had an election to win and Western support was going to be vital, particularly as the number of seats in Manitoba, Saskatchewan, and Alberta had been increased from twenty-seven to forty-three since 1911. The Unionists had to keep the support of those dedicated to non-partisan politics, and convince any who were lukewarm about Borden's version of Union government that it was the genuine article. The Unionists accomplished this in four ways, by incorporating solutions to traditional Western problems into their platform, by reacting to Western pressure for "conscription of wealth," by tailoring the operation of the Military Service Act to meet farmers' specifications, and by absorbing as Union government candidates independent nominees of the Grain Growers' Associations. Finally, to convince voters unmoved by these techniques, Unionist campaigners appealed to the bigotry of English-speaking Protestants to drive a wedge between those of British descent and the French Canadians and those immigrants who were not deprived of the franchise.

At the same time that the date for the election was announced, the Union government issued a platform designed to have particular appeal in the West. The first of its twelve planks called for "the vigorous prosecution of the war," while seven of those remaining were directed at specific Western demands. Sections two, three, four, and nine promised political and economic reform through "the abolition of patronage," the introduction of woman's suffrage, "increased taxation of income," and "effective measures to prevent excessive profits." Section five promised "a strong and progressive policy of immigration and colonization" designed to achieve "settlement upon the land." Section seven promised a solution to the railway problem through "co-operative management of the various railway systems so as to secure economy in operation," while section ten promised government support for co-operative marketing ventures "so that the price paid by the producer may conform more closely to that paid by the consumer." Small wonder that the *Grain Growers' Guide* could gush that "it can be truly said that this is the most progressive program put out by any government actually in power in the last twenty-five years."[33]

A platform alone could not deliver the forty-three Western seats. The new government had to demonstrate that it intended to carry out this program, and its supporters had to make the public aware that it was being carried out. Most important was action to effect the tax reforms vaguely described as "conscription of wealth." It was important to the West for two reasons: first because it showed that the government was seeking new revenue from direct taxation which might make possible future tariff reductions; and, second, because it proved that the Union government had the courage to confront the "big interests" supposed by the public to be reaping enormous windfall profits through wartime profiteering. The first steps toward "conscription of wealth" were taken before the public pressure for Union government succeeded. In July, 1917, the Borden government had introduced Canada's first income tax and in August had begun the process of railway nationalization that led eventually to the Canadian National Railway system.

Both these measures attracted favourable comment in the West, although it was somewhat grudgingly given. The *Grain Growers' Guide* interpreted the income tax as "an adjunct of the conscription bill...the natural result of the demand for conscription of wealth as well as manpower," but was unhappy that the tax was to be substituted for the excess profits tax rather than added to it. Similarly mixed feelings existed in the West about the nationalization of the Canadian Northern. The government's decision to nationalize rather than to extend further loans brought "general gratification among the farmers of Western Canada," but the inevitable decision to compensate Mackenzie and Mann was described as "graft—no other word will suit the case." Westerners, whether Liberal, Conservative, or independent politically, believed that neither entrepreneur had invested much in the road beyond time and audacity, and argued that "the country does not owe the two belted knights a single dollar."[34]

Despite these grumblings, railway nationalization and the income tax provided a solid basis on which the Union government could claim to be conscripting wealth. To demonstrate that these actions were only a beginning, the government introduced a system of profit controls on the packing and milling industries, the "middlemen" so despised by the Western farmer. These controls convinced skeptics that "at last the government appears to recognize the seriousness of the situation." To make certain that the public was aware of the controls, the news was trumpeted in the press and by Unionist speakers and campaign literature. "Critics of Union Government who aver that there has been no conscription of wealth...must either be densely ignorant or are willfully misrepresenting the facts," wrote the *Calgary Herald*, listing the income tax and the new profit controls as evidence. In one Unionist pamphlet a "Union supporter" describes the same measures to a disbeliever and concludes that "the Union Government has taken these things in hand....Why, man, they have *only begun* to conscript wealth."

The idea that more drastic measures would be taken to reform taxation after the Unionists were re-elected continued to be dangled before the Western voter. J.A. Calder told an audience in Moose Jaw that "as far as the Union Government is concerned the whole question of taxation must be revised...proper methods must be devised to place the burden of the war where it should be placed." The unspoken implication was that "it should be placed" on Central Canadian industry and its wartime profits, not on the farmer or the working class consumer through the protective tariff.[35]

The most potentially dangerous issue for the Unionists was the conscription of men, not that of money. Western Canada supported conscription in part because of the expectation that it would equalize the drain on the manpower resources of each of Canada's regions. Since "the rest of Canada except Quebec is bled already," Westerners expected that the Military Service Act would be applied most vigorously in that province. But enforcement of the Act was in the hands of local tribunals. In Quebec and in French-speaking areas of the West these tribunals seemed quick to dispense exemptions, while in English-speaking areas officials were more reluctant to let men escape service. "I am a Unionist worker and supporter" wrote A.A. Langford of Biggar, Saskatchewan, to Sir Robert Borden,

...but talking to a number of our workers this morning, they are entirely provoked at the way the exemption boards in Montreal and other places are exempting the French Canadians....What is being done? Brace up and show these people that they can't carry on this stuff. Failure to do so will ruin the Unionist cause quicker than anything else I know off [sic] as the workers will soon become restless.

In some Western districts, the tribunals were as rigid with regard to exemptions as the Quebec tribunals were flexible. A Portage la Prairie farmer complained that there were "so many cases of almost robery [sic] that the Portage plains is in an uproar." The problem, he maintained, was that "this local tribunal is composed of one coal merchant, an Insurance Agent, and a Ticket Agent, and two of them have each lost a son making them very bitter." Another farmer demonstrated the Western attitude to conscription by complaining that "the Military Service Act which is now being enforced (which I am heartily in sympathy with) is draining our district of all available men." The *Grain Grower's Guide* found it "impossible to understand" the failure of the Union government to exempt farmers and farm workers, and warned that "the present conscription policy" could have "serious political consequences for the Unionists."[36]

Before this angry editorial could reach its readers, the Union government had acted. Protests against the conscription of farm labour had been particularly virulent in rural Ontario, and on November 20 General Mewburn announced in Dundas that tribunals were being instructed to exempt all genuine farmers, farmers' sons, and farm workers. This decision was taken primarily with rural Ontario in mind but it had a beneficial effect on the Unionist cause in the West as well. To make certain that farmers were aware of Mewburn's promise, the Unionists placed a full-page advertisement in agricultural newspapers and rural weeklies, with large headlines shouting "FARM HELP WILL NOT BE DRAFTED."[37]

The fourth technique used by the Union government in its wooing of the West was the careful selection of candidates, since both the candidates themselves and the techniques by which they were selected had to reflect as scrupulous a non-partisanship as could be achieved. As soon as the election writs were issued there was a scramble among Western Liberals and Conservatives for nominations, since in most constituencies a Union government label seemed to mean certain success at the polls. The Unionists had to be careful not to step on the toes of the indepen-

Women haying, Souris, Manitoba, 1916.
Manitoba Archives.

dent candidates who had already been placed in the field, particularly those nominated by farm organizations. The Grain Growers' Associations objected to the "old time" methods of candidate selection and demanded as the price of their support "a goodly number of men from Western Canada who have not only been elected as win-the-war representatives but also as loyal supporters of the farmers' platform."[38]

Obviously a candidate like John A. Maharg, the president of the Saskatchewan Grain Growers who had been nominated as an independent in Moose Jaw, had to be granted a Unionist endorsement. Three other men who held office in farmers' organizations were given Union endorsement as candidates. The candidate nominated originally in Marquette in Manitoba was asked to step aside, but for T.A. Crerar, not a professional politician. The other independent challenged by the Unionists was Salem Bland, the Social Gospel Methodist minister who had been nominated by a non-partisan convention to contest the seat of Winnipeg Centre. Bland lost a second nominating convention to Major G.W. Andrews in a meeting packed with returned veterans, but despite his defeat became an active supporter of the new Unionist candidate, campaigning at Andrews' side when he met working-class audiences. This co-option of the farmers' movement and of previously nominated independents failed only once, in Mackenzie, Saskatchewan, where two would-be supporters of a national government opposed each other.[39]

V

While candidates were being nominated, the Unionist campaign was continuing to take shape. Unionist Liberals were waved before the public on every possible occasion. C.A. Dunning, provincial treasurer of Saskatchewan, was a particular favourite because of his close connection with the farm movement. Liberals from outside politics took the platform as well, like popular novelists Nellie McClung and Ralph Connor. T.A. Crerar, however, was the new government's most important Western prize. His role was to prove that the Union government was genuine. "The Grain Growers have always believed in Union Government," he reminded Western farmers. "Personally I have believed in it....At the last two Grain Growers' Conventions, resolutions were passed approving the principle." Crerar also emphasized the economic policies of the Union government, pointing out that they went a long way towards meeting traditional Western complaints.[40]

In the West, as in the rest of English Canada, Unionist speakers stressed the importance of Canada's continued effective participation in the Great War, participation that could only be maintained by the Unionist policy of conscription. Campaign literature contained accounts of German atrocities in Belgium and asked Western women, "...would you have the Germans land their unclean hordes on Canadian soil?" The newly enfranchised women became a special target of the campaign and were told to "keep in mind that every ballot is a bullet...see to it that the ammunition is got to the polls on December 17th." One speaker told a meeting of women that "each vote cast for Union Government will be a wreath laid on the graves of the boys who have given their lives,...a drop in the cup of blessings which we would like to hand to every man in Khaki." The Allied cause, especially since the United States had entered the war, had become endowed in the mind of the public with the qualities of a crusade. The tangle of European power politics had slipped into the background and the confrontation became one between good and evil, democracy against "Kaiserism." Unionists did not tell the West that Canada was fighting for the Empire alone, but for "the rights of ourselves and our children to live as a free community." Canada had an obligation, said R.C. Henders to the electors of Macdonald, "to do her share in the great conflict in which her own freedom is involved as well as that of the rest of the empire and the civilized world in general." This obligation could only be carried out by returning a Union government.[41]

The Protestant churches supported the Union as firmly as they had stood behind the Great War itself. The election became part of the effort which had to be expended to win the "holy war." Church groups passed official resolutions endorsing the Unionists and individual ministers campaigned on behalf of candidates. In those areas in which it was regarded as an asset, particularly in the West, Union candidates implied that federal prohibition, long sought by the churches, would come soon after a Unionist victory. In this way the Union government was able to portray itself as an instrument of social and moral reform, the source of the social regeneration which many reformers hoped for as the domestic counterpart of the war effort.[42]

The campaign of 1917 was not fought exclusively on such noble themes. It was one of the most bitterly fought in Canada's electoral history, and both Unionists and Laurier Liberals played on the aroused prejudices of French and English. In its official statement of policy, the Union government specifically requested "moderation in speech and action on the part of its supporters during the election," and asked them not to use "inflammatory or abusive language toward those who may think differently" because "seldom is anything of real value gained by sectional, racial or religious appeals." Borden and most of his ministers avoided "inflammatory or abusive language" from the platform but their restraint was not emulated among Unionist candidates and newspaper editors. Because of this, and because the Laurier Liberal campaign in Quebec used racial animosity as its principal theme, the months of November and December "witnessed a descent into the abyss of French-English violence and prejudice to a depth without precedent in Canadian history."[43]

The Unionists used this appeal to the prejudices of Western workers and farmers as a technique of preventing regional or class interests from manifesting themselves, and an anti-French theme can be found throughout Unionist speeches, advertisements, and editorials. To G.W. Allan, Unionist candidate for Winnipeg South, there were only two issues facing Canadians, "first, the winning of a decisive victory over the Hun, and second, ever lambasting the Province of Quebec on the 17th December." He urged T.A. Crerar to use this argument and to fight "to the limit against the French Canadians damned traitors that they are." The Unionist press, which included all Western dailies except the *Edmonton Bulletin* and the *Calgary News-Telegram*, was open in its identification of Sir Wilfrid Laurier's position on conscription with support for the Central Powers. Bob Edwards' *Calgary Eye Opener* asked its readers if they were

...going to let this hoary four-flusher [Laurier] get away with this? Not on your tin-type! Canada shall not desert her defenders to please any whited Sepulchre from Quebec....One would almost imagine that Wilfrid as a child had been raised on saurkraut instead of pea soup.

The *Winnipeg Telegram* identified Laurier with the anti-war *nationalistes*, Henri Bourassa and Armand Lavergne, and proclaimed on its editorial page that "a vote for a Laurier, Bourassa and Lavergne candidate is a vote to establish tyranny, lawlessness and terror in the place of law, order, and decency such as we have long enjoyed."[44]

The Unionists fought hard, despite confident predictions that virtually all of the West would fall easily into their hands. The reason for the fierceness of the campaign was their concern over the personal attraction that Sir Wilfrid Laurier still held for many farmers. He had gone down to defeat in 1911 in defence of reciprocity, and because of this had remained popular, particularly in Saskatchewan and Alberta. But while Laurier was personally popular, the collection of ward-heelers and bag men who represented him on the ballot in many constituencies in the West were not. Only three of the sitting Liberal MPs chose to run again as Laurier candidates, Frank Oliver in Edmonton West, J.P. Molloy in Provencher, and W.H. White in Victoria. In two Winnipeg seats, in Saskatoon, in Moose Jaw, in Regina, and in Calgary East, the Liberals simply endorsed Labour nominees. In Dauphin, Nelson, Souris, Maple Creek, Last Mountain, and Qu'Appelle, the remnants of the party could not find candidates. In most of the remaining ridings the Liberals turned to any nonentity willing to bear the Laurier colours, whatever his background or principles. Fred Shirtliff, Arthur Meighen's opponent in Portage la Prairie, had even pledged himself to the enforcement of the Military Service Act!

Frances Beynon, although a strong opponent of the Union government, admitted that the alternative was unpleasant and that "a lot of the Laurier candidates were a stiff dose to swallow." The Unionists exploited this Liberal weakness to the fullest extent possible. A widely circulated cartoon contrasted a "Union Liberal" with a "Laurier Liberal." The former is represented by a young farmer carrying the Union Jack and a "stand by the Army" pennant, while the Laurier Liberal is old and bent, with a top hat, a high collar, spectacles, and spats. In his hands are the white flag and a pennant with the words "Quit the War," the Unionist interpretation of Laurier's policy on Canadian participation.[45]

VI

As the date of the election drew closer, a massive Unionist victory in the West became more and more a certainty. There was some Unionist concern about Alberta, where Frank Oliver and C.W. Cross had joined forces to prevent a total collapse of the Liberal Party and the Non Partisan League was presenting three candidates. But in Manitoba and Saskatchewan the Unionists' strategy of reform and racism had been more effective and campaign workers were confident of all seats but Provencher and North Battleford, which had large French-Canadian populations. Their confidence was justified. On December 17, the Union government swept to an overwhelming victory between the Red and the Rockies. Forty of the forty-three Western seats fell to Unionists, six by acclamation. One of the three Liberal seats, Edmonton West, was reversed when the military vote was counted. Twenty-four Liberal candidates lost their deposits by failing to gain half as many votes as the Unionist victor. The Unionist majority in the popular vote was equally one-sided as they swept 68 per cent of the civilian vote and 71 per cent of all votes cast. Even those who had predicted a great victory were surprised by its dimensions.[46]

When analyzed in detail, however, the results of the 1917 general election are an effective yardstick for measuring variations within the West which suggest conclusions about the West itself and its attitudes to the issues raised by the Great War. The first impression to emerge from a closer examination of the popular vote is that support for Unionist candidates was much stronger in Manitoba and Saskatchewan than in Alberta. In Manitoba the Unionists received 80 per cent of the popular vote and in Saskatchewan 71 per cent, while Alberta gave them less than 60 per cent of its votes. Only six Laurier Liberals retained their deposits in Manitoba and Saskatchewan, whereas nine of the twelve Alberta candidates were successful in doing so.

This relatively better showing in Alberta occurred for three reasons. First, in that province Laurier retained the allegiance of a large part of the Liberal "machine," and of two daily newspapers, the *Calgary News-Telegram* and the *Edmonton Bulletin*. Both these pieces of good fortune came because two former enemies, C.W. Cross and Frank Oliver, felt strongly enough about Laurier to bury their differences and pull together in a last-ditch attempt to turn back the Unionists. Oliver's loyalty also provided Laurier with his only candidate of any stature, although the military vote prevented Oliver's success in Edmonton West. The second Liberal advantage in Alberta was the fact that the Non Partisan League nominated candidates in four Alberta ridings. This undermined the Unionist claim to be the sole true representative of non-partisanship, a new and independent party rather than simply a coalition of the "old" parties which had earned the disapproval of the organized farmers of Alberta. Finally, almost a quarter of Alberta's population was American-born, and those former Americans who were naturalized were more impervious to the patriotic appeals of the Unionists. The constituencies with large numbers of American residents gave the Unionists their narrowest victories in the West.[47]

Despite the opposition of trade union leaders to conscription and thus to the government created to impose it, Unionist majorities were better in urban areas than in rural ones. The most spectacular victory of the election was that of C.W. Andrews in Winnipeg Centre—won four years later by Socialist J.S. Woodsworth—who out-polled his Liberal-Labour opponent by almost 21,000 votes. In combined rural-urban ridings, Unionists won much larger majorities in cities than they did in the countryside. Arthur Sifton swept the city of Medicine Hat by a five-to-one margin but in the surrounding farm area his majority was only three-to-two. In Calgary East, Unionist Lee Redman won 70 per cent of the urban vote and only 57 per cent of the rural. When the West as a whole is considered, urban areas gave the Unionists 76 per cent of their popular vote, rural areas 66 per cent. This result suggests that Unionist strategy was spectacularly effective with the urban working class, predominantly of English-Canadian or of British origin.[48]

The strong support for Union government in urban areas reflects the poor treatment which anti-conscriptionist Labour candidates received at the hands of the voters. Seven such candidates were nominated, two in Manitoba by the Canadian Labour Party, three in Saskatchewan by the Independent Labour Party, and two in Alberta, one by a local Calgary group and the second by the Socialist Party of Canada. Only Joe Knight, who ran for the Socialists in Red Deer, failed to receive the endorsement of the Laurier Liberals as well. All Labour candidates lost their deposits and the seven constituencies went to the government by wide majorities. William Irvine, Labour candidate in Calgary East, came closest to victory with 32 per cent of the vote. R.A. Rigg, who had resigned his seat in the legislature to contest Winnipeg North, was able to draw 26 per cent, while James Somerville in Moose Jaw received 22 per cent. The other four candidates were crushed by more humiliating margins.

The new women voters of the War-time Elections Act padded the Unionist totals, as did the pro-conscriptionist soldiers' vote, but the results for the Labour nominees were disheartening nonetheless. If one counts the civilian vote only, R.S. Ward, candidate in Winnipeg Centre, failed to take a single poll, losing even in solidly working-class Brooklands by 319 votes to 98. Martin Robin, in "Registration, Conscription, and Independent Labour Politics," concedes that "many workers voted Unionist" and suggests that "others expressed their opposition to the Union Government...through support for Laurier Liberals." This generalization does not seem to apply to Western Canada. In ridings with large numbers of working-class voters which had no

Labour candidate, workers by and large voted Unionist rather than for anti-conscriptionist Liberals. G.J. Charette, Laurier Liberal candidate in Springfield, could not even carry the town of Transcona, whose delegates had introduced two motions against conscription at the 1917 Trades and Labor Congress Convention. Charette lost the town's four polls to Unionist R.L. Richardson by 632 votes to 249.[49]

In its comment on the results of the election, *The Voice* admitted that the Unionist victory had been remarkable and could not be explained away by the War-time Elections Act. Working-class opposition to conscription had simply not materialized. Instead *The Voice* pointed to the obvious fact that for the most part Canadians, in the West as elsewhere, had voted according to race and ignored the interests of economic class. What the election of 1917 revealed was "a distinct cleavage of the country on racial lines—a condition that every thoughtful citizen must deplore as regrettable."[50]

When seen in this perspective, the election results in Western Canada are really just the national results reduced in scale. In Manitoba, Saskatchewan, and Alberta the strongest electoral opposition to the Union government came from French Canadians, who provided the Laurier Liberals with their victory in Provencher. In that constituency, at polls in English-speaking districts like Emerson, Sanford, and Dominion City, the Unionist candidate received heavy majorities. In Francophone areas, however, Liberal candidate J.P. Molloy gained almost unanimous support. He won La Broquerie 101 votes to 4, St. Jean Baptiste 202 votes to 8, St. Pierre 210 votes to 11, and St. Malo 100 votes to 2! This pattern repeated itself in other Western seats with concentrations of French Canadians, although only in Victoria in northern Alberta did it help turn the seat away from the Unionists. French settlements in Swift Current endorsed the Laurier candidate by 125 votes to 20, in Springfield by 1,318 votes to 243. In Edmonton East, votes in Lac la Biche, Doucette, Charon, and Lafond rejected the Unionists, 109 votes to 26. In Marquette, T.A. Crerar carried every poll but St. Lazare and campaign workers attributed the loss there to "the large French and half Breed vote." Arthur Meighen won in Portage la Prairie by a four-to-one margin, yet lost St. Eustache, St. François Xavier, and St. Laurent 502 votes to 84.[51]

The other group of voters which rejected the Unionists, although not as emphatically as did the French Canadians, were those naturalized citizens who had not been deprived of their votes by the War-time Elections Act. Anti-Unionist feelings were noticeable among Scandinavians–Icelanders, Swedes, and Norwegians–and among some American immigrants as well. This hostility cost the Unionists only one seat, Victoria in northeastern Alberta, but reduced the margin of victory in other ridings where there were large numbers of naturalized citizens. This can be demonstrated by comparing the Unionist percentage of the civilian popular vote in these ridings with their percentage of that vote in the province as a whole. In Manitoba, Unionist candidates received 76 per cent of the civilian popular vote but only 61 per cent in Selkirk, which contained most of Manitoba's Icelandic community. Saskatchewan's Unionist civilian popular vote was 71 per cent of the total. In Swift Current, which had many American settlers, and in Humboldt, which had a large Scandinavian population, Unionist percentages were significantly smaller, 63 per cent and 59 per cent respectively. This tendency can be demonstrated by an examination of the figures from individual polling stations. In Marquette, for example, the settlements of Scandinavia and Erickson gave T.A. Crerar only 51 votes as compared with 179 for his Liberal opponent. In Selkirk, Gimli and Arborg went to the Liberal candidate by 200 votes to 59.

Any analysis of the results of the 1917 general election must consider the importance of the alteration of the franchise in the outcome. In addition to the changes made by the War-time Elections Act there was also the Military Voters' Act, which allowed soldiers in Europe to choose the constituency in which they wanted to vote, or to become "voters at large" whose votes for the "government" or the "opposition" could be applied in any constituency. The Unionists have been accused of using the special legislation to carry out "electoral villainy of the first order," but it seems unlikely that the overall results of the 1917 election would have been very different in Manitoba, Saskatchewan, or Alberta had no such legislation existed.[52] The military vote overturned the civilian result in only one Western constituency, Frank Oliver's seat of Edmonton West. Oliver's civilian majority had been 80 votes, but the soldiers' ballots gave Unionist W.A. Griesbach a majority of 2,698. The Edmonton area had sent thousands of men to war, and the size of the military vote in Edmonton West does not seem unusual. In fact results throughout the West suggest that if the Unionists were indeed bent on "electoral villainy" they were remarkably shortsighted. The outcome in both Laurier Liberal seats, Provencher and Victoria, could have been changed by the judicious application of less than 450 soldiers' ballots.

More significant in the West was the War-time Elections Act, since it simultaneously removed a group of naturalized citizens from the electors' lists and added new women voters. It is impossible, however, to determine precise numbers in either case and it is difficult to make meaningful estimates. Since the previous election of 1911, sixteen new constituencies had been created, five in Alberta, six in Saskatchewan, and five in Manitoba. Because of this, and because of the mobility of the Western population in this period, attempts to estimate what the election results might have been without the alterations made to the franchise are little more than conjecture.

J.A. Boudreau makes such an attempt in "The Enemy Alien Problem in Canada, 1914-21" and concludes that, had naturalized citizens of enemy alien origin been allowed to vote, Unionists would have been defeated in ten Western seats in addition to Victoria and Provencher. Boudreau bases this conclusion on a comparison between the number of residents of enemy alien origin listed in these constituencies in the 1916 *Census of the Prairie Provinces* with the majority enjoyed by the Unionist candidate. On this basis he argues that eleven constituencies in the Prairie West would have changed hands. The flaw in Boudreau's argument is his use of the *total* "enemy alien" population of a constituency, rather than the number of naturalized males over the age of twenty-one. There were 6,042 persons of enemy alien origin in Edmonton West, but were enough of them eligible to vote to reverse a Unionist majority of 2,968 votes? Unfortunately, figures as to the number of naturalized males of voting age of enemy alien origin are not available for each individual constituency. The total number of such persons in the Western Provinces was 37,014; 31,949 Austro-Hungarian Ukrainians and 5,075 Germans. The Unionist majority, not including the military vote, was 112,327. With the military vote included, it rises to 158,786. In the constituencies Boudreau singles out, Unionist majorities were in most cases substantial. Only in Bow River, where H.H. Halliday edged out J.E. Gouge by 312 votes, could the results have been reversed easily.[53]

The War-time Elections Act was a double-edged sword. Obviously a large number of women voted for the first time and, equally obviously, most of them voted for Unionist candidates. But any attempt to qualify this statement further immediately becomes vulnerable to greater difficulties than the ones which handicap any analysis of those who lost the ballot. It is not difficult to calculate the number of women in any one constituency but it is impossible to estimate accurately the number who were wives, widows, or mothers of soldiers. Many Western recruits were bachelors from the British Isles, without relatives to claim ballots on their account. Thus the number of women who enthusiastically cast ballots in Manitoba, Saskatchewan, and Alberta will never be known. The probable result of their votes was to add to Unionist majorities, particularly in the cities, where it was easier to get out the vote in a midwinter election. The staggering Unionist victories in Winnipeg Centre, Winnipeg South, Brandon, Regina, and Saskatoon were in part the result of women voters. The loss of the woman's vote would probably not have altered the final results appreciably, because the Unionists did not gain these votes in the same ridings in which alien voters were lost to the Laurier Liberals. Ridings with large enemy alien populations were generally in the relatively early stages of agricultural development. They had smaller female populations than ridings in older, more developed areas, and many of the homesteaders were bachelors. Considering both effects of the Wartime Elections Act together, only Bow River and perhaps Edmonton West could have shown different results on election day without it.

The real effect of the War-time Elections Act did not come on December 17, the day of the election. It came on October 12, when Prime Minister Borden was able to announce that he had formed a Union cabinet. The controversial franchise legislation is important in that it pushed reluctant Western Liberals on their path towards coalition. Once Union government had been achieved any possibility of the formation of a new regional party was averted.

VII

What did the overwhelming support of the West for Union government mean? Undoubtedly, many Westerners were motivated by a desire to enforce conscription when they cast ballots on December 17. To vote for a Laurier Liberal would have meant denying support to the CEF, "an army which has brought forth praise from military experts of other countries" and was "deserving of all the support which a grateful and resourceful people can give." To reject conscription would not only have broken faith with Canada's soldiers, it would have allowed French Canadians to dictate the nation's position on the Great War. To the English-speaking West this was unacceptable and "the Union Government was the only thing to save Canada...from the plots of the French Jesuit Priests." By touching this raw racist nerve in the West, the Union government won the support of a substantial part of the West's English Protestant majority.[54]

But there was more substance behind the West's support of Unionism than this determination to make Quebec "do its duty" with regard to the Great War through the means of the Military Service Act. The idea of a non-partisan national government had strong appeal in Western Canada, both in war and peace, since it seemed to promise an end to a two-party system in which Central Canada was able to dominate both parties. The West had been skeptical that true Union government could come from men so identified with that party system, but the new Union platform and the ostentatious measures to control profits seemed to suggest that Borden and his colleagues sincerely intended to listen to the voice of the West. In late November Irene Parlby wrote to Violet McNaughton that "the Union Government has made a good beginning, and if it gets the confidence of the people behind it, should be able to deal with things much more firmly."[55]

On December 17, Westerners gave the new government their confidence in the hope that it could live up to it. Some saw Union not simply as a war measure but as something which would be more enduring. The editorials which interpreted the election results spoke of a permanent end to partisan politics. Not only the *Grain Growers' Guide* and other farmers' papers talked this way. The *Swift Current Sun*, once a solid Liberal sheet, expressed satisfaction that "the party politics which we have known has passed away, we hope never to return." The *Calgary Herald*, an equally committed Conservative organ, was also enthusiastic. "The people of this part of Canada are not wedded to any party," wrote the *Herald*'s editor, "and have hailed the opportunity to try a non-partisan government with enthusiasm." One of the most emphatic presentations of Western expectations of the Union government is contained in *Deep Furrows*, a history of the Western Canadian Grain Growers' Movement published early in 1918. Its author, Hopkins Moorhouse, wrote:

> Not since Confederation has such a thing happened in this country. The vampire methods with which our political system has been cursed have been thrown underfoot and thinking Canadians everywhere have drawn a breath of relief. The en-

ergies which have been wasted in jockeying for party position are now concentrating upon effective unity of action.

It was not going to be easy for any government to meet such expectations, as the Union government was to discover in the final, bitter year of the Great War.[56]

CHAPTER SEVEN

1918
Wartime Controls
and Domestic Discontent

I

As Canadians quietly welcomed the New Year there was little evidence of the unity and enthusiasm that had poured forth in that long ago August of 1914. The unity of French and English had eroded gradually, its passing proclaimed by the election campaign concluded only two weeks earlier. The enthusiasm had been replaced, for English Canadians, by a determination that Canada must fight on to the utmost of her ability until Germany was defeated. "It would appear that there is nothing to do but prepare for a still more strenuous year," the editor of the *Farmer's Advocate* told his readers, for "that's our part." No one—soldier, statesman or, civilian—imagined that victory was a certainty in the coming year, and total victory was the only conclusion to the Great War that was acceptable after three years of sacrifice.[1]

In France the opposing armies occupied almost the same positions as they had in April, 1915, when the first battalion of the Canadian Expeditionary Force had arrived at the front. Although the United States had entered the war on the side of the Allies, the Americans had not yet fully mobilized and had only a token army in Europe. Determined to strike before more Americans could arrive, the German General Staff spent the first days of the new year designing a devastating series of offensives which would smash the British and Canadian positions and bring the German army within a half-day's march of the channel ports. Like their soldiers on the Western Front, the Canadian people faced 1918 with the grim understanding that the Great War had not been won and that it could yet be lost.

Despite the fact that 1918 brought the war's conclusion, it was a year of bitterness and disappointment for most Canadians. This was especially so in the Canadian West. Because so many Prairie sons were overseas, the cost in life for Manitoba, Saskatchewan, and Alberta was particularly heavy, and each day this cost was spelled out in the newspaper columns of dead and missing, and in the accompanying photos of local boys among the fallen. For Western farmers the effects of inadequate tillage combined with hostile nature to produce drought conditions in parts of the Prairie area that were almost as severe as those of 1914. For wage-earners inflation became the biggest enemy as the cost of living leapt to twice its pre-war level. But most disappointing to the residents of Western Canada was the failure of the Union government to fulfil the hopes they had placed upon it. In both its domestic and its war policies, the new government came to be regarded as a failure by a majority of its former Western supporters.

II

Because the war overshadowed so much of Canadian life it is somewhat arbitrary to speak of a domestic and a war program for the Union government in 1918. Domestic policy was in most cases inextricably connected with the problems of maintaining the Canadian Corps in the field and of providing the Allies with food and munitions. To understand the change in Western attitudes to the Union government, however, it is useful to examine in detail the enforcement of the Military Service Act, a military decision with important domestic implications. The manner in which Westerners responded to the new conscription policies introduced in the first months of 1918 illustrates both the degree of their support for the Allied cause and one of the reasons for the deterioration of their relationship with the Union government.

Conscription had been a cornerstone of the Unionist campaign. During the autumn of 1917 the West had found fault with the operation of the Military Service Act, and Westerners expected that operation to become more efficient once the government had received its mandate. "All the slackers will get their marching orders now," was the triumphant prediction of one of T.A. Crerar's campaign workers. To an English-speaking Westerner the most obvious "slackers" were the French Canadians, and Quebec's refusal to "do her duty" was one of the important reasons why the West had come to accept conscription as necessary. The creation of a Canadian Army had imposed "an awful strain on the human resources of the West" and selective service seemed to be the best means of levelling the burden between Canada's regions.[2]

In this respect the West was to be disappointed. The Military Service Act, as Arthur Meighen had pointed out during the course of the debate on the bill, called bachelors before married men and the tendency toward early marriage in Quebec meant that conscription fell comparatively lightly on that province. As this fact became apparent, Westerners voiced their disillusion. "I worked my head off for Union Government and would do it again," a Manitoban wrote to his member of Parliament. "But the operation of this Military Service Act has been the greatest disappointment. When are the hangings going to start in Quebec? Shooting is too good for those devils, hang 'em, starting with Bourassa." His hopes, and the less extreme expectations of others, were not to be carried out.[3]

Although it failed to conscript the French Canadians at whom the West had hoped it would be directed, the Military Service Act left farmers, farmers' sons, and most agricultural labourers untouched during the winter of 1917-18. The Union government respected General Mewburn's promise made to the farmers of Ontario during the election campaign. But on March 21, 1918, the German General Staff took the situation out of the hands of the Canadian government by launching a full-scale offensive aimed directly at that part of the front held by British and Canadian troops. The British Fifth Army was shattered and for the next two months there continued what military historians have referred to as the "Great Retreat." The casualty rate of the Canadian Corps became higher than the rate at which it could be reinforced. On April 20, the government rescinded its policy of agricultural exemptions for men between the ages of twenty and twenty-three and amended the Military Service Act to enable the conscription of nineteen-year-olds, should it become necessary.

The cancellation of the agricultural exemption created an immediate reaction among the Canadian farming community, English- and French-speaking alike. Rural Ontario became "a seething mass of dissatisfaction...almost insurrection," and the United Farmers of Ontario denounced the Union government and joined farmers from Quebec in a pilgrimage of protest to Ottawa. The reaction from Western farmers and from their organizations was different, however. The Manitoba and Saskatchewan Grain Growers and the United Farmers of Alberta refused to lend their official support to the UFO in its attack on the government, a decision which led Ontario farmers to develop "a

"To Hell with the Kaiser," Calgary, 1918.
Glenbow-Alberta Institute, Calgary, Alberta.

strong feeling against the West." The Western farm movement was, of course, unhappy about the loss of the agricultural exemption but its members were prepared to "accept the decision of the government [although] they did not necessarily approve of it."[4]

The UFA executive went so far as to urge that farmers "loyally abide by the decision of the Government," although they warned that the shortage of labour which would result from the conscription of farm workers would handicap Western production. Mrs. Irene Parlby, president of the United Farm Women of Alberta, realized that the cancellation would cause "great hardship" to farm families but was certain that the decision had only been made out of military necessity and because the government "had information that made them think it was necessary." The *Grain Grower's Guide* also accepted the new regulations, arguing that "Canada must provide all the assistance in her power to stay the onward march of the Hun." The *Guide*'s editor, George F. Chipman, confided to T.A. Crerar that the Western public would support the government "to almost any length" in view of the serious situation created by the German advance.[5]

While Quebec erupted in anti-conscription riots and Ontario farmers invaded Ottawa, the registrars responsible for implementing the Military Service Act in Western Canada reported that the residents of their districts were quietly accepting the cancellation of exemptions as "inevitable" and as "a necessary measure in view of the existing conditions on the Western Front." Not only was popular protest almost nonexistent, but the percentage of defaulters–those who failed to report when called–was smaller in the West than in any other region in Canada. In Manitoba, Saskatchewan, and Alberta 6.7 per cent of those eligible for conscription refused to report as compared with 9.3 per cent in Ontario, 40.8 per cent in Quebec and 19.4 per cent in Canada as a whole.[6]

This remarkable acceptance of the burden of conscription illustrates the region's acceptance of the avowed objectives of the Canadian war effort and was taken as evidence of Western superiority. Editors pointed proudly to the "war record" of the West and particularly to that of its farmers, which they felt stood out "in bold contrast to that of the farmers of the East." In his *Edmonton Bulletin* Frank Oliver suggested that the reaction of Ontario farmers to the cancellation of the agricultural exemption was typical of the attitude of that province throughout the war.

The young men from the farms of Ontario flocked to the munitions factories, while the young men from the farms of Alberta flocked to the recruiting stations. What could be got out of the war has been all too prominent in Ontario's calculations....What could be put into the war has been the all-compelling question in the minds of Albertans.

Western farm leaders themselves were less vitriolic. The farmers of Central Canada had "hurt their case...by the manner in which they have presented it and the extreme statements they have indulged in," explained T.A. Crerar to Norman Lambert of the Canadian Council of Agriculture.[7]

Western farmers who protested against the cancellation of exemptions did so on the grounds that conscription of farmers would reduce the Canadian contribution to the Allied cause. The Order in Council introducing the new regulations was issued at the beginning of the seeding period and coincided precisely with a campaign by the Canada Food Board to secure "Greater Production." Western farmers argued that it was impossible for their sons and hired hands to serve simultaneously in the trenches and in the fields. The Moose Jaw local of the Saskatchewan Grain Grower's Association, for example, promised that "the fullest possible cooperation will be given to any measures necessary to winning the war" but warned that the new conscription policy would reduce the amount of grain produced in their district. A Manitoba farmer assured the provincial minister of agriculture that "we do not wish to evade military duty" but asked, "who is going to harvest the coming crop?" One especially poignant letter came to C.A. Dunning, director of the Greater Production Campaign, from a Saskatchewan farmer whose last son was about to be conscripted, leaving him unable to work his farm. "If he has to go," wrote Alex Delgarno, "I do not want him to wait until he is conscripted. If it had not been for the shape I am in he would have been there long ago. None of us wants anybody else to fight our battles for us."[8]

Westerners felt that they did not have to be told to do their duty. This made them particularly resentful of the techniques used to enforce the Military Service Act. The detection and capture of defaulters was made the responsibility of the military itself and of the Dominion Police. "Swaggering impudent fellows," the police alienated "thousands who were heart and soul for enforcing the Act" with their arbitrary arrests of young men unfortunate enough to be caught without proof of their exempt status. This, as much as the cancellation of the agricultural exemption, angered Westerners since their region had such a low percentage of defaulters. T.A. Crerar felt that any Western opposition to conscription was based largely on "*the manner* in which it is being carried out and administered." But whatever the reason for the existence of discontent over conscription, it was not the most fundamental cause of the West's alienation from the Union government.[9]

III

To many of those Westerners who gave it support, the Union was more than just a "win the war" government pledged only to compulsory service. As Ramsay Cook and Craig Brown have pointed out, the Unionist victory was "in many ways the culmination of ideas and impulses at work in Canadian society for more than a decade." To Western Canadians it was seen as a major step in the attempt to reform the Canadian political, social, and economic system. These exalted expectations were satirized by the *Alberta Non Partisan* in January, 1918. Under the headline "EXPECTATIONS," a cartoon showed a farmer breaking sod. Six fresh-cut furrows were marked with Western aspirations: "Government ownership of railways, Taxation of exempted lands, Government control of public utilities, No duty on farm machinery, Electoral reform, Abolition of the liquor traffic." Meanwhile the farmer urged his straining team to "Speed up there!" since "1918 will be a great year...Borden said so." The importance of these reforms to continued Western support was understood by W.A. Buchanan, the Unionist member for Lethbridge. "The West will stay Union," he told J.W. Dafoe, "provided the government makes good in other respects."[10]

Of the six items spelled out in the cartoon, only "abolition of the liquor traffic" was carried through quickly and unequivocally. The West had helped point out the dry path in 1916 but action by the dominion government was necessary to put a stop to the manufacture of liquor for interprovincial sale. With two Orders in Council issued on December 24, 1917, and March 11, 1918, the Union government made it illegal to import liquor into Canada or to transport it across a provincial boundary. The imposition of prohibition on a national scale was at once taken as evidence that the Unionists would live up to Western expectations. "The new Union Government could not have begun its tenure of office with more popular legislation," was the conclusion of the *Farmer's Advocate*, a conclusion echoed in other parts of the West. Prohibition was "only a sample of what Union Government can do," evidence that the West had at last found a government which would accept its prescription for Canada's domestic health. The extension of the federal franchise to women, promised as part of the work of the new Parliament, seemed further evidence that this belief was justified. But as 1918 continued, the enthusiasm generated by prohibition evaporated as further reforms failed to materialize.[11]

The most longstanding goal of Westerners, in particular of the organized farmers, was a substantial reduction in the tariff as it applied to their tools of production. For two reasons they were confident of relief from the new government. The first was political, since the West had played such an important part in the Unionist victory and because several Unionist members, most notably Minister of Agriculture T.A. Crerar, had committed themselves to the Farmers' Platform of the Canadian Council of Agriculture. But the Western farmer also felt that he had a better case for a tariff reduction on farm machinery than at any previous time. The government was sponsoring a Greater Production Campaign, urging that farmers "fight with food" by making "the utmost effort to produce food for our soldiers and allies." Was it not obvious that if food production was to be encouraged the price of agricultural machinery had to be kept as low as possible? "This is not a matter of free trade or protection," wrote F.S. Jacobs of the *Farmer's Advocate.* "It is a matter of war. The thing is to get food for our allies, and to this end no encumbrances should be placed in the way of the farmers of Western Canada." "We ask no favours," wrote Elza Buck, a Saskatchewan farmer. "We are every ounce patriotism."[12]

But rather than reduce the general scale for agricultural implements, the Union government adopted a selective policy. An Order in Council issued February 8, 1918, provided that farm tractors with a value of less than $1,400 would be allowed to enter the country free of duty. Although this action was greeted as "a very good start" and as perhaps the harbinger of "better things to come," the Order in Council did little to meet the real problems of the Western farmer. Few of them had the capital or the experience to begin tractor farming, and the light tractor was not yet sufficiently developed to be effective on most Prairie farms. It was the duty on other machinery that was the obstacle to most farmers, and the effects of the duty were made even more harsh by an inflation that had affected machinery prices as it had everything else. Disc harrows increased in price almost 50 per cent, and some ploughs almost doubled in cost. As one farmer complained, "A great many of our farmers will have to rig up their old machinery and make them do because these new machinery prices are not within their reach."[13]

Parliament opened on March 18, 1918, but the new budget was not introduced until April 30, after almost six weeks had passed. Western critics of the Union government laughed at Western farmers for their hopes and predicted that the tariff issue would be "the real test of the Government...the rock on which the ship of state will be wrecked." The budget contained no tariff reductions for machinery but predictions of the government's collapse proved incorrect. Grain Grower Unionists protested the absence of tariff reductions but did not withdraw their support for the government. Somewhat unfairly, they found themselves subjected to considerable criticism for even daring to raise the question of the tariff during wartime. In their speeches to Parliament J.A. Maharg, Andrew Knox, and R.C. Henders spent as much time making clear the desire of themselves and their constituents to "push the war to a successful finish" as they did attacking the budget.[14]

Patriotism won out over economic principle, and Westerners accepted the fact that "in all probability we will see little change in the tariffs until after the war." The Western farmer did not change his mind about the tariff; he simply put aside his aspirations for economic reform until Germany could be defeated. What he did begin to change his mind about was the Union government itself, as he realized that in war as well as in peace the same economic issues remained to divide Western and Central Canada. In its 1918 budget the Union government demonstrated to the West that, on that one critical issue, Central Canada was not about to change its mind.[15]

The second traditional source of Western discontent was the operation of the Canadian railway system, and in this area the Union government gave a somewhat more satisfactory performance. Although Westerners voiced the usual objections to the rate increases approved by the Board of Railway commissioners in December, 1917, and announced five days *after* the dominion election, it was obvious to most of them that the new rates were a realistic response to the pressure of inflation, and necessary to meet pay increases awarded rail workers. There was general Western approval of the decision to nationalize Mackenzie's and Mann's Canadian Northern Railway. Some objected to the compensation paid to William Mackenzie and Donald Mann, or complained that the Canadian Pacific should have also become a part of the new national system, but on the whole the *Grain Grower's Guide*'s attitude of "so far, so good" probably summarized Western attitudes to the Union government's approach to the transportation problem in 1918.[16]

IV

Perhaps as equally damaging as the tariff issue to the government's reputation in the West was its inability to deal with rapid inflation, an issue popularly described as the "high cost of living." The conscription of young farmers and the continuation of high tariffs undermined the Union government's popular base, but Western support for the war effort led to acceptance of the former as a military necessity and the latter as a temporary economic inevitability. Inflation, however, was a visible and constant problem to every consumer. During 1915 and 1916 the prices of food, clothing, fuel, and housing had remained almost stable. F.C. Acland, deputy minister of labour, was able to report in 1916 that any inflationary tendencies had been "purely local," and been "remedied by natural causes." Statistics compiled by the provincial government of Saskatchewan demonstrate that the cost of living for an "average" Regina family increased by only 8 per cent between August, 1914, and the same month in 1916. When combined, the rural prosperity created by the bountiful harvests of 1915 and 1916, the decline in unemployment, and the tendency for wages to increase as a result probably caused the standard of living for some people to improve slightly in those two years. The cost of housing for the West's urban working class actually *declined* between 1913 and 1916.[17]

During the subsequent winter, however, an upward movement of prices began that did not reverse itself until 1920. It is difficult to measure the exact amount of this inflation, as estimates sometimes vary, but the *Canadian Annual Review*, anxious to describe the Union government in the most favourable terms possible, admitted that between 1914 and 1919 the cost of living in Canada had increased by 100 per cent, with most of this increase occurring in the last two years of the war. There is disagreement among historians as to the degree to which this increase was offset by higher incomes. Two detailed studies based on the city of Winnipeg come to different conclusions. While Harry Sutcliffe maintains that real wages for most workers declined precipitously, David Bercuson argues that complaints about inflation were "a blanket generalization based on popular misconception." Bercuson does admit, however, that most workers *believed* that their standard of living had declined by 1918. A useful concept which helps clarify this question is the idea of "reference groups" used by Arthur Marwick in his work on Britain during the Great War. Marwick contends that British workers experienced a somewhat improved standard of living during the war which made them want further improvements and which produced fierce resistance to any threats to gains already achieved. Similarly, any gains made by the Western wage-earner or farmer in the first two years of war must have either disappeared or seemed threatened by 1918. One thing is very clear. By 1918 newspapers regularly voiced the general concern about "the lessened buying power of money" and reported that "this climbing up and up of prices is having an unsettling effect upon the wage earning masses of the people." The Canadian public considered inflation to be a serious problem.[18]

Because the greater part of the inflationary spiral was confined to the last two years of the war it tended to be particularly noticeable, and the public blamed increases in the price of necessities on "profiteering," the gouging of the consumer and the producer by "middlemen"–the meat packer, the miller, the wholesaler. This interpretation of inflation was particularly popular in Western Canada. It followed naturally from the Western distrust of the Eastern "Big Interests," and absolved the West, as a region of producers rather than processors or manufacturers, from any of the responsibility for the increase in prices. Prairie farmers were particularly self-righteous about inflation, for the price of wheat had been fixed well below the level to which a free market would have carried it.

The West demanded that inflation be checked, and suggested that it was the responsibility of the Union government to do this by placing rigorous controls on the "huge profits made by corporations in almost every line." "Is it not about time," they grumbled, "that price setting was carried outside the matter of [wheat], and an independent board looked into the setting of prices on all commodities?" When it complained that "the public have been soaked good and plenty" by Central Canadian manufacturers of boots and shoes, the *Swift Current Sun* was only expressing the prevailing Western understanding of inflation, and when it concluded that "there is a·little job there for Union Government" it also spoke the public mind. W.F.R. Turgeon, attorney general for Saskatchewan, warned J.A. Calder that inflation was the most serious threat to the government's popularity during the summer of 1918, and urged that the cost of living receive "serious and immediate consideration."[19]

The Union government never gave inflation the consideration the public thought that it deserved. A Royal Commission created by the Borden Conservative government reported without much effect, and the Unionists were not anxious to impose price controls since the increased consumption that such a step might have caused would have decreased surpluses available for export. For action against inflation the public began to look toward two agencies created in June, 1917, the Food Controller's Office and the Fuel Controller's Office. These positions had been established to facilitate conservation of resources in short supply during wartime, and it is quite clear that reduced prices for food and fuel would have had precisely the opposite effect. Despite this fact many Canadians came to expect them to be a sort of consumer protection service, and neither the Borden Conservatives nor the Union government really tried to erase this misconception. During October, 1917, for example, the food controller was given responsibility for the regulation of the profits of millers and packing houses. Thus the food and fuel controllers came under criticism, most notably in the West, when the cost of living continued to climb in 1918 as it had the preceding year.

Food Controller W.J. Hanna, an Ontario Conservative, was unpopular from the first in Western Canada. Described as the "Eastern Canadian Food Dictator," he quickly added substance to this innate Prairie prejudice by issuing a series of regulations which failed to take into account Western conditions. A ban on the canning of fruits and vegetables worked particular hardship in Manitoba, Saskatchewan, and Alberta, where fresh produce was difficult or impossible to obtain. An appeal to consumers to "save beef," which recommended veal as an alternative, was regarded as sheer idiocy by Western stockmen. Hanna attempted to obtain better co-operation and understanding in the West by appointing provincial advisory committees, but misunderstanding and public hostility could not be made to disappear. Instead, the first six months of the food control program only convinced Westerners that, as in the case of recruiting, they were being asked to carry more than their share of the war's cost. After a tour of the province of Ontario a correspondent to *The Voice* reported that in his hotels "the bill of fare was a yard long, and was crowded with items comprising the richest and choicest of viands imaginable." Far from conserving food, the people of the food controller's native province seemed to be "indulging in an orgy of eating." After a visit to Ottawa, W.R. Motherwell confirmed that at the Chateau Laurier "afternoon teas were gorgeous affairs patronized by swarms of beautiful and well-groomed ladies that did not seem to be very much in need of the food then eaten."[20]

Shortly after the election of the Union government, Hanna resigned and was replaced by H.B. Thomson, a British Columbian. The Food Controller's Office became the Canada Food Board and was placed under the Department of Agriculture. J.D. MacGregor of Winnipeg was appointed as Western food controller and C.A. Dunning became the director of the board's program to encourage "Greater Production." The changes were felt to be overdue in Western Canada, and were accepted with the hope that "the chance for further mistakes has been eliminated." Only a few weeks passed, however, before the new board was receiving as much criticism as Controller Hanna had. Despite MacGregor's appointment, new regulations for conserving food seemed no more attuned to Western needs than the old ones. Although there was no attempt to set up a domestic rationing system, Canada Food Board Order 31, for example, placed limits on the amount of flour and sugar which could be stored by any one household. The amounts allowed were too small to provide adequately for the needs of rural families, particularly in areas not well serviced by retail stores and where travel was often difficult. The result, according to the secretary of the Saskatchewan Grain Growers Association, was "a tremendous amount of unrest, disturbance and resentment...created amongst our locals and members all over Saskatchewan."

Moreover, the board received the blame when incidents of hoarding and profiteering were uncovered. When a company associated with Sir Joseph Flavelle was implicated in one such scandal, it was not surprising that the *Edmonton Bulletin*, an opponent of the Union government since its inception, should denounce the board as "an official attempt to help the Flavelle fraternity corner the nation's food supply." But when Unionist papers began to repeat the same charges, the depth of Western distrust of the Canada Food Board became serious.[21]

The situation reached a climax in June when the entire executive of the board's advisory committee for Saskatchewan resigned. They summed up the West's charges against the Canada Food Board in their letter of resignation, charging that regulations were ''too numerous, complicated and promulgated without due consideration," that substitute foods were not available in the West and that "many regulations which may be entirely workable in the East are not so in the West, and very often inflict hardship on the dealer or the consumer here." They also scored the Union government for its unwillingness to let the board go to work to regulate the cost of living, arguing that investigation by any other means was "far too cumbersome and slow." The *Farmer's Advocate* reported the resignations and commented upon them in an editorial. The *Advocate* saw the problem of the board as further evidence of the failure of the Union government to appreciate the uniqueness of the West: "If the Canada Food Board is to hold the confidence of the people of Western Canada, and particularly the people of our farms," the *Advocate* concluded, "then any orders affecting the people of Western Canada must be suitable to the conditions of Western Canada, whether those same orders apply over the whole of Canada or not."[22]

The Office of the Fuel Controller was more removed from the public eye and was never the subject of the abuse heaped upon the Canada Food Board. Still, Controller C.A. Magrath was hardly a popular figure, particularly in Manitoba and Saskatchewan. Residents of the two provinces had been accustomed to heating their homes with imported Pennsylvania anthracite during the long sub-zero Western winter. Magrath had the unpleasant job of telling them that because of the need for this coal for industrial purposes they would be forced to convert to domestically produced lignite. Lignite was dirtier, gave less heat per ton, and burned poorly in some types of furnaces. Worse yet, the Manitoba and Saskatchewan consumer found himself asked to pay a higher price than he paid for anthracite, and to stock up by midsummer or run the risk of being caught by shortages during the winter. Not surprisingly, the controller was blamed for his unwillingness or inability to fix prices and to guarantee supplies, and the Western conviction that the West was making most of the necessary sacrifices was further amplified. In Manitoba, wrote an angry home owner, "hard coal is more necessary than in any other part of the world." In the end the fuel controller compromised. Manitoba and Saskatchewan were allowed 65 per cent of the anthracite they had imported in 1916-17. But the Western consumer grumbled nonetheless as he stockpiled soft coal for his furnace.[23]

The most disturbing direct outcome of the increased cost of living was an increase in the number of labour disputes. During 1918 there were 169 strikes in Canada, more than the total for the first three war years. Those suspicious of the labour movement connected the unrest as "co-incident with the growth of the I.W.W. and One Big Union and Bolshevist propaganda." Trade unions had grown during the war, and by 1918 the number of organized workers in Canada was 248,000 as compared with 166,000 five years before. The most likely cause for the increase in militance, however, was a concern with the spectacular rate of inflation rather than the influence of radical ideas. Most disquieting about the labour troubles of 1918 was the fact that strikes began to occur in traditionally quiescent sectors of the work force. The coal miners of Alberta and eastern British Columbia, represented by the United Mineworkers of America, had by 1918 gained a 45 per cent pay increase over 1915 rates and a cost of living indexation which was to prevail for the remainder of the war. It was not class-conscious coal miners who made 1918 a record year for industrial unrest. Much to the consternation of municipal governments, civic employees in many Canadian cities went to the picket lines in the spring and summer of 1918. This occurred in both Calgary and Winnipeg, and in Winnipeg it reached almost the proportions of a general strike, a portent of the situation a year later.[24]

Westerners who were not part of the labour movement generally reacted to these strikes with disfavour. The farmer in particular found it difficult to understand the position of the urban worker. "When they have accepted with good grace a fixed price for their largest and most important cash crop, wheat," wrote an economist at the University of Saskatchewan, farmers "fail to understand why certain elements among labour do not scruple to take advantage of a temporary and accidental monopoly in the labour market." During the Winnipeg strike a correspondent informed R.A. Rigg that "never was labour in this city on so unpopular a side as this time." But despite the fact that the general public was often hostile to the strikers, it was the Union government that received most of the criticism for labour unrest. "People will hold the Dominion Government to account," was the *Swift Current Sun*'s conclusion to an editorial entitled "Public Sympathy opposed to Strikes." "They have the labour situation in a muddle, particularly in the West," complained the lieutenant governor of Alberta to Walter Scott. Even a newspaper like the *Calgary Daily Herald*, which continued to support the Union government strongly throughout 1918, admitted that the Unionists were responsible for "serious trouble" with Canadian labour.[25]

T.W. Crothers, first Unionist minister of labour, was probably the least popular member of the cabinet, disliked by labour and not respected by the public. Described variously as a "square peg" and a "futile fool," Crothers was an Ontario corporation lawyer unsuited to his cabinet post. After a postal strike demonstrated his inability to deal with such situations, the *Grain Grower's Guide* advised Borden to "find a minister of labour who can handle the job." Crothers was replaced eventually by Senator Gideon Robertson, a former official of the Brotherhood of Railway Telegraphers. This did little to placate the West, for Robertson's background in a conservative craft union did not win the favour of either the general public or the Western labour movement. To deal with the threat that work stoppages posed to the economy, however, the Union cabinet issued a series of Orders in Council under the authority of the War Measures Act which were designed to bring recalcitrant workers into line. The most far-reaching of these was PC 2825. Issued in October, 1918, it denied the right to strike and made violators subject to fine and imprisonment. The order did little to increase Western confidence in the government's ability to deal with labour and, although it was rescinded less than a month after its enactment, it brought the government's relationship with labour itself to a new low just as the war ended in Europe.[26]

V

The task of the Union government was made more difficult by the fact that the Canadian public had an external yardstick by which to measure its effectiveness. In the West and elsewhere, editorialists compared the Canadian war effort with that of the United States. Invariably Canadian political leadership and the policies of the Union government were found wanting when such comparisons were made. As individuals set side by side with Lloyd George and Woodrow Wilson, Sir Robert Borden and his cabinet seemed colourless and uninspiring. "Too bad we have not a Wilson in Canada" or "Oh for a Lloyd George" ran the complaints. When the *Farmer's Advocate* invited its readers to complete a list of "Great Leaders of Today," Borden went unmentioned. Woodrow Wilson enjoyed a wide margin over David Lloyd George as the West's first choice, while Herbert Hoover, American food controller and director of Belgian Relief, came third.[27]

It was not surprising that the public was so aware of Hoover and Wilson. America's mobilization for war received widespread and favourable coverage in Canadian newspapers. The speeches of Wilson, Hoover, and other prominent Americans were often reprinted for Canadian readers for, as the *Swift Current Sun* commented, "the thoughts of these people are very important to our own thoughts just now for our problems are very much akin." More than leadership was compared. American programs for food and fuel conservation, the nationalization of railways and telegraph lines for the duration of the war, the enforcement of the Selective Service Act and campaigns to control profiteering were described in glowing terms in the news columns, while the editorials suggested that "the Union Government take these object lessons to heart." The unfairness of these comparisons to the United States should have been obvious. Wilson led a nation that was fresh from three years of prosperous neutrality, a nation without the division of opinion between French and English to be considered at every turn. But the critics of the Union government did not take these facts into account and suggested instead that "when we contrast Canada with our neighbor the United States...we cannot but stand ashamed" with regard to such diverse issues as food control and veterans' pensions.[28]

However, the Union government was prepared to admit that it was not matching the success of its American counterpart in one respect–communication with the nation's public. Here the government's attempts to maintain public enthusiasm and to explain its policies fell far short of the work done in the United States by the Committee on Public Information. In September, 1918, N.W. Rowell bluntly told Borden that the government was "out of touch with the people," and suggested the American domestic propaganda machine as an example of what constituted more effective communication. The informal network of editors, ministers, and educators which had publicized the Bryce Report and helped maintain the public's awareness of the justice of Canada's cause could not be expected to explain the complicated directives of the food controller or the reason for Orders in Council amending the Military Service Act. After warnings that a more effective instrument of communication was necessary, the Directorate of Public Information was established in November, 1917. Under Director M.E. Nicholls a system of volunteer speakers patterned after the Committee on Public Information's "four minute men" was initiated and an attempt was made to co-ordinate the press releases of all departments.

But the problem of explaining its policies to the public was one the Union government was never really able to solve. The Canada Food Board, to illustrate this, had its own publicity budget and was able to advertise its "Greater Production" campaign even after the Order in Council conscripting farmers' sons and agricultural labourers had been issued. During April and May, 1918, farm journals carried advertisements urging that extra acres be seeded opposite announcements that farmers were to report for military duty. In July, 1918, T.A. Crerar confided to A.L. Sifton that he was convinced that "our Department of Public Information is NG," and that because of this "the Government is failing to carry opinion with it as it should in Western Canada," even though "a very considerable body of public opinion...wants the Government to succeed."[29]

Openness in government was one of the objectives of Western Canadian reformers, and one of the reasons for the popularity of the various versions of Direct Legislation in the West. Most Westerners believed that "there is nothing better on earth than to trust the people, educate them, take them into confidence." If this were done they would then "respond wholeheartedly to the right appeal." The Union government seemed to operate in secrecy, without feeling the need to explain its actions. An Order in Council issued in June, 1918, made it an offence to criticize the Allied war effort publicly, and generally tightened the censorship of the press. The *Swift Current Sun* warned that as far as the West was concerned this was "a serious mistake." George F. Chipman complained to T.A. Crerar that "it is one of Borden's crowning mistakes that he has not kept the people of Canada well informed and taken them into his confidence." In an editorial in his *Grain Grower's Guide* entitled "The People Should Know," Chipman made this complaint public.

> The Union Government has lost the confidence of an immense number of people who supported it at the last election. This loss of confidence is due almost entirely to the failure of the Government to give the people the information and the facts which they should have.

This image of an aloof, secretive government isolated from public opinion was reinforced by the Union government's method of dealing with situations by means of Orders in Council rather than through Parliament. The parliamentary majority that the Unionists had sought was assembled only once during the remainder of the war, and for a session that lasted only a little over nine weeks. As a steady stream of cabinet directives was issued, the opponents of the Union were able to charge that the Commons was being ignored, that government had been taken "out of the hands of the people" and a "veil of secrecy" thrown around its operations. "Whither are we being shoved?" asked a

Winnipeg labour leader after an Order in Council had banned several left-wing political organizations and made strikes illegal for the duration of the war.[30]

But, as Craig Brown has pointed out, the Union government was criticized as often for *lacking* direction and decisiveness as it was for arbitrary behaviour. The same critics who decried the Order in Council as undemocratic could demand in the name of "national efficiency" the "appointment of efficient specialists who will diagnose our troubles and tell us what must be done." The contradiction contained in this criticism reflects the ambivalent attitudes displayed by both government and public toward the expansion of governmental power which took place during the Great War. It was this ambivalence that made some of the Union government's attempts to intervene in the wartime economy less effective than they might have been. When compared with the laissez faire economy of pre-war Canada, such things as the Canada Food Board or the Board of Grain Supervisors seem dramatic innovations, yet the government never fully abandoned the principle of voluntarism. The income tax, the attempts at food and fuel control, and, most significant, the nationalization of two transcontinental railways were undertaken more out of necessity than because of any change in governmental philosophy. All attempts to regulate the economy were carried out by "a combination of large amounts of persuasion with small doses of compulsion."[31]

Nor were there any indications that the Union government had any conceptions of the "welfare state" which emerged from the Second World War. This essential belief in voluntarism can be seen clearly in the policy adopted toward soldiers' dependents and then toward the veterans themselves when they began to return from the front. The needs of soldiers' families were met essentially by private charity through the Patriotic Fund, which raised money through donations and distributed it as the fund's directors felt necessary. The fund put working-class mothers and their families in a humiliating position. "Before a soldier's wife can draw an allowance she must subject herself to a sort of inquisition," reported *The Nutcracker* of the situation in Calgary. "Hints are given that soldiers' wives should not buy a new hat, or go to the theatre." An army officer told *The Voice* that he daily encountered "many women, heartbroken over the indignities they have suffered." This system was condemned almost universally as "notoriously unfair" and as a "nightmare relic of barbarism," but the Patriotic Fund continued to provide the basic source of support for the impoverished next-of-kin of Canada's soldiers. Discharged veterans were provided with pensions if they had been wounded, but the pensions were universally described as inadequate "even coupled with what they can earn in a disabled condition." Rehabilitation and retraining programs were created on a limited scale in June, 1916, but were available only to those permanently disabled. "He saved his blooming country, will his country now save him?" asked Robert Stead in a wartime poem called "The Veterans." The answer seemed to be no, and it was not until June, 1918, that a Department of Soldier's Civil Re-establishment began to deal seriously with the problem.[32]

VI

As far as most of its Western supporters were concerned, the Union government had failed to "make good in other respects" and its mandate of the previous December was steadily eroded throughout 1918. One Saskatchewan resident commented that "no Government was ever returned with a stronger mandate" but that everywhere he went throughout the West he heard nothing but "a great deal of criticism of the Union Government." The Western editors who had been among its most enthusiastic supporters and spokesmen began to suggest that they had been mistaken and that they were "still waiting for a new era in governmental circles." The war was going to come to a successful conclusion but "in matters of domestic policy the Union Government is falling down badly." Even some of the government's own ministers could recognize that they had lost much of the popular support they had once enjoyed in the West and admit that they were "fully entitled to all the bricks coming our way."[33]

The disillusionment that the one-time supporters of Union government felt was as much a product of their own overinflated expectations as it was an accurate assessment of the government's record. Westerners had expected that their support of Unionist candidates would give their region a stronger voice in government and that the achievement of long-sought objectives would be the result. When these hopes proved unrealistic and as the war came to an end, they turned away from the Unionists as rapidly as they had turned towards them. Because of this reversal of Western attitudes the enthusiasm with which the West originally supported the Union government is sometimes dismissed as illusory: as the creation of a wave of propaganda and the imposition of discriminatory electoral legislation. Richard Allen does this in *The Social Passion*, arguing that "1918 began for Canada with the spurious unity of Union Government" and that "the Western vote, although overwhelmingly for Union candidates was nevertheless half-hearted." No doubt the economic, political, and social objectives of many Western supporters of the Unionists were not shared by their Central-Canadian counterparts, but this did not make Western hopes any less sincere. And there was unanimity of feeling behind the Union government in the sense that it represented the determination of English Canadians that Canada do her part in a struggle for freedom and democracy, and that her role be that of a "principal, not a colony." The important fact about Union government is its original popularity, not its eventual dissolution.[34]

The Western rejection of the Union government's domestic policy must not be interpreted as a change in Westerners' attitude to the Great War, or as the weakening of their determination to bring Germany and her rulers to their knees. After an examination of domestic problems in the nations of Europe during the war, A.J.P. Taylor concludes that although "social discontent and political unrest" existed in all countries,

> ...the surprising thing is how slowly and how late this was turned into war weariness. For much of the period, men were demanding instead that the war should be waged more fiercely and more completely....In fact fiercer war was from first to last the popular cause.

This same attitude was exhibited by most English-speaking Westerners, whatever they came to think of the Union government. Because "the fate of democracy was balanced on the issue," they demanded "mobilization, co-operation of every interest—national effort in short." Germany's attempts to negotiate a peace in the autumn of 1918 were rejected as nothing more than verbal "poison gas." Instead, Canadians, as one of the "free peoples of the world" should continue "fighting this war to a finish." No outcome short of "unconditional surrender" could be accepted for "No other termination will make the world safe for democracy." It had been the "Banner of Democracy" which had rallied the Canadian West and it was the "Banner of Democracy" that kept it fighting. "Some objections there are to the proceedings," said *The Voice*, one of the Union government's constant critics, "but the fact is that the Canadian Expeditionary Forces go with all the might of Canadian Democracy behind them." To those "Easterners" who charged the West with disloyalty for its stand on the tariff, the *Grain Grower's Guide* flung back the West's record of sacrifice and added that "the whole people of the West, farmers and town people, are as determined to see the war through to a finish as any group of protectionists that ever flourished upon a tariff." True, the West rejected some parts of the national policy but as far as the war was concerned "they stand exactly where they did last December, devoted to the country and the issue at stake."[35]

VII

On the morning of November 11, 1918, units of the Canadian Corps entered the Belgian city of Mons, the very point from which the tenacious retreat of the British Army had begun in 1914. The German forces which had occupied the city withdrew, and at 11:00 o'clock that morning an armistice ended the fighting. For Canada and her soldiers the Great War was over. The reaction was restrained. Instead of engaging in the wild celebration that many had looked forward to, the fighting men responded with quiet relief. To Western Canada "the great news came unexpectedly." Many had expected at least another year of war and, "even up to the hour of its announcement," hopes of an armistice "seemed almost too good to be possible." Spontaneous demonstrations like those which had greeted the war's beginning celebrated its conclusion, but there the similarity ended. Gone was the bombast of the editorial pages. In its place was a soft-spoken pride in Canada's contribution to victory. "The end has come and come our way," said the Calgary Daily Herald, "it was surely worth waiting and fighting for."[36]

In 1914, before the end of innocence, war had held out the promise of excitement, glory, and adventure for individuals as well as relief from depression for the West itself. The war had had a sobering effect, however, and by 1918 pride in what had been accomplished was mixed with foreboding about the future. Some Westerners, at least, now realized that "the problems of peace may be quite as perplexing as the problems of war." It was these "problems of peace" that occupied the thoughts of some of them in the days after the armistice. Premier Martin of Saskatchewan, for one, confided to General J.F.L. Embury that he had "no doubt that for the next few years we will have problems and conditions to face in this country...which will perhaps be more serious than even those which we have had to deal with over the past five years."[37]

For Canada the Great War had been both a source of unity and of division. French Canada interpreted the war as a blood sacrifice made on the altar of the British Empire, and as a confirmation of Canada's colonial status. English Canada saw instead a crusade for justice, freedom, and democracy in which Canada was able to demonstrate her national maturity by participating as a partner of Great Britain rather than as a dependent. In this way the war brought English Canadians together as surely as it drove French and English apart. The newly created unity of purpose was reflected by the decision to conscript manpower for the Canadian Corps and to sink party differences in support of a Union government to direct the national war effort. Nowhere in English Canada was this sense of purpose more apparent than in the Prairie West, and Manitoba, Saskatchewan, and Alberta made a contribution to Canada's part in the Great War that was out of proportion to their share of the total population.

The West did this despite the fact that on the eve of war it had been beset by serious social and economic problems. Smarting from their lack of ability to influence the direction of national policy, Westerners had a long list of accounts to settle with Central Canada. Convinced by the outbreak of war that this accounting would have to be postponed, Westerners rallied to the "Banner of Democracy" with an enthusiasm unmatched in the older provinces. As the war continued, they saw the hope that Union government might satisfy their economic grievances while it sought a victory against Germany, but the new government demonstrated during 1918 that this hope had been chimerical. More than four years of war did not shake Western confidence that Canada's goal was a worthy one, that it was "Canada's war as well as that of the other Allies" and that it was "our own battle line which our men held so nobly."[38]

Proud as they were of the Canadian contribution to Allied success, Westerners took particular satisfaction in the major part their own provinces had played making that contribution possible. "How nobly Winnipeg and all the West did!", wrote a soldier's widow to the president of the Manitoba IODE. "We shall always feel pride in being Westerners." As a corollary to this regional pride came a sense of superiority to the East, strengthened by the West's conviction that it had been asked to make a greater sacrifice and that it had made it willingly. "It is a curious fact that the West which is supposed to be less loyal than the East has done far more than the East in proportion to its population," observed Henry Marshall Tory, President of the University of Alberta. When Lt. Col. W.A. Griesbach of the 49th Edmonton Battalion sent his men into battle with the admonition to "Show 'em you're Westerners," he was addressing his remark to Central Canada as much as to the enemy. Griesbach's words to his troops became the theme of a poem by an Edmonton boy. Fourteen-year-old Spencer Race concluded "Over the Top" with the lines:

Of shot and shell, the German yell
Of bullets they took no heed
For the words their Colonel uttered
Had now become their creed
And they showed they were Westerners.

The emergence of a sense of regional identity in Westerners predated the Great War, but the years of war heightened their feelings of identity. In this sense Western Canada "came of age" within the Dominion in the same way that Canada itself matured within the Empire and the international community.[39]

As dramatic as the four years of war had been, they had not solved the West's long term problems. Prohibition and woman's suffrage were part of the war's legacy, but the dry millenium was to last only until 1924 and the new women voters did not produce the purification of Canadian politics that the reform movement had promised from it. The school systems of Manitoba and Saskatchewan had been turned into effective tools for the nationalization of the European immigrant, but this change had occurred during the war more than because of it. Two transcontinental railways had been nationalized, but the problems of the Canadian transportation system were as yet unresolved and the new income tax had supplemented the tariff as a source of revenue without replacing it.

As the Prairie West looked ahead to 1919 it saw many of the same problems that had confronted it in the summer of 1914. Drifting soil and poor yields reminded farmers of the debts that remained to be paid for their decision to increase production to take advantage of wartime demand and inflated wartime prices, and drought threatened an agricultural economy still overly dependent on one major grain crop. The readers of the Christmas number of *The Farmer's Advocate* would have found several differences between the issue of 1918 and that of 1913, the last pre-war Christmas. There were references to "the glorious chapter of Canadian History which had closed on November 11th 1918," and on a full page of pictures of Western war dead, "dedicated to the immortal memory of all Western Agriculturalists who fell on the field of battle in freedom's cause," were reprinted the final lines of Lincoln's Gettysburg Address. No advertisements for beer or liquor appeared, save for non-alcoholic Maltum Stout. A Canada Food Board symbol was displayed in the lower right corner of the advertisement for Purity Flour, and advertisements for tractors and automobiles had increased fivefold, to the point that they challenged the prominence of those for draft horses and breeding services. But in other ways the special holiday issue must have seemed unchanged from the one published five years earlier.

In his lead editorial entitled "What Are Our National Resources?" F.S. Jacobs proposed tariff reform to shift the burden of taxation away from the producer and the consumer and on to "inanimate forms of wealth." A second theme was the West's lack of agricultural diversification, and articles suggested livestock and poultry as alternatives to the monoculture of wheat. Prominently featured was an updating of the Farmers' Platform passed at a meeting of the Canadian Council of Agriculture held in Winnipeg shortly after the armistice. In response to the conclusion of the Great War, the platform called for the establishment of "an international organization to give permanence to the world's peace" and for "the exercise [of] all due diligence for the future well-being of the returned soldier and his dependents." But the other issues outlined—the tariff, tax reform, the transportation problem, and "other democratic reforms"—were the same ones that had appeared in the original platform of 1910.

Early in 1919 Norman James, a private soldier returning to the small Alberta community from which he had enlisted, was invited to address a public meeting called to welcome himself and his comrades home. During the speech of welcome the town's mayor expressed the hope the veterans would be able to "straighten things out" and to create "the New Order in Canada." On behalf of his fellow soldiers, James declined to accept this challenge. "To be frank with you," he told the crowd, "we were hoping that *you* would do something about that while we were away."[40]

James's biting remark was most unfair. The Great War had not caused those Westerners who had stayed at home to put aside aspirations for a "new order." Within the West and within Canada as a whole some of the foremost objectives of the pre-war social reform movement had been achieved, and the years of conflict had not changed the West's mind about its economic objectives. The response to peace was a renewal of Western political protest in a new and more virulent form. During the 1919 session of Parliament nine Grain Grower Unionists left the government in protest against its failure to reduce the tariff, and the independent farmer's party so long proposed by the *Grain Grower's Guide* at last existed. In Winnipeg later that same spring, a general strike gave evidence that Western labour was as discontented as the Western farmer. Westerners, both rural and urban, were profoundly dissatisfied with the effects of basic national policies and with certain features of the socio-economic system they believed those policies supported. This mood, in some ways strengthened during the war, found more open expression with the end of hostilities in Europe, and was demonstrated in the general election of 1921 as both national parties were spurned by a large part of the Western electorate.

But the political protest which emerged in the post-war years was not a negation of the ideal of democracy for which Westerners had felt themselves to be fighting. By no means. It was instead a sign of the West's new maturity and of its determination to leave as deep an imprint on the period of reconstruction as it had on the Canadian war effort.

Appendix

Table 1

Distribution of the Labour Force,
Manitoba, Saskatchewan, and Alberta, 1911-21

Males

	1911		1921	
	Number	Percentage	Number	Percentage
All Occupations	500,834	100	620,852	100
Agricultural	279,724	55.8	369,107	59.5
Mining	6,695	1.3	9,298	1.4
Manufacturing and Mechanical	22,437	4.5	31,565	5.0
Construction	30,167	6.0	22,122	3.6
Transportation	29,120	5.8	35,480	5.7
Trade and Finance	37,600	7.5	51,098	8.2
Professional Service	9,874	1.9	15,488	2.5
Personal Service	14,057	2.8	16,781	2.7
Clerical	13,851	2.7	23,994	3.9
Labourers	48,296	9.6	33,741	5.4
Other	10,517	2.1	13,038	2.1

Females

	1911		1921	
	Number	Percentage	Number	Percentage
All Occupations	47,404	100	77,536	100
Agricultural	3,748	7.9	5,215	6.7
Manufacturing	4,639	9.8	4,225	5.4
Transportation	928	2.0	2,246	2.9
Trade and Finance	3,212	6.8	7,360	9.5
Professional Service	6,452	13.6	16,589	21.4
Personal Service	22,366	47.2	25,546	32.9
Clerical	5,760	12.2	16,062	20.7
Other	237	0.5	388	0.5

Source: *Census of Canada*, 1911, 1921.

Table 2

Average Yields of Principal
Western Field Crops, 1912-21

Wheat_____ Oats_ _ _ _ _ _ _ Barley_____ _ _____

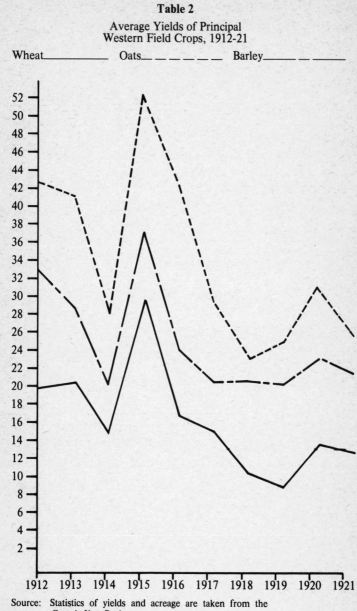

Source: Statistics of yields and acreage are taken from the
Canada Year Book.

Table 3

Monthly Wages and Board of Farm Labourers, Manitoba, Saskatchewan, and Alberta, 1909-19

Males

	Manitoba		Saskatchewan		Alberta	
	Wages	Board	Wages	Board	Wages	Board
1909	35.95	11.00	38.30	16.00	40.08	15.00
1910	40.00	14.70	40.00	14.00	40.00	16.70
1914	39.13	15.49	40.51	16.50	40.26	16.36
1915	45.00	15.00	42.00	17.00	44.00	17.00
1916	48.00	18.00	49.00	18.00	52.00	20.00
1917	68.00	21.00	73.00	23.00	76.00	23.00
1918	78.00	23.00	86.00	25.00	86.00	26.00
1919	89.00	26.00	94.00	28.00	95.00	28.00

Females

	Manitoba		Saskatchewan		Alberta	
	Wages	Board	Wages	Board	Wages	Board
1909	23.97	9.00	24.23	10.00	26.16	12.00
1910	25.00	11.30	24.50	13.00	27.50	13.90
1914	22.35	12.98	22.96	13.96	23.63	13.91
1915	27.00	13.00	24.00	14.00	24.00	14.00
1916	27.00	15.00	26.00	15.00	29.00	16.00
1917	40.00	17.00	41.00	18.00	44.00	19.00
1918	45.00	19.00	49.00	20.00	50.00	22.00
1919	52.00	20.00	55.00	23.00	58.00	24.00

Source: *Canada Year Book*, 1914, 1921.

Table 4

Farms of Minority Groups as Compared to All Prairie Farms 1917-21

Total Farm Acreage

	1916	1921	Percentage of Increase
Four Minority Groups*	2,563,299	3,397,248	32.5
Prairies as a Whole**	73,300,135	87,931,804	20.0

Total Improved Acreage

	1916	1921	Percentage of Increase
Four Minority Groups*	1,357,619	1,854,148	36.6
Prairies as a Whole**	34,330,246	44,863,266	30.7

Total Field Crop Acreage

	1916	1921	Percentage of Increase
Four Minority Groups*	1,068,274	1,436,091	34.4
Prairies as a Whole**	24,595,915	32,203,806	30.9

*The four minorities considered are Doukhobors at Blaine Lake and Kamsack, Saskatchewan; French Canadians at Ray, Hazelwood, and St. Rose, Alberta; German Catholics at St. Peter's and St. Joseph's, Saskatchewan, and Mennonites on the West Reserve, Manitoba. Figures for these groups were computed from information in C.A. Dawson, *Group Settlement in the Prairie Provinces*, pp. 50, 124, 308-12, and 359.

**Figures for Manitoba, Saskatchewan, and Alberta are taken from *Census of the Prairie Provinces, 1916*, pp. 284-89 and from Canada, *Sixth Census*, 1921, pp. 4-5.

BIBLIOGRAPHICAL NOTE

The most important sources for this study were manuscript collections in the Public Archives of Canada, the Archives of Saskatchewan and Manitoba, and the Archives of the Glenbow-Alberta Institute in Calgary. Also consulted were the University Archives of Saskatchewan and Alberta, the Provincial Archives of Alberta, and the Archives of Queen's University which contain the invaluable T.A. Crerar Papers. It would be impossible to list all those collections which contain pertinent material, and specific references can be found in the notes which follow. Worthy of special attention, however, are the R.L. Borden Papers in the Public Archives of Canada. The papers of Canada's wartime prime minister can provide information on all aspects of the war's domestic consequences.

Also indispensable was the periodical press of Western Canada. Four dailies and a dozen weeklies were consulted throughout the war period, as well as a number of specialized journals. Particularly useful were *The Voice*, a labour paper published in Winnipeg; three farm papers, the *Grain Grower's Guide, Farmer's Advocate*, and *Farm and Ranch Review*; and the *Western School Journal*, a teacher's magazine. *The Nutcracker*, later the *Non Partisan Leader*, expressed the point of view of the Non Partisan League. Four French-language weeklies, *Le Manitoba, Le Patriote de l'Ouest, La Liberté*, and *Le Courrier de l'Ouest* were also published in the Prairie Provinces during this period. Microfilmed copies of these papers are available in the Provincial Libraries of Manitoba, Saskatchewan, and Alberta.

Post-graduate theses are providing Canadian historians with important information on which to base larger studies, and readers will find more than twenty of these cited in the notes. For those who wish a more detailed documentation of material available for the study of the Prairie West during the period of the Great War I would suggest the notes and bibliography of my own doctoral dissertation completed at Queen's University in 1975.

NOTES

Abbreviations Used in the Notes

AS: Archives of Saskatchewan
CAR: *Canadian Annual Review*
CYB: *Canada Year Book*
Glenbow: Archives of the Glenbow Foundation
GGG: *Grain Grower's Guide*
MFP: *Manitoba Free Press*
PAC: Public Archives of Canada
PAM: Provincial Archives of Manitoba
QUA: Queen's University Archives
USA: University of Saskatchewan Archives

Chapter One

[1]Nellie McClung, *The Stream Runs Fast* (Toronto, 1945), p. 136, and C.W. Gordon, *Postscript to Adventure* (New York, 1938), p. 154.

[2]Donald Creighton, *Dominion of the North* (Boston, 1944), p. 463; J.M.S. Careless, *Canada: A Story of Challenge* (Toronto, 1964), pp. 326-27; and W.L. Morton, "The 1920's" in J.M.S. Careless and R.C. Brown, eds., *The Canadians 1867-1967* (Toronto, 1967), pp. 205-9.

[3]The combined value of the wheat and oats crops in 1912 was $179 million compared with $195 million in 1911, despite the fact that both the yield and the acreage seeded to wheat and oats increased. In 1914 the acreage seeded to wheat, oats, and barley declined to 15.6 million acres from the previous year's total of 16.8 million. Calculations based on figures in *The Canada Yearbook 1913*, pp. 136-44, and *The Canada Yearbook 1915*, pp. 161-67. Public Archives of Canada (PAC), Sir Robert L. Borden Papers, George Hoadley to Martin Burrell, August 13, 1914, p. 103957; R.B. Bennett to Borden, July 27, 1914, pp. 103835-36.

[4]A more detailed discussion of the pre-war recession can be found in Chapter 3.

[5]W.L. Morton, *The Progressive Party in Canada* (Toronto, 1950), p. 26. In the 1911 election the Liberals captured 17 of 27 Prairie seats and 53 per cent of the popular vote, as compared with the Conservative's 44 per cent. It is interesting to note that in Manitoba, where the Conservatives gained all but two of their Prairie members, the principal campaign issue was not reciprocity as much as a demand for a northward extension of the provincial boundaries, a second traditional theme of Western discontent. Thus in a way the Conservative majority in that province represented "regional protest" as much as did the Liberal majorities in Saskatchewan and Alberta.

[6]*Grain Grower's Guide* (GGG), April 15, 1914. For an indication of Western opinion about further government aid to railways see PAC, Borden Papers, pp. 11461-97.

[7]George F. Chipman, "Winnipeg: The Melting Pot," *Canadian Magazine*, September 1909, pp. 409-16. On the "foreign navvy" and his role in the history of Canadian immigration see D.H. Avery, "Canadian Immigration Policy and 'The Foreign Navvy'," in Canadian Historical Association, *Historical Papers, 1972.*

[8]These quotations, in order of their appearance, are from: Provincial Archives of Manitoba (PAM), Canadian Club of Winnipeg *Annual Report*, 1913, p. 24; E.B. Mitchell, *Western Canada before the War* (London, 1915), p. 183; Alberta, Department of Education *Annual Report 1912*; the *Vegreville Observer*, September 1914; and the *Manitoba Free Press* (MFP), July 29, 1914.

[9]*GGG*, April 15 and June 10, 1914.

[10]PAC, Borden Papers, Sam Hughes to Borden, June 10, 1914, OC/4281.

[11]*GGG*, July 29, 1914.

[12]*Saskatoon Phoenix*, June 25, 1914 and *Dauphin Herald*, July 2, 1914.

[13]Paul F. Sharp, *The Agrarian Revolt in Western Canada* (St. Paul, 1948), pp. 74-75. Sharp argues that "the crusade for peace enlisted the devotion of the ablest prairie radicals." This is contradicted effectively by D. Page, who demonstrates that these "prairie radicals" were few in number and ignored the attempts of peace movements to make use of their services. Page, "The Development of a Western Canadian Peace Movement," in S.M. Trofimenkoff, *The Unknown Decade: Western Canada during the 1920's* (Ottawa, 1972), pp. 75-78.

[14]Mack Eastman to UFA Convention, reported in *GGG*, May 20, 1914. The other quotations are taken from "Who Organizes

War Scares," *GGG*, September 18, 1912, and "The Incubus of Militarism," *Dauphin Herald*, September 11, 1913.

[15] *Dauphin Herald*, May 28, 1914.

[16] Information on the cadet movement is taken from PAC, Borden Papers, Militia Orders, November 23, 1914, p. 23087; Alberta, Department of Education, *Annual Report 1914*, p. 24; *Lloydminster Times*, July 1914; *Swift Current Sun*, July 24, 1914.

[17] This information is taken from the *Saskatoon Phoenix*, August 4, 1914.

[18] PAC, Borden Papers, OC/192, "War Gifts from the Provinces"; *The Voice*, August 14, 1914; and D.J. Goodspeed, *The Road Past Vimy* (Toronto, 1969), p. 11.

[19] For examples of these stories, see the *Lloydminster Times*, August 6, 1914; Cypress River *Western Prairie*, August 6, 1914; *Swift Current Sun*, August 11, 1914; *Saskatoon Phoenix*, August 6, 1914.

[20] PAC, Woodside Papers, George Huestis to Mrs. Henry J. Woodside, October 3, 1914, vol. 10; Sir Clifford Sifton Papers, J.M. Robinson to Sifton, August 7, 1914.

[21] University of Alberta Archives, H.M. Tory Papers, A.C. Rankin to Tory, August 26, 1914, Box 42, f. 1402.

[22] PAM, Colin H. Campbell Papers, E.H. Bennest to Campbell, August 4, 1914, Box 3.

[23] "A Trooper at Valcartier" to the editor of the Cypress River *Western Prairie*, September 10, 1914.

[24] G.F.R. Stevens, *A City Goes To War* (Brampton, 1964), p. 210.

[25] *Swift Current Sun*, November 24, 1914; PAC, Borden Papers, memo H.B. Ames to Borden, May 27, 1915, pp. 108586-93; and Harold Baldwin, *Holding the Line* (Chicago, 1918), p. 4. One reason for the large number of British recruits was the fact the veterans of the Imperial forces were given preference for the much sought after places in the first contingent.

[26] The first phrase is taken from *The Voice*, November 13, 1914, the second from PAM, R.P. Roblin Papers, Roblin to T.W. Crothers, October 6, 1914, p. 82.

[27] This account is taken from the *Dauphin Herald*, "Volunteers Get Right-Royal Send Off," August 27, 1914, but virtually the same ceremony took place in other Prairie towns. In Lloydminster, Saskatchewan, the volunteers were given a "3B briar pipe and a tin of tobacco" as the town's token of appreciation, but in most other aspects the departure was handled in precisely the same fashion.

[28] Archives of Saskatchewan (AS), Walter Scott Papers, Scott to S.G. Hill, November 7, 1914, p. 12711.

[29] *MFP*, August 6, 1914. For the reasoning behind the decision, see, for example, AS, Scott Papers, Scott to R.H. McDonald, September 28, 1914, p. 12808, or Scott to G.B. Johnston, October 1, 1914.

[30] Canada, House of Commons, *Debates*, Special Session 1914, pp. 39-42, 96.

Chapter Two

[1] Premier Scott of Saskatchewan wrote that "In Canada there is only one voice. Even in this province where we have tens of thousands of Germans and Austrians the same is true. Whatever their hearts say, they keep to themselves–their heads tell them they must uphold the flag they have adopted and they are doing it." AS, Scott Papers, Scott to D.H. Ross, August, 1914, p. 12969.

[2] A.R.M. Lower, *My First Seventy-five Years* (Toronto, 1967), p. 229; and Charles F. Harrison, "Sons of the British Empire Unite–Your Country is Calling" (Vancouver, 1916), in Archives of the Glenbow Foundation (Glenbow), World War I Song Collection.

[3] Winnipeg City Council, *Minutes, 1914*, August 11, 1914.

[4] PAM, Canadian Club of Winnipeg, *Annual Report 1913-14*, p. 71; and AS, Scott Papers, Scott to L.B. Cochran, August 20, 1914, pp. 12619-21.

[5] University of Saskatchewan Archives (USA), *The Sheaf*, vol. 3, no. 2, November, 1914.

[6] "Ralph Connor" (C.W. Gordon), *The Sky Pilot in No Man's Land* (New York, 1917), p. 142.

[7] For a further explanation of their concept of "democracy," see Chapters 4 and 5.

[8] *The Voice*, "What About Russia?" September 11, 1914.

[9] *Lloydminster Times*, August 13, 1914, and the *Alberta Non Partisan*, September 12, 1918.

[10] PAC, Clifford Sifton Papers, A.E. Philp to Sifton, January 27, 1915, p. 160491; and Baldur Jonsson, MSS. of an unpublished novel quoted at length in W.J. Lindal, *The Icelanders in Canada* (Winnipeg, 1971), pp. 224-25.

[11] Bland's speech was reported in *The Voice*, January 8, 1915. The other quotations are from the *Dauphin Herald*, "An Empire of Ideas," October 8, 1914 and the *Western School Journal*, "Edi-

tor's Chat," May 1918, pp. 176-77.

[12]Dafoe's comment is from *MFP*, August 26, 1917; Neely's from House of Commons, *Debates*, 1917, vol. 3, p. 2779; and Henders' from *MFP*, January 11, 1917. Gordon reprints his speech in his autobiography, *Postscript to Adventure* (New York, 1938), p. 207.

[13]The quotation is from AS, Scott Papers, J.H. Heffernan to Scott, September 23, 1914, pp. 12692-93.

[14]*Ibid.*; and Sifton, "Foundations of the New Era" in John O. Miller, ed., *The New Era in Canada* (Toronto, 1917), p. 37.

[15]R.J.C. Stead, "Manhood's Estate," in *Kitchener* and *Other Poems* (Toronto, 1917), pp. 42-43.

[16]Russel B. Nye, *The Unembarrassed Muse* (New York, 1970), p. 4.

[17]J.M. Roberts, ed., *History of the Twentieth Century* (Toronto, 1969), p. 430. In *Atrocity Propaganda 1914-1919* (New Haven, 1941), pp. 1-3, J.M. Read points out that propaganda techniques were described more than two thousand years earlier in Sun Tsu's *Art of War*, but argues that they "were first organized in a scientific manner" during the Great War.

[18]Harold D. Lasswell, *Propaganda Technique in the World War* (London, 1938), p. 9; J.M. Read, *Atrocity Propaganda*, p. 2.

[19]For a detailed description of American and British propaganda operations see Lasswell, *Propaganda Technique*, pp. 14-47, and J.R. Mock and C. Larson, *Words that Won the War* (Princeton, 1939).

[20]See PAC, Borden Papers, OC/343, "Canadian War Records and Censorship," especially Col. E.J. Chambers to Arthur Meighen, December 19, 1916, pp. 39576-77.

[21]PAC, Borden Papers, Ames to Borden, February 18, 1915, pp. 108468-70; Borden to A.E. Kemp, February 26, 1915, pp. 108488; RLB/709, "War Publicity 1914-16," pp. 108345-9288.

[22]Right Hon. Viscount Bryce, Chairman, *Report of the Committee on Alleged German Outrages* (New York, 1915), p. 61.

[23]These headlines are from *The Western Prairie*, April 29, 1915 and May 20, 1915; the *Dauphin Herald*; and the *Lloydminster Times*, June 10, 1915.

[24]PAC, Borden Papers, P.E. Blondin to Borden, April 7, 1916, pp. 109067-70; Borden to Blondin, April 8, 1916, p. 109079. Cf. *Lloydminster Times*, December 7, 1916.

[25]John Lewis, "Canada at War" in *Canada and the Great World War* (Toronto, 1919), vol. 2, p. 26; and Nellie McClung, *The Next of Kin: Those Who Wait and Wonder* (Boston, 1917), p. 44.

[26]For a discussion of the attitudes of two denominations towards the war see Michael Bliss, "The Methodist Church and World War I," in C. Berger, ed., *Conscription 1917*(Toronto, n.d.); and E.A. Christie, "The Presbyterian Church in Canada and Its Official Attitude toward Public Affairs and Social Problems" (unpublished MA thesis, University of Toronto, 1955). Also valuable is Richard Allen, *The Social Passion: Religion and Social Reform in Canada 1914-1928* (Toronto, 1971). The concluding quotation is from Reverend Wellington Bridgman, *Breaking Prairie Sod* (Toronto, 1920), p. 156.

[27]Bliss, "The Methodist Church and World War I," pp. 44-45; PAM, T.C. Norris Papers, Rev. Alex Hamilton to Norris, November 22, 1917, Box 2; and AS, C.A. Dunning Papers, "Church Bulletin of the Canada Food Board," pp. 41855.

[28]K.W. McNaught suggests in *A Prophet in Politics* (Toronto, 1959), p. 79, that Bland lost his teaching position at Wesley College because of his stand on political and social issues during the war. Richard Allen has demonstrated that this dismissal came about because of the serious financial difficulties the war caused for Wesley College, and in fact for all colleges and universities. *The Social Passion*, pp. 45-60.

[29]PAC, Borden Papers, Methodist Ministerial Association of Winnipeg to Borden, October 26, 1915, p. 39512-13.

[30]*Dauphin Herald*, November 12, 1914.

[31]The quotation is from the *Western School Journal*, February, 1915, p. 76. See also AS, Scott Papers, Scott to George McCraney, November 19, 1914, p. 34244; and *Canadian Annual Review*, 1915 (CAR), pp. 676-77.

[32]AS, Department of Education Collection, R.F. Blacklock to Teachers of Saskatchewan, May 27, 1917. See also PAM, Norris Papers, R. Fletcher to T.C. Norris, December 6, 1917, Box 1; and *Western School Journal*, October, 1917, and March, 1918.

[33]Ida M. Davidson, "An Original Program," *Western School Journal*, January, 1918, pp. 19-21; Lena G. Shay, "An Arithmetic Suggestion," *ibid.*, June, 1918, p. 261; and *CAR*, 1916, pp. 676-77.

[34]James H. Gray, *The Boy From Winnipeg* (Toronto, 1969), p. 91; Wallace Stegner, *Wolf Willow* (New York, 1966), p. 33; J.G. MacGregor, *North West of Sixteen* (Tokyo, 1968), p. 180. Student essays are from *Western School Journal*, February, 1915, pp. 58-59, April, 1915, pp. 146-47, December, 1915, pp. 384-85, September, 1917, pp. 282-83.

[35]This paragraph is based on material in the Henry Marshall

Tory Papers, University of Alberta Archives and the Walter C. Murray Papers, University of Saskatchewan Archives (USA). Specific references are from Murray Papers, Mrs. J.R. Dillon to Murray, February 1916. PAM, Clifford Sifton Papers, Crummy to Sifton, February 21, 1917; and *MFP*, July 5, 1917.

[36]University of Alberta Archives, Tory Papers, W.A.R. Kerr to H.B. Ames, January 20, 1916, and Tory to H.C. Rankin, August 31, 1915.

[37] *Western School Journal*, May 1917, pp. 193-98. For a further discussion of the effect of the war on the education of immigrants see Chapter 4.

[38]PAC, Borden Papers, H.P. Blackwood to Borden, May 17, 1915, pp. 315-24. File OC/278, "Recruiting 1915," pp. 31, 533-626, contains other letters demanding increased effort on the part of Canada, the majority of which are from Manitoba, Saskatchewan, Alberta, and British Columbia. Demands for a larger CEF can also be found in the Western press. See, for example, *Saskatoon Phoenix*, November 18, 1914, and the *Swift Current Sun*, May 7, 1915, as well as Ramsay Cook, *The Politics of John W. Dafoe and the Free Press* (Toronto, 1963), p. 68.

[39]PAC, Borden Papers, Borden to R.H. Smith, May 29, 1915, p. 31550. Norris' speech was reported in *MFP*, November 15, 1915, and an example of Western approval of a contingent of 500,000 can be found in AS, Scott Papers, Scott to John A. Reid, January 8, 1916, p. 14304.

Chapter Three

[1]Adam Shortt, *Economic Effects of War upon Canada* (Ottawa, 1916), p. 74.

[2]These quotations are from Donald Creighton, *Canada's First Century* (Toronto, 1970), p. 136; and K.W. McNaught, *The Pelican History of Canada* (London, 1969), p. 124. Similar statements may be found in many other works.

[3]Ramsay Cook, J.T. Saywell, and John C. Ricker, *Canada: A Modern Study* (Toronto, 1963), p. 169.

[4]My calculations, *Census of the Prairie Provinces*, 1926, p. xi, and *Census of 1951*.

[5] *Winnipeg City Council Minutes*, May 26, 1914 and GGG, July 15, 1914.

[6]PAC, Borden Papers, Sir W. Mackenzie to Borden, November 23, 1915, pp. 11994-12003, and November 24, 1915, pp. 12006-9. See also G.R. Stevens, *Canadian National Railways* (Toronto, 1960), vol. 2, p. 462.

[7]Glenbow, CPR Collection, P.L. Naismith to J.S. Dennis, September 18, 1914, Box 5, f. 52. The figures cited to not take into account employees of construction companies laid off when railway construction was cut back.

[8]PAC, Borden Papers, W.A. Johnson to Borden, June 9, 1916, pp. 9294-95; Borden to Johnson, July 1, 1916, p. 9301; Queen's University Archives (QUA), C.A. Dunning Papers, R.F. Thompson to Sir Henry Drayton, March 21, 1918, p. 16708.

[9]Statistics are from the CYB and AS, W.F.R. Turgeon Papers, Box 31, pp. 44-63; PAC, C. Sifton Papers, May 22, 1916, p. 160895.

[10]PAC, Borden Papers, OC/195, "War Camps 1914-16."

[11]Ibid., March 22, 1915, p. 16981; Swift Current Sun, September 21, 1915.

[12]PAC, Borden Papers, "Work of the Department of Militia and Defence," p. 22893.

[13]Farm and Ranch Review (Calgary), December 20, 1915; Swift Current Sun, May 23, 1916; The Voice, April 16, 1915; and MFP, October 27, 1915. The Manitoba Free Press claimed that orders given to Winnipeg failed to make use of even half of the plants already available within the community. PAC, Borden Papers, pp. 23640-44.

[14]PAC, Borden Papers, Memo by R.H. Carr, October 10, 1915, p. 23662; W. Hearst to Sam Hughes, October 26, 1915, p. 23753, R.D. Waugh to Borden, June 5, 1915, pp. 23024-25.

[15]Ibid., Sir J.W. Flavelle Papers, R.B. Bennett to General Bertram, November 2, 1915, and March 11, 1915, vol. 1, f. 2; Shell Committee to Bennett, November 3, 1915, vol. 1, f. 2.

[16]Ibid., Borden Papers, Memorandum, September 24, 1915, pp. 23544-47; Borden to G.H. Perley, January 14, 1916, p. 24079; ibid., Flavelle Papers, Memorandum, December 15, 1915, vol. 1, f. 2; Carnegie to Sir Frederick Black, January 18, 1916.

[17]Ibid., Flavelle Papers, S.B. Hillocks to R. Rogers, September 6, 1915; F.L. Willis to Rogers, January 31, 1916; Flavelle to Meighen, April 7, 1916, and April 19, 1916; Irish to Flavelle, March 17, 1917.

[18]Ibid., Borden Papers, Notes of Conversation, October 10, 1915, p. 23663; Flavelle Papers, Irish to Flavelle, March 17, 1917 and "Department of Labour 1916-18," vol. 2, f. 11.

[19]Ibid., Borden Papers, Flavelle to Borden, April 18, 1916, p. 24405; W.H. Hearst to Hughes, October 26, 1915, p. 23753.

[20]Ibid., Flavelle Papers, Report by F.C. Hirsch, January 25,

1919, vol. 36; *The Voice*, April 16, 1915.

[21]PAC, Flavelle Papers, Irish to Flavelle, March 17, 1917.

[22]PAM, R.P. Roblin Papers, J.B. Walker to M.V. Roche, April 22, 1915; *Labour Gazette*, 1915, p. 275; GGG, August 30, 1916; PAC, Flavelle Papers, E.G. Sterndale Bennett to Arthur Meighen, January 14, 1916.

[23]Figures for Edmonton are from a city census quoted in J.G. McGregor, *Edmonton* (Edmonton, 1967), p. 313. The figures for Prince Albert are from AS, Turgeon Papers, Box 31, pp. 44-63. It should be mentioned, however, that civic population figures are somewhat less reliable than those of the Dominion Census.

[24]PAC, H.J. Woodside Papers, T.T. Huestis to Woodside, April 26, 1915, vol. 10; Glenbow, Calgary Brewing and Malting Co. Collection, A.E. Cross to P.N. de Vries, December 27, 1915, Box 71, f. 560; Bradstreet's *Book of Commercial Ratings*, as cited in C.A. Dawson and E.R. Younge, *Pioneering in the Prairie Provinces* (Toronto, 1940), p. 53; *Farmer's Advocate* (Winnipeg), "What of the Country Stores?", May 17, 1916; PAC, H.J. Woodside Papers, Charles Woodside to Mrs. H. H.J. Woodside, May 27, 1916.

[25]R.M. Haig, *Taxation in Urban Municipalities of Saskatchewan* (Regina, 1917), pp. 24-25; John Appleton, "Broadening the Basis of Municipal Taxation," *Journal of the Canadian Banker's Association*, vol. 25, no. 4, July 1918, pp. 284-88.

[26]AS, W.M. Martin Papers, J.G. Colmer to G.H. Perley, July 5, 1918, p. 34261; J.H. Sutcliffe, "The Economic Background of the Winnipeg General Strike" (MA thesis, University of Manitoba, 1972).

[27]Quoted in John Appleton, "After-War Financial Problems of Western Municipalities," *Journal of the Canadian Banker's Association*, vol. 27, no. 2, January 1920, pp. 162-67.

[28]Stephen Leacock, "Our Organization for War," in Miller, *New Era*, p. 413.

[29]PAC, Woodside Papers, Fred Boyd to Woodside, July 22, 1916.

[30]These calculations are based on figures from the CYB 1910-21.

[31]PAC, Borden Papers, George Hoadley to Martin Burrell, August 13, 1914, p. 103957.

[32]Calculations based on CYB, 1913-14; Saskatchewan Department of Agriculture, *Acreage and Yields of Grain Crops*, 1913; USA, Dean W.J. Rutherford Collection, "Articles and Addresses," 1914.

[33] *Census of 1921*, vol. 4, pp. 4-5; *The Sheaf,* February, 1915; CYB, 1920, p. 657.

[34] *Journal of the Canadian Banker's Association*, January 1918, p. 91; Glenbow, CPR Collection, "Land Sales," Box 40, f. 465; R.W. Murchie, *Agricultural Progress on the Prairie Frontier* (Toronto, 1936), p. 103.

[35] John Proskie, "Financial Progress of Settlers with Special Reference to the Vulcan-Lomond Area" (MA thesis, University of Alberta, 1937).

[36] See Appendix, Table 3; QUA, T.A. Crerar Papers, J.M. Carson to Crerar, March 3, 1918.

[37] QUA, Dunning Papers, John Wick to Dunning, February 28, 1918, pp. 42118-19; Merrill Denison, *Harvest Triumphant: The Story of Massey-Harris* (Toronto, 1948), pp. 214-21; Seager Wheeler, *Profitable Grain Growing* (Winnipeg, 1919), pp. 177-90.

[38] Saskatchewan, *Royal Commission on Agriculture and Rural Life* (Regina, 1955), vol. 2, *Mechanization and Farm Costs*, pp. 1, 16-17. Because the tractor received so much attention from agricultural periodicals during this period, there is a natural tendency for historians to over-emphasize its importance, as Dr. Grant MacEwan does in *Power for Prairie Plows* (Saskatoon, 1971), pp. 71-83. The best way to measure the actual effect on the use of horse power is to compare the acreage of field crops with the number of horses. Such a comparison gives a figure of 13.73 acres/horse in 1913 and 13.74 acres/horse in 1919.

[39] *Farm and Ranch Review*, September 6, 1915; *Swift Current Sun*, May 26, 1915, and February 26, 1918; *Calgary Herald*, January 24, 1918; USA, Murray Papers, Murray to A.K. MacLean, April 24, 1918; R.M. Wik, *Henry Ford and Grass-Roots America* (Ann Arbor, 1972), Chapter 5.

[40] *Farm and Ranch Review*, September 20, 1915; CYB, 1921, p. 552.

[41] *Journal of the Canadian Banker's Association*, January 1917, p. 162; *Farmer's Advocate*, June 14, 1916.

[42] *Farmer's Advocate*, March 15, 1916, and August 1, 1917.

[43] *Ibid.*, May 10, 1916.

[44] *Census of 1921*, vol. 4, pp. 4-5; *Farmer's Advocate*, May 31, 1916. A "section" is 640 acres and the basic homestead unit is 160 acres, one quarter-section.

[45] John Bracken, *Tillage of Stubble Land* (Regina, 1917), pp. 7-8; USA, Rutherford Collection, "Articles and Addresses," 1916; QUA, Dunning Papers, "Farm Production War Policy,"

February 26, 1918, pp. 42070-75; A.R. Turner, "W.R. Mother-well and Agricultural Development in Saskatchewan, 1905-1918" (MA thesis, University of Saskatchewan, 1958), Chapter 7. In 1915 and 1916 the dominion Department of Agriculture published *Agriculture War Books*, which contained advice of mixed quality. Sir Thomas White was the worst offender, and his speeches–reprinted in these books–urged that "every man with a plot of land should plant it," since wheat exports would ease potential balance of payments problems.

[46]See Appendix, Table 2; Wheeler, *Profitable Grain Growing*, p. 102.

[47]*MFP*, November 21, 1917; *Farmer's Advocate*, March 22, 1916, and December 26, 1917.

[48]Saskatchewan, *Report of the Live Stock Commission* (Regina, 1917), p. 47; *Farm and Ranch Review*, October 5, 1915; *Journal of the Canadian Banker's Association*, October, 1916, p. 62; *Farmer's Advocate*, March 15, 1916, and April 5, 1916.

[49]*Farm and Ranch Review*, January 20, 1915; *Farmer's Advocate*, June 14, 1916; *Journal of the Canadian Banker's Association*, January, 1917, p. 183; Murchie, *Agricultural Progress*, p. 94.

[50]See Appendix, Table 1; W.W. Thompson, *Suggested Lines of Cooperative Production* (Regina, 1919), p. 14.

[51]W.L. Morton, *The Progressive Party in Canada* (Toronto, 1950), pp. 297-305; PAC, John W. Dafoe Papers, Dafoe to G.M. Wrong, October 16, 1916.

Chapter Four

[1]W.L. Morton, *The Canadian Identity* (Toronto, 1962), p. 111; Victor Turek, *The Poles in Manitoba* (Toronto, 1967), p. 241; Allan Smith, "Metaphor and Nationality in North America," *Canadian Historical Review*, vol. 51, no. 3, September, 1970, pp. 247-75.

[2]Vera Lysenko, *Men in Sheepskin Coats* (Toronto, 1947), p. 115.

[3]These figures are for the provinces of Manitoba, Saskatchewan, and Alberta combined, and are compiled from R.H. Coats, "The Alien Enemy in Canada: Internment Operations" in *Canada and the Great World War* (Toronto, 1919-21), vol. 2, p. 146. The exact figures are 94,325 "Austrians" and 18,606 Germans.

[4]John Higham, *Strangers in the Land: Patterns of American Nativism* (New York, 1965), Chapter 1; J.S. Woodsworth, *Strangers within Our Gates* (Toronto, 1909), p. 100; J.P. McConnell, "The

Northwest: Its People and Prospects," *MFP*, July 17, 1905; Canada, House of Commons, *Debates*, 1901, p. 2934; Glenbow, Alberta WCTU Collection, Mrs. Louise McKinney in *Report of the Annual Convention*, 1913, Box 6, f. 35; *GGG*, January 29, 1913.

[5]Rev. W. Wyman reported in *The Western Prairie* (Cypress River, Manitoba), September 3, 1914; *The Voice*, August 8, 1914.

[6]*Swift Current Sun*, June 18, 1915; *The Voice*, May 14, 1915; PAC, Borden Papers, Calgary City Council to Borden, December 16, 1918, pp. 89689-90.

[7]*Winnipeg Telegram*, June 10, 1919, cited in Morris Mott, "The Foreign Peril: Nativism in Winnipeg, 1916-33" (unpublished MA thesis, University of Manitoba, 1970), p. 41; Rev. Wellington Bridgman, *Breaking Prairie Sod* (Toronto, 1920), p. 173; *Winnipeg Tribune*, March 26, 1920.

[8]Ralph Connor (C.W. Gordon), *The Major* (New York, 1917).

[9]E.B. Mitchell, *In Western Canada before the War* (London, 1915), p. 11.

[10]Paul Yuzyk, *Ukrainians in Manitoba* (Toronto, 1953), pp. 186-87; Ol'ha Woycenko, *Ukrainians in Canada* (Winnipeg, 1967), pp. 205-6; J.A. Boudreau, "Western Canada's Enemy Aliens in World War I," *Alberta Historical Review*, Winter, 1964, p. 6; *MFP*, August 11, 1914.

[11]F. Heap, "Ukrainians in Canada," *The Canadian Magazine*, May, 1919; G.A. Davidson, *The Ukrainians in Canada* (Ottawa, 1947), pp. 10-11; M.H. Marunchak, *The Ukrainian Canadians: A History* (Winnipeg, 1970), p. 325; J.S. Woodsworth, "Ukrainian Rural Communities" (mimeographed research paper, copy in Douglas Library, Queen's University, 1917), pp. 121, 144.

[12]AS, Scott Papers, J.E. Case to Scott, July 10, 1915, p. 59629, and reply July 13, 1915, p. 59632.

[13]Anon., *Two Years of War as Viewed from Ottawa* (Ottawa, 1916), pp. 73-74; *Lloydminster Times*, June 3, 1915.

[14]For detailed accounts of internment operations see Sir William Otter, *Internment Operations 1914-20* (Ottawa, 1921); Desmond Morton, "Sir William Otter and Internment Operations," *Canadian Historical Review*, vol. 55, no. 1, March, 1974; and J.A. Boudreau, "The Enemy Alien Problem in Canada, 1914-1921" (unpublished Ph.D. dissertation, UCLA, 1965), pp. 35-40. A description of day-to-day life in the camp at Castle, Alberta, can be found in the camp journal in Glenbow.

[15]AS, W.F.R. Turgeon Papers, Calder to Turgeon, August 6,

1918, Box 32, pp. 315-20; Dunning Papers, Dunning to Calder, September 3, 1918, pp. 43422-43.

[16]PAC, Borden Papers, OC/304, "Dominion Elections Act 1917," pp. 33482-502; OC/357, "Union Government 1917," pp. 39689-40040; G.L. Dodds to Borden, January 15, 1918, pp. 53375-77.

[17]E.K. Francis, *In Search of Utopia* (Glencoe, 1965), p. 190; PAC, C. Sifton Papers, copy of Peter Makaroff to Arthur Meighen, September 6, 1917; Boudreau, "Enemy Alien Problem," pp. 155-56.

[18]PAM, Valentine Winkler Papers, H.H. Ewart to Winkler, May 17, 1915, Box 2; *Swift Current Sun*, February 9, 1917; AS, Dunning Papers, Thomas White to Bishops of Mennonite Church, October 11, 1918, p. 41328; E.K.Francis, *In Search of Utopia*(Glencoe, 1965), p. 189; and Aaron Sawatzky, "The Mennonites of Alberta and their Assimilation" (unpublished MA thesis, University of Alberta, 1964), pp. 69-70.

[19]*MFP*, September 9, 1918.

[20]PAC, Borden Papers, F.W. Law to Borden, September 18, 1918, p. 121122; Victor Peters, "The Hutterian Brethren" in D. Swainson, *Historical Essays on the Prairie Provinces* (Toronto, 1971), p. 135. The inflow of Hutterites was matched in 1920 by the emigration of 6,500 conservative Mennonites to Mexico and Paraguay. They left not because they feared another war but because of the legislation of the Manitoba government which threatened their educational system. See I.A. Friesen, "Emigration in Mennonite History, with Special Reference to the Conservative Mennonite Emigration from Canada to Mexico and South America after World War I" (unpublished MA thesis, University of Manitoba, 1960).

[21]W. Kristjanson, *The Icelandic People in Manitoba* (Winnipeg, 1965), pp. 386-87; J.H. Haslam, "The Canadianization of the Immigrant Settler," *Annals of the American Academy of Political and Social Science*, vol. 107, May, 1923, p. 47.

[22]Turek, *Poles in Manitoba*, pp. 137-39; Howard Palmer, "Responses to Foreign Immigration: Nativism and Ethnic Tolerance in Alberta, 1880-1920" (unpublished MA thesis, University of Alberta, 1971), p. 238; PAM, M.J.B. Campbell Papers, M.G. Wright to Campbell, June 19, 1915, Box 8.

[23]PAC, Borden Papers, General Gwatkin to Loring Christie, June 21, 1916, p. 16617; Turek, *Poles in Manitoba*, pp. 71-76.

[24]PAC, C. Sifton Papers, A.E. Philp to Sifton, January 27, 1915, p. 160491.

[25]PAM, Winkler Papers, W.S. Linnell to T.H. Johnson, September 14, 1915, Box 3; Canada, *Annual Report of the Department of the Interior, 1915-16*, p. 74.

[26]Cf. C.H. Young, *The Ukrainian Canadians: A Study in Assimilation* (Toronto, 1931), pp. 60, 80-82; T.C. Byrne, "The Ukrainian Community in North Central Alberta" (unpublished MA thesis, University of Alberta, 1937), p. 35; J.G. MacGregor, *Vilni Zemli* (Toronto, 1969), p. 252. For an illustration of these different attitudes on the parts of English-Canadian and immigrant farmers, see Frederick Philip Grove's *Fruits of the Earth* (Toronto, 1933), Chapters 15 and 18. For statistics on farm growth, see Appendix, Table 4.

[27]See Appendix, Table 3.

[28]AS, Violet McNaughton Papers, July 7, 1917; Morton, "Sir William Otter...," p. 55; *Farm and Ranch Review*, December 5, 1917.

[29]See, for example, Raymond Huel, "L'Association Catholique Franco-Canadienne de la Saskatchewan: A Response to Cultural Assimilation" (unpublished MA thesis, University of Saskatchewan, 1969), p. 105. See also Francis, *In Search of Utopia*, pp. 179-80, p. 205.

[30]J.S. Woodsworth, "Ukrainian Rural Communities," p. 49, emphasis added; *Regina Evening Province and Standard*, May 26, 1915.

[31]George Weir, "The Evolution of Separate School Law in the Prairie Provinces" (unpublished D.Ped. thesis, 1917); Hon. R.S. Thornton, *Bilingual Schools: Address to the Legislature* (Winnipeg, 1916); Manitoba, Department of Education, *Special Report on Bilingual Schools in Manitoba* (Winnipeg, 1916); MFP, January 24, 1916.

[32]*CAR*, 1918, p. 687; Weir, "Separate School Law," p. 107; and Harold W. Foght, *A Survey of Education in the Province of Saskatchewan* (Regina, 1918), p. 33.

[33]J.G. MacGregor, *Vilni Zemli*, p. 232; *Edmonton Bulletin*, January 4, 1914; H.T. Sparby, "History of the Alberta School System to 1925" (unpublished Ph.D. dissertation, Stanford, 1958), p. 144.

[34]Thornton, *Bilingual Schools*, pp. 10-11; *The Voice*, February 18, February 25, March 3, and March 10, 1916.

[35]Foght, *Survey of Education*, pp. 59-62, 152; Raymond Huel, "The French Canadians and the Language Question," *Saskatchewan History*, vol. 23, no. 1, Winter, 1970.

[36]AS, Martin Papers, Martin to A.J. Sparling, March 8, 1916,

p. 14808; Foght, *Survey of Education*, p. 5, emphasis added.

[37]PAM, Manning Papers, Printed speech by G.R. Coldwell in response to motion to eliminate bilingual education, 1914, f. 20; G.T. Daly, *Catholic Problems in Western Canada* (Toronto, 1921), p. 170; George M. Weir, "Canada's Golden Jubilee of Confederation" (Regina, 1917), pp. 42-44; PAC, Dafoe Papers, J.W. Dafoe to Thomas Côté, April 17, 1916.

[38]*Le Courrier de l'Ouest* (Edmonton), August 13, 1914; *Le Patriote de l'Ouest* (Prince Albert), February 24, 1915; *La Liberté* (St. Boniface), July 11, July 18, and August 1, 1917.

[39]*Regina Daily Post*, December 18, 1918, cited in Huel, "ACFC," p. 137; AS, Turgeon Papers, Raymond Denis to Turgeon, May 6, 1918, Box 32, p. 468.

[40]Turek, *Poles in Manitoba*, pp. 220-22; PAM, Manning Papers, P.A. Talbot to Manning, June 11, 1917, p. 32; PAC, Dafoe Papers, Dafoe to Thomas Côté, April 4, 1916; Laurier Papers, Talbot to Laurier, January 29, 1916, p. 190924.

[41]*Swift Current Sun*, February 26, 1918; J.E. Hughson, "Introduction" to W.J. Bridgman, *Breaking Prairie Sod* (Toronto, 1920), p. xiv.

Chapter Five

[1]A. Richard Allen, *The Social Passion* (Toronto, 1971); Lionel Orlikow, "The Reform Movement in Manitoba" in Swainson, *Historical Essays on the Prairie Provinces*.

[2]PAM, Colin H. Campbell Papers, R.P. Roblin to Colin H. Campbell, January 9, 1914.

[3]*CAR*, 1914, p. 598.

[4]Mrs. Louise McKinney, "President's Address," in Alberta WCTU, *Report of the Annual Convention 1915*; Nellie L. McClung, *In Times Like These* (New York, 1915), p. 161; Clifford Sifton, "Foundations of the New Era," in J.O. Miller, *The New Era in Canada* (Toronto, 1918), pp. 37-38; AS, Saskatchewan Grain Growers' Association, *Convention Report*, December 12, 1917.

[5]Mrs. H.V. Plumptre, "Some Thoughts on the Suffrage," in Miller, *New Era*, pp. 328-29; Glenbow, Alberta WCTU Collection #1, f. 35, *Report of the Annual Convention, 1915*, p. 30.

[6]McClung, *In Times Like These*, p. 5; R.E. Spence, *Prohibition in Canada* (Toronto, 1919), p. 71, p. 165; Sara Rowell Wright, "The WCTU Program," in *The Social Service Congress of Canada* (Ottawa, 1914), p. 322; MFP, March 6, 1916; GGG, June 16, 1915.

[7]Frances M. Beynon in *GGG*, May 30, 1917.

[8]Ralph Connor, *The Sky Pilot in No Man's Land* (New York, 1917), pp. 149-50; AS, Martin Papers, Ladies of North Battleford Methodist Church to W.M. Martin, November 7, 1916, p. 31654; Motherwell Papers, Mrs. W.R. Motherwell, Address at Lemberg, Saskatchewan, December 5, 1916, f. 123.

[9]Glenbow, Calgary Brewing and Malting Collection, W. Towers to A.E. Cross, January 1, 1918, f. 577; *MFP*, March 7, 1916.

[10]*Edmonton Bulletin*, July 20, 1915; *Regina Leader*, February 24, 1915.

[11]*MFP*, March 7, 1916; McClung, *In Times Like These*, p. 170.

[12]Resolution of the Manitoba Rural Deanery, Church of England, reported in *MFP*, March 1, 1916.

[13]AS, Scott Papers, Scott to Willoughby, December 1, 1914, p. 48455; Levi Thomson to Scott, April 8, 1915, p. 48503; Motherwell to Scott, December 18, 1914, p. 12889; Scott to S.G. Hill, July 1, 1915, p. 13300; Scott to J.H. Ross, April 12, 1915, p. 13650; AS, J.A. Calder Papers, Calder to G.H.V. Bulyea, March 23, 1915, G4, p. 11.

[14]Detailed accounts of these referenda can be found in Erhard Pinno, "Temperance and Prohibition in Saskatchewan" (unpublished MA thesis, University of Saskatchewan, 1971); John H. Thompson, "The Prohibition Question in Manitoba, 1892-1928" (unpublished MA thesis, University of Manitoba, 1969); and R.I. McLean, "Temperance and Prohibition in Alberta, 1875-1915" (unpublished MA thesis, University of Calgary, 1970).

[15]*MFP*, March 6, 1916; *Canadian Farmer*, November, 1916, translation in AS, Martin Papers, pp. 31616-68; Glenbow, Alberta WCTU Collection, *Annual Report 1915*, p. 60; *MFP*, March 14, 1916.

[16]Glenbow, Calgary Brewing and Malting Collection, A.E. Cross to D.R. Ker, March 24, 1915, f. 550; *Edmonton Bulletin*, July 6, 1915.

[17]A.S., Motherwell Papers, Liquor Advertisement, f. 71; *Calgary Eye Opener*, July 8, 1916.

[18]Province of Manitoba, *Annual Report on the Temperance Act*, Sessional Paper #13, 1917; AS, Martin Papers, Mrs. G.V. Jewett to Martin, April 23, 1917, p. 31759; R.E. Popham and W. Schmit, *Statistics of Alcohol Use and Alcoholism in Canada* (Toronto, 1958), pp. 48-53. See also James H. Gray, *The Boy From Winnipeg* (Toronto, 1970), p. 126; *Red Lights on the Prairies* (To-

ronto, 1971), pp. 149-51; and *Booze* (Toronto, 1974).

[19]AS, Scott Papers, Levi Thomson to Scott, April 8, 1915, p. 48503; *Saskatoon Phoenix*, March 19, 1915. Richard Allen has suggested that prohibition was "almost predictable" in Manitoba and Saskatchewan before the war began in 1914 (*Social Passion*, p. 22). This judgment seems exaggerated, given the lack of success of local option ballots, the defeat of the Norris Liberals in Manitoba, and comments such as those of Calder and Scott.

[20]McClung, *In Times Like These*, p. 14. See also Carol Lee Bacchi Ferraro, "The Ideas of the Canadian Suffragists, 1890-1920" (unpublished MA thesis, McGill University, 1970), pp. 109-11.

[21]McClung, *In Times Like These*, p. 27.

[22]Kenneth Haig, *Brave Harvest* (Toronto, 1945), pp. 192-93. There were exceptions, most notably Frances M. Beynon, women's editor of the *Grain Growers' Guide*, and her sister, Mrs. A.V. Thomas.

[23]Aileen S. Kraditor, *The Ideas of the Woman Suffrage Movement* (New York, 1965), pp. 38-63.

[24]PAC, Dafoe Papers, Clifford Sifton to Dafoe, September 21, 1914; W.L. Morton, "The Extension of the Franchise in Canada: A Study in Democratic Nationalism," *Canadian Historical Association Report*, 1943, p. 79; PAC, Sifton Papers, Ida Sifton to Clifford Sifton, August 13, 1917, p. 161845.

[25]R.J.C. Stead, *The Cow Puncher* (Toronto, 1918), p. 342; *Non Partisan Leader*, June 13, 1917.

[26]USA, Murray Papers, B38/7; Glenbow, United Farmers of Alberta Collection, f. 35; MFP, February 27, 1915.

[27]McClung, *In Times Like These*, pp. 28-29; PAM, United Farmers of Manitoba Collection, United Farm Women Report, 1918.

[28]The Census of 1921 revealed a 63 per cent increase in the number of women in the Western provinces employed outside their homes. For comparative figures see Canada, *Fifth Census, 1911*, vol. 6, p. 10, and *Sixth Census, 1921*, vol. 4, p. 10. The statistics on women teachers in Alberta are taken from Alberta, Department of Education, *Annual Report*, 1916, pp. 16-17; MFP, October 4, 1917.

[29]Wilson Macdonald, "The Girl Behind the Man Behind the Gun," in *Song of the Prairie Land* (Toronto, 1918), pp. 124-26.

[30]Arthur Marwick, *The Deluge* (London, 1965); *Winnipeg Tribune*, October 9, 1915; Provincial Archives of Alberta, Miriam Elston Scrapbooks, "The Home Shall be an Honoured Place,"

Everywoman's World, November, 1916; AS, Scott Papers, Ella B. Carroll to Scott, February 1, 1916, p. 59492; Norris Papers, W.R. Wood to T.C. Norris, January 26, 1918, Box 2.

[31]University of Alberta Archives, Henry Marshall Tory Papers, F.W. Rolt to H.M. Tory, May 15, 1915, f. 14082A; Canada, House of Commons, *Debates*, 1917, vol. 2, pp. 1515-19.

[32]C.L. Cleverdon, *The Woman Suffrage Movement in Canada* (Toronto, 1950), pp. 46-83; June Menzies, "Votes for Saskatchewan's Women" in Norman Ward, *Politics in Saskatchewan* (Don Mills, 1968).

Chapter Six

[1]The standard interpretation of conscription as a crisis in French-English relations can be found in Elizabeth Armstrong, *The Crisis of Quebec, 1914-18* (New York, 1937) and Mason Wade, *The French Canadians* (Toronto, 1956).

[2]AS, W.F.R. Turgeon Papers, P.E. Myre to Turgeon, July 2, 1917, Box 30, pp. 335-38.

[3]Charles F. Lipton, *The Trade Union Movement of Canada, 1827-1959* (Montreal, 1967), pp. 169-80; Martin Robin, "Registration, Conscription and Independent Labour Politics," in C. Berger, ed., *Conscription 1917*, p. 60. Both Lipton and Robin see British Columbia and the West as the centre of this opposition to the war and to conscription. Lipton, p. 170; Robin, p. 64.

[4]*Labour Gazette*, vol. 17, no. 8, August, 1917; *Calgary Herald*, April 9, 1919; Lipton, *Trade Union Movement*, p. 170; Canada, *Report on Organized Labour* (Ottawa, 1917), pp. 24-26; *The Voice*, September 11, 1914; *The Nutcracker* (Calgary), November 17, 1916.

[5]*The Voice* (Winnipeg), August 14 and October 30, 1914, and January 1, 1915; Lipton, p. 163; *Ottawa Citizen*, April 26, 1918; and *Winnipeg Tribune*, ND.; clippings in PAM, Rigg Papers, "Correspondence and Clippings, 1918-1953."

[6]*Proceedings of the Thirty-first Annual Convention of the Trades and Labor Congress* (Vancouver, 1915), p. 14; *The Voice*, December 10, 1916.

[7]J.S. Woodsworth to the editor, *MFP*, December 28, 1916; AS, Martin Papers, J.W.S. Eddy to Martin, January 27, 1917, pp. 29779-81.

[8]PAC, Borden Papers, OC/313, "National Service," pp. 34640-61. See also W.J.C. Cherwinski, "The Formative Years of the Trade Union Movement in Saskatchewan, 1905-1920" (un-

published MA thesis, University of Saskatchewan, 1966), p. 121; *MFP*, December 16, 1916; Canada, House of Commons, *Debates*, 1917, vol. 6, pp. 6086-91; *MFP*, January 11, 1917.

[9]*MFP*, May 28, 1917; Robin, "Registration, Conscription...," pp. 69-70; *Edmonton Bulletin*, September 21, 1917.

[10]*MFP*, January 1, 1917; *Winnipeg Telegram*, January 8, 1917; PAC, Borden Papers, G.A. Shewfelt to Borden, January 15, 1917, p. 34662; *Winnipeg Tribune*, January 26, 1917, emphasis added.

[11]*The Voice*, January 28, 1916.

[12]W.L. Morton, *The Progressive Party in Canada* (Toronto, 1950), pp. 57-58, 73; *GGG*, January 17, 1917.

[13]QUA, Crerar Papers, T.A. Crerar to Gordon Waldron, August 3, 1917; Crerar to H.B. Cowan, August 27, 1917; Gordon Waldron to Crerar, July 28, 1917.

[14]*Ibid.*, Resolution of the MGGA, January 10, 1917; PAC, Borden Papers, OC/391, "Conscription of Wealth."

[15]PAC, Borden Papers, p. 32185.

[16]*MFP*, August 8, 1914.

[17]PAC, Borden Papers, OC/285, OC/357, OC/363, "Union Government"; *The Voice*, December 29, 1916; Cherwinski, "Trade Union Movement," p. 126; *The Nutcracker*, December 29, 1916.

[18]*GGG*, May 30, 1917; PAC, C. Sifton Papers, J.W. Dafoe to Sifton, February 12, 1917, pp. 161401-15; AS, McNaughton Papers, Violet McNaughton to Mrs. M. Robertson, April 23, 1917.

[19]Duff Spafford, "Independent Politics in Saskatchewan before the Nonpartisan League," *Saskatchewan History*, June, 1965; *Swift Current Sun*, April 6, 1917; *MFP*, July 4, 1917; *Maclean's Magazine*, July, 1916.

[20]*MFP*, July 5, 1917; PAC, Borden Papers, W.J. Coleman to Borden, June 8, 1917, pp. 39720-21, Thomas McKay to Borden, June 9, 1917, p. 39727; *GGG*, July 11, 1917. See also *Farmer's Advocate*, August 22, 1917.

[21]*Swift Current Sun*, August 31, 1917; PAC, Borden Papers, Lorne Molloy to Borden, June 21, 1917, pp. 40519-21, 40768.

[22]John W. Dafoe, *Sir Clifford Sifton* in *Relation to His Times* (Toronto, 1931), p. 418; PAC, Dafoe Papers, Dafoe to N.W. Rowell, July 25, 1917; Ramsay Cook, "Dafoe, Laurier, and the Formation of Union Government," in Berger, ed., *Conscription, 1917*, p. 32; QUA, Crerar Papers, Crerar to J.B. Parker, October 3, 1917; *MFP*, August 13, 1917; AS, J.A. Calder Papers, C.P. Klombies to Calder, ND, G9, pp. 92-95; PAC, Borden Papers,

C. Sifton to Borden, July 25, 1917, pp. 40337-39; *MFP*, August 16, 1917; AS, Martin Papers, Martin to Lt. Col. A.T. Thompson, August 22, 1917, p. 26219; AS, Turgeon Papers, Laurier to Turgeon, August 11, 1917.

[23]PAC, Borden Papers, H.L. Montgomery to Borden, August 18, 1917, p. 40669; *GGG*, August 15, 1917; *Non Partisan Leader* (Calgary), August 15, 1917; *The Voice*, August 10, 1917; *GGG*, August 15, 1917; *MFP*, August 15, 1917; PAC, Borden Papers, F.C. Bennet to Borden, September 10, 1917, pp. 39929-35; J.B. McLaren to Borden, September 14, 1917, pp. 39945-46; *Swift Current Sun*, August 31, 1917; PAC, Borden Papers, H.C. Ellis to Borden, September 20, 1917, pp. 399957-58.

[24]J.S. Willison, "Immigration and Settlement," in J.O. Miller, ed., *The New Era in Canada* (Toronto, 1917), p. 103; J.S. Woodsworth, *Strangers within Our Gates* (Toronto, 1909), p. 208. For examples of these proposals see: Canada, House of Commons, *Debates* 1917, vol. 2, p. 1515; PAC, C. Sifton Papers, G. Barrett to Arthur Meighen, August 1917, p. 161271, and Borden Papers, G.M. Newton to G.H. Bradbury, May 18, 1917, pp. 33507-78. The resolution of the Equal Franchise Board is reported in *The Non Partisan Leader*, June 13, 1917.

[25]*Swift Current Sun*, September 11, 1917; *MFP*, October 5, 1917; AS, McNaughton Papers, Parlby to McNaughton, November 20, 1917.

[26]Ramsay Cook and Craig Brown, *Canada 1896-1921: A Nation Transformed* (Toronto, 1974), p. 272.

[27]*La Liberté* (St. Boniface), October 17, 1917; PAC, Dafoe Papers, G.W. Allan to Dafoe, October 12, 1917; *Edmonton Bulletin*, October 18, 1917.

[28]Paul F. Sharp, *The Agrarian Revolt in Western Canada* (St. Paul, 1948), pp. 90-97.

[29]*The Nutcracker*, June 7, 1917; PAC, Borden Papers, Ford to Borden, August 21, 1917, p. 39885, and reply August 25, 1917, p. 39886, Ford to Borden, August 31, 1917, p. 39917 and reply, September 6, 1917, p. 40734, Ford to Borden, September 12, 1917, p. 40749.

[30]*Alberta Non Partisan*, October 26, 1917, and November 9, 1917; AS, Violet McNaughton Papers, Frances Beynon to McNaughton, October 5, 1917.

[31]*The Voice*, October 26, 1917.

[32]QUA, T.A. Crerar Papers, J.B. Hugg to Crerar, October 12, 1917; PAC, Dafoe Papers, J.A. Aitken to Dafoe, October 11, 1917; QUA, Crerar Papers, Bland to Crerar, October 18, 1917;

ibid., McWilliams to Crerar, October 20, 1917; *GGG*, October 31, 1917.

[33] *GGG*, October 24, 1917.

[34] *Farmer's Advocate*, August 8, 1917; *GGG*, August 1, 1917; *ibid.*, August 8, 1917; *Swift Current Sun*, August 28, 1917.

[35] PAC, Borden Papers, Memorandum, November 15, 1917, p. 40802; *Farm and Ranch Review*, November 20, 1917; *Calgary Herald*, December 13, 1917; PAM, R.A.C. Manning Papers, "What the Man in the Street Hears about Union Government," f. 137; *MFP*, December 15, 1917.

[36] PAC, Borden Papers, A.A. Langford, Biggar, Saskatchewan, to Borden, November 27, 1917, p. 44422; PAM Valentine Winkler Papers, J.G. Smith to Winkler, November 19, 1917; QUA, Crerar Papers, Murdock Young to H.A. Mullins, November 21, 1917; *GGG*, November 21, 1917.

[37] W.R. Young, "Conscription, Rural Depopulation and the Farmers of Ontario, 1917-19," *Canadian Historical Review*, September, 1972, pp. 305-6; *Lloydminster Times*, December 13, 1917; *Farmer's Advocate*, December 5, 1917.

[38] AS, John A. Maharg Papers, J.B. Musselman to secretaries of SGGA locals, November 8, 1917; QUA, Crerar Papers, W.J. Short to Crerar, October 25, 1917.

[39] *MFP*, December 4, 1917.

[40] *GGG*, December 5, 1917; C.W. Gordon, *Postscript to Adventure* (New York, 1938), p. 337; QUA, Crerar Papers, E.J. Tarr to Crerar, December 18, 1917.

[41] PAM, Manning Papers, "Union Bulletin," December 12, 1917; PAC, A.E. Kemp Papers, "An Eyewitness," vol. 120, f. 21; *MFP*, December 4, 1917.

[42] See J.M. Bliss, "The Methodist Church and World War I", pp. 46-48; and Allen, *The Social Passion*, pp. 41-43.

[43] PAC, Borden Papers, *Union Government* (Ottawa, 1917), p. 15, p. 40777; Roger Graham, *Arthur Meighen* (Toronto, 1960), vol. 1, p. 188.

[44] QUA, Crerar Papers, G.W. Allan to Crerar, December 4, 1917; *Calgary Eye Opener*, November 24, 1917; *Winnipeg Telegram*, December 14, 1917.

[45] *GGG*, December 12, 1917; AS, McNaughton Papers, Beynon to McNaughton, January 11, 1918; *MFP*, December 6, 1917.

[46] PAC, C. Sifton Papers, J.W. Dafoe to Sifton, December 10, 1917, p. 161401, and Borden Papers, Charles Ireland to A.E. Blount, December 10, 1917, p. 88998. These and all subsequent

electoral statistics are from Canada, House of Commons, *Sessional Papers 1920*, no. 13.

[47] American-born made up 22.5 per cent of the Alberta population in 1911. *CYB*, 1913, p. 72.

[48] POPULAR VOTE IN THE WEST, RURAL/URBAN, 1917

	% Union	% Opposition
Manitoba	76/83.5	24/16.5
Saskatchewan	67.9/77.5	32.1/22.5
Alberta	52.3/64.5	47.7/35.5
TOTAL	65.9/76.3	34.1/23.7

Source: Canada, *Sessional Papers*, 1920, no. 13.

[49] Robin, "Registration, Conscription," p. 76.

[50] *The Voice*, December 21, 1917.

[51] QUA, Crerar Papers, W.C. O'Keefe to Crerar, December 18, 1917.

[52] This phrase is taken from W.T.R. Preston, *My Generation of Politics and Politicians* (Toronto, 1927), p. 235 and is repeated by J.M. Beck in *Pendulum of Power* (Scarborough, 1968), pp. 145-46. A similar charge is made by O.D. Skelton in his *Life and Letters of Sir Wilfrid Laurier*, vol. 2, pp. 198-99.

[53] Boudreau, "Enemy Alien Problem in Canada," pp. 150-53; Canada, *Census of the Prairie Provinces 1916*, p. xxxix.

[54] *Farmer's Advocate*, December 5, 1917; QUA, Crerar Papers, H.L. Montgomery to Crerar, December 20, 1917.

[55] AS, McNaughton Papers, Parlby to McNaughton, November 20, 1917.

[56] *Swift Current Sun*, December 18, 1917; *Calgary Herald*, December 20, 1917; Hopkins Moorhouse, *Deep Furrows* (Winnipeg, 1918), pp. 290-91.

Chapter Seven

[1] *Farmer's Advocate*, January 2, 1918.

[2] QUA, Crerar Papers, W.C. O'Keefe to T.A. Crerar, December 18, 1917; *Swift Current Sun*, June 17, 1917; *Edmonton Bulletin*, May 22, 1917.

[3] Q.U.A., Crerar Papers, John Williams to T.A. Crerar, April 25, 1918.

[4] QUA, Dunning Papers, J.J. Morrison to Roderick McKenzie, May 4, 1918, p. 42250; *ibid.*, George F. Chipman Papers, Chipman to T.A. Crerar, June 3, 1918; *GGG*, May 25, 1918.

[5]*Calgary Daily Herald*, May 16, 1918; Glenbow, UFA Executive Minutes, May 30, 1918; AS, Violet McNaughton Papers, Irene Parlby to McNaughton, May 19, 1918; *GGG*, April 24, 1918; QUA, Chipman Papers, Chipman to T.A. Crerar, April 23, 1918.

[6]Canada, Department of Justice, *Report of the Director of the Military Service Branch* (Ottawa, 1919), pp. 132, 149.

[7]*Edmonton Journal*, June 13, 1918; *ibid.*, May 21, 1918; QUA, Norman Lambert Papers, Crerar to Lambert, June 15, 1918.

[8]QUA, Dunning Papers, Thomas Allcock to C.A. Dunning, April 25, 1918, pp. 42585-86; PAM, Valentine Winkler Papers, J.W.R. Lukin to Winkler, May 6, 1918; QUA, Dunning Papers, Alex Delgarno to Dunning, May 2, 1918, pp. 42611-12.

[9]PAC, A.L. Sifton Papers, Sam Hughes to J.C. Doherty, April 3, 1918; *ibid.*, T.A. Crerar to A.L. Sifton, July 6, 1918. Paul F. Sharp suggests that the cancellation of agricultural exemptions from conscription was the basic cause of Western alienation from the Union government and that the Western farm movement expressed solidarity with the UFO during its protest rally in Ottawa. "The conscription issue," he contends, "unquestionably created an opposition to the union government that forever discredited it in the [Western] farmer's eyes." *Agrarian Revolt in Western Canada*, p. 126. This seems to be an overstatement. There is no evidence that Western reaction was as hostile as that of the Ontario farmer, and W.L. Morton suggests that conscription was a much less important issue to Westerners. *Progressive Party in Canada*, p. 73. An explanation for the more violent response of the UFO has been proposed by W.R. Young, who attributes the attitude of Ontario farmers to the fact that the rural population of Ontario was steadily declining in real and proportional terms. Thus conscription of farmer's sons and farm workers was perceived as a factor which could further accelerate this decline. Young, "Conscription, Rural Depopulation and the Farmers of Ontario, 1917-19."

[10]Cook and Brown, *Canada: A Nation Transformed*, p. 294; *Alberta Non Partisan*, January 18, 1918; PAC, Dafoe Papers, W.A. Buchanan to J.W. Dafoe, December 21, 1917.

[11]*Farmer's Advocate*, January 16, 1918.

[12]*Ibid.*, February 13, 1918; QUA, Dunning Papers, Elza Buck to C.A. Dunning, January 22, 1918, p. 42040.

[13]QUA, Dunning Papers, C.A. Hoffmann to Dunning, February 22, 1918, pp. 42458-61; John Wick to C.A. Dunning, February 28, 1918, pp. 42118-19.

[14] *Alberta Non Partisan*, April 12, 1918; *Farmer's Advocate*, May 22, 1918, May 29, 1918.

[15] *Farmer's Advocate*, May 1, 1918.

[16] *GGG*, September 11, 1918.

[17] Canada, *Report of the Department of Labour*, Sessional Paper 36, 1916, p. 8; AS, W.M. Martin Papers, Memorandum, p. 14406; *CYB*, 1921, p. 650; Appendix, Table 3.

[18] *CAR*, 1918, p. 573; Harry Sutcliffe, "The Economic Background of the Winnipeg General Strike: Wages and Working Conditions" (unpublished MA thesis, University of Manitoba, 1972); D. Bercuson, *Confrontation at Winnipeg* (Montreal, 1974), p. 33; Marwick, *The Nature of History* (London, 1970), p. 126; *Farmer's Advocate*, July 31, 1918.

[19] *Farmer's Advocate*, April 24, 1918; *Swift Current Sun*, April 12, 1918; AS, W.F.R. Turgeon Papers, Turgeon to Calder, July 27, 1918, Box 22, pp. 315-3201.

[20] *Alberta Non Partisan*, July 4, 1917; AS, McNaughton Papers, Memorandum, September 8, 1917; *The Voice*, November 2, 1917; AS, Motherwell Papers, Motherwell to Crerar, April 17, 1918.

[21] *GGG*, January 2, 1918; QUA, Dunning Papers, J.B. Musselman to Saskatchewan Grain Grower's Association Locals, May 18, 1918, pp. 41805-8; *Edmonton Bulletin*, January 26, 1918; *Swift Current Sun*, June 15, 1918.

[22] USA, College of Agriculture Collection, Saskatchewan Board of Food Controllers to H.B. Thomson, June 15, 1918; *Farmer's Advocate*, July 10, 1918.

[23] PAC, C.A. Magrath Papers, Final Report of the Fuel Controller, vol. 4, file 12, pp. 25-27, *GGG*, July 10, 1918.

[24] *CAR*, 1918, pp. 330-31; *Labour Gazette*, 1917, pp. 612-15; 1918, p. 367.

[25] *Farmer's Advocate*, October 2, 1918; PAM, R.A. Rigg Papers, T.J. Murray to Rigg, May 28, 1918; *Swift Current Sun*, May 24, 1918; AS, Scott Papers, G.H.V. Bulyea to Scott, December 7, 1918, p. 14640; *Calgary Daily Herald*, November 2, 1918.

[26] AS, McNaughton Papers, Irene Parlby to McNaughton, August 7, 1918; *GGG*, August 7, 1918.

[27] R.C. Brown, "'Whither are we being shoved?': Political Leadership in Canada during World War I," in R.D. Cuff and J.L. Granatstein, eds., *War and Society in North America* (Toronto, 1971), p. 106; *The Voice*, May 31, 1918; *Swift Current Sun*, December 15, 1916; *Farmer's Advocate*, February 13, 1918.

[28] *Swift Current Sun*, July 30, 1918; *GGG*, January 2, 1918;

Farmer's Advocate, December 26, 1917.

[29]PAC, Rowell Papers, Rowell to Borden, September 2, 1918, pp. 2868-71; *ibid.*, Borden Papers, Memorandum, pp. 50893-95; *ibid.*, A.L. Sifton Papers, T.A. Crerar to Sifton, July 6, 1918.

[30]*Farmer's Advocate*, August 28, 1918; QUA, Chipman Papers, Chipman to Crerar, June 13, 1918; GGG, June 19, 1918; *Alberta Non Partisan*, April 26, 1918; QUA, Crerar Papers, F.J. Dixon to Crerar, October 12, 1918, cited in Brown, "Political leadership...," p. 104.

[31]See Brown, "Political Leadership...," pp. 108, 112; David E. Smith, "Emergency Government in Canada," *Canadian Historical Review*, vol. 49, 1969, pp. 429-48; and Cook and Brown, *Canada: A Nation Transformed*, Chapter 12.

[32]*The Nutcracker*, May 10, 1917; *The Voice*, October 16, 1914; *Farm and Ranch Review*, October 5, 1917; *Farmer's Advocate*, December 26, 1917; H.S. Beland, "The Returned Soldier," in *Annals of the American Academy*, May, 1923; R.J.C. Stead, "The Veterans," in *Kitchener and Other Poems* (Toronto, 1917).

[33]AS, Scott Papers, W.B. Cumming to Walter Scott, June 27, 1918, p. 14730; *Farmer's Advocate*, August 28, 1918; *Swift Current Sun*, October 8, 1918; PAC, Dafoe Papers, J.A. Calder to J.W. Dafoe, August 16, 1918.

[34]R. Allen, *The Social Passion*, pp. 63, 204.

[35]A.J.P. Taylor, "War Weariness and Peace Overtures," in J.M. Roberts, ed., *History of the Twentieth Century* (London, 1970), p. 815; Moorhouse, *Deep Furrows*, pp. 288-89; GGG, October 30, 1918; *Alberta Non Partisan*, September 12, 1918; *The Voice*, October 23, 1918.

[36]GGG, July 3, 1918; J. Castell Hopkins, *Canada at War* (Toronto, 1919), p. 422; *Farmer's Advocate*, December 11, 1918; *Calgary Daily Herald*, November 11, 1918.

[37]Glenbow, Alberta WCTU Collection, L.C. McKinney, "Presidential Address" in *Report of the 1919 Annual Convention*, p. 32; AS, W.M. Martin Papers, Martin to Embury, November 12, 1918, p. 8537.

[38]AS, Martin Papers, p. 26267.

[39]PAM, M.J.B. Campbell Papers, Annabelle Walker to Campbell, February 23, 1917; University of Alberta Archives, H.M. Tory Papers, Tory to A.C. Rankin, August 31, 1915, file 42: 1402; PAC, W.A. Griesbach Papers, Box 2, file 15.

[40]Norman B. James, *Autobiography of a Nobody* (Toronto, 1947), p. 114.

Index